THE ARTE OF RHETORIQUE

THE ARTS OF MANKIND

The Arte

of

Rhetorique

(1553)

BY

THOMAS WILSON

A FACSIMILE REPRODUCTION

WITH AN INTRODUCTION

BY

ROBERT HOOD BOWERS

Fellow of the Newberry Library

GAINESVILLE, FLORIDA

SCHOLARS' FACSIMILES & REPRINTS

1962

SCHOLARS' FACSIMILES & REPRINTS
118 N.W. 26TH STREET
GAINESVILLE, FLORIDA, U.S.A.

HARRY R. WARFEL, GENERAL EDITOR

L. C. CATALOG CARD NUMBER: 62-7014

MANUFACTURED IN THE U.S.A.

LETTERPRESS BY J. N. ANZEL, INC.
PHOTOLITHOGRAPHY BY EDWARDS BROTHERS
BINDING BY UNIVERSAL-DIXIE BINDERY

Introduction

I

Thomas Wilson's *The Arte of Rhetorique* (1553) is an important book: it is the first complete rhetoric in the English language. Its significant predecessors: Leonard Cox's *The Arte or Crafte of Rhetoryke* (1524?) was largely confined to an exposition of rhetorical invention, and Richard Sherry's *A Treatise of Schemes and Tropes* (1550), a work from which Wilson borrowed, was largely confined to an exposition of stylistic rhetoric and literary ornament. Furthermore, Wilson's rhetoric is an eminently readable and sensible discussion of Ciceronian rhetorical doctrine. The most recent historian of rhetoric in Renaissance England, Wilbur S. Howell, in his authoritative *Logic and Rhetoric in England, 1500-1700* (1956) has called it "The greatest Ciceronian rhetoric in England short of a direct translation of the works of the Latin master himself" (p. 98). Understandably enough the content of Wilson's book has often been studied, notably by the late Russell H. Wagner in *Speech Monographs*, XXVII (March, 1960), to which the interested student is at once directed for a full analysis.

Wilson's tripartite treatise may justly be called complete because it is concerned with the whole process of oratory; it is concerned with the moral end of persuasion, with the proper qualifications of an orator, with the kinds of orations and effective means of strengthening them, and with the actual ways of rendering delivery attractive. Hence the "five great arts" of the Ciceronian tradition (invention, disposition, elocution, memory, and utterance) required of a properly trained orator are at once set forth in Book I. Also the treatise is remarkable for the amount and caliber of exemplary material which it provides: for example on fol. 21^v-34^v the full text of Erasmus' *An Epistle to perswade a young gentleman to Mariage* is given as an example of deliberative oratory. This was a popular text: about 1530 R. Tavenour made an English translation of the Latin original under the title *A ryght frutefull epystle in laude and prayse of matrymony* (*STC* 10492). As further evidence of the enormous popularity of Erasmus in Tudor England, it is interesting to note that Richard Sherry appended his translation of Erasmus' essay "On the Education of Children" to his *Treatise of Schemes and Tropes*.

Invention receives considerable emphasis in Book I probably because Wilson felt what serious rhetoricians have always felt: excessive preoccupation with stylistic rhetoric adulterates content. Then he carefully discriminates between demonstrative, deliberative, and judicial oratory, and includes examples of each type. Book II treats the various methods of developing and organizing a speech and describes the steps of entrance or beginning, narration, division, proposition, and conclusion. A final section deals with amplification:since Wilson is convinced that "the beautie of amplifying standeth most in apt mouing of affections" (fol. 71^r), instruction in how to move an audience to pity or laughter follows. Book III, which begins with an account of elocution (i.e., diction and tropes), contains the famous attack on "ink-horn terms," the plea for the use of words drawn from one's "mother's language" (fol. 86ʳ). This objection to the use of diction derived from Latin, French, or Italian was voiced also by a number of Wilson's intellectual peers, such as Sir John Cheke, Provost of King's College, Cambridge. Actually the illustrative matter which Wilson introduces at this point includes many malapropisms; one suspects that an important reason for the attack on "ink-horn terms" was the actual misuse of words by persons affecting a speech beyond their control. We learn also that some affected persons "will talke nothing but Chaucer." Book III concludes with a succinct account of memory and utterance (i.e., how to memorize a speech effectively; and how to develop effective pronunciation and gesture). This sketch of the entire book's content does no justice to the rich expressiveness of Wilson's own language.

II

During the sixteenth century, English readers owned more Continental books than English books; books for scholars, such as text-books of rhetoric and logic, were mainly written in Latin and produced at the great European publishing centers of Amsterdam, Paris, Basel, and Lyons. One wonders if works like Jacobus Publicius' *Ars Oratoria* (Venice, 1490) or Albrecht von Eyb's *Margarita Poetica* (Basel, 1503) were known in the England of Henry VIII. Our knowledge whether these Continental books were owned by Englishmen is fragmentary and impressionistic despite the admirable work of Sears Jayne in *Library Catalogues of the English Renaissance* (1956), since Jayne was handicapped by numerous vague, imprecise entries in the catalogues. The inventory of Abraham Tilman's books, made in 1589, contains such vague entries, impossible to identify, as "A Spanish Bible" and "Florales in greeke." Also, apart from Sir Robert Cotton's famous private library in Westminster, which got under way during the 1590's and was soon opened to Sir Francis Bacon and other qualified readers, there was no great central library in England during the sixteenth century with a surviving general or union catalogue which might afford us some accurate notion of what Continental books were available in Tudor England.

Wilson's *Rhetorique*, then, must have been in competition with the numerous Latin rhetorics which Continental dealers supplied to the English market. But it had several advantages: it was written in the vernacular and hence was presumably easier to read than a Latin text. Furthermore, its frequent illustrations drawn from English history and culture helped to domesticate its Ciceronian precepts and render the text attractive to Elizabethan readers. For instance, Wilson, with good Tudor prejudice, remarks that Richard III was "cruell of heart, ambiciouse by nature, enuiouse of mynde, a depe dissembler, a close man for weightie matters" (fol. 95ᵛ). Finally, the simple fact that Wilson's rhetoric went through eight editions, in 1553, 1560, 1562, 1563, 1567, 1580, 1584, 1585, surely argues that his book enjoyed marked success. Yet it is not mentioned in Mark H. Curtis, *Oxford and Cambridge in Transition: 1558-1642* (1959).

Although a good deal of rhetoric was doubtless taught at Oxford and Cambridge, and certainly practised in the constant disputations and determinations which formed the principal academic exercise in the arts course, rhetoric was generally regarded in Tudor England as a school rather than a university subject. Thus we find that T. W. Baldwin in his massive survey of Elizabethan school education, *William Shakespeare's Smalle Latine & Lesse Greeke* (1944), discusses Wilson's rhetoric in company with a number of school rhetorics. But this seems a mistaken classification because in his illustrative material Wilson deals primarily with lawyers and their task of pleading in courts, and secondly with preachers and their task of delivering sermons in churches. This substance is precisely what we should expect from Wilson since he was a lawyer as well as a militant Protestant. His book is not addressed to ushers and tutors or to schoolboys who provided the audience for whom senior schoolmasters composed hundreds of Renaissance rhetorics in Western Europe. Nor do we know if Wilson's book was prescribed reading at Oxford or Cambridge (the very title of a work such as the anonymous *Libellus sophistarum ad vsum Cantibrigiensium* of 1510; STC 15576, suggests that it was prescribed). Because of a paucity of reliable evidence, Craig R. Thompson's gracefully written *Universities in Tudor England* (1959) provides few specific facts about the actual content of the arts courses at those great universities, although the general outlines of the arts curriculum are sharply sketched. It is pleasant to speculate that Wilson's rhetoric was used by teachers and students of the common law at the Inns of Court in London. But we need not speculate about two essential facts: Wilson's rhetoric is a remarkable product of Tudor humanism as well as a book of permanent interest and information to generations of students of public address.

Through the kind permission of Dr. Stanley Pargellis, Newberry's Librarian, the basis for the present facsimile of the *editio princeps* of Wilson's *The Arte of Rhetorique* (STC 25799) is the copy donated to the Newberry Library by the late Professor Frederic Ives Carpenter. Mrs. Gertrude L. Woodward, the Custodian of Newberry's rare books, informs me that the donation was made in 1914 when Professor Carpenter was a Newberry trustee. The only modern edition of Wilson's book, that edited by G. H. Mair for the Oxford University Press in 1909 on the basis of a 1560 second edition rather than the first edition of 1553, has long been out of print. Mair was apparently under the misapprehension that the second edition represented a more complete version of Wilson's ideas: actually it merely adds a few pages of illustrations.

ROBERT HOOD BOWERS

University of Florida

A Table of Contents

The seconde Booke

The third Booke

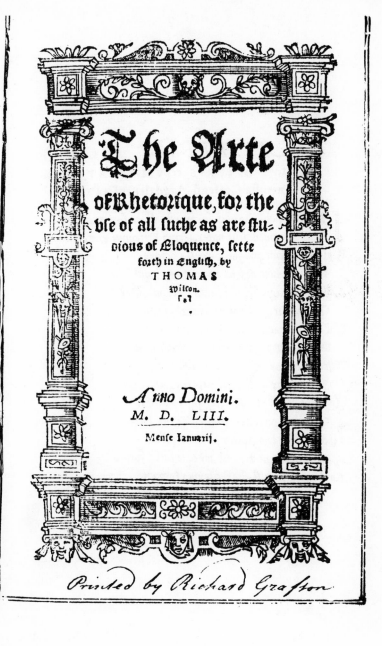

The Arte

of Rhetorique, for the
vse of all suche as are studious of Eloquence, sette
forth in English, by
THOMAS
Wilson.

Anno Domini.
M. D. LIII.

Mense Ianuarij.

Printed by Richard Grafton

GVALTERVS HAD-
DONVS D. IVRIS CIVILIS, ET OXO-
niensis Collegij Magdalenensis Præses.

R̔ητορικὴ, λογικὴ soror, est affata sororem:
   Quem didicit nuper, sermo Britannus erat.
R̔ητορικὴ tacuit, magno perculsa dolore:
   Nam nondum nostro nouerat ore loqui.
Audijt hæc, λογικῆς, Vuilsonus forte, magister
   Qui fuerat, nostros addiderat q; sonos:
R̔ητορικὴ mutam, uerbis solatus amicis
   Se uocat, & rogitat num esse Britanna uelit.
Deijciens oculos respondit uelle libenter,
   Sed se, qua possit, non reperire, uia.
Ipse uias (inquit) tradam, legesq; loquendi:
   Quomodò perfectè uerba Britanna loces.
Liberat ille fidem, nostro sermone politur
   R̔ητορικὴ, nostra est utraque facta soror.
Anglia, nobilium si charus sermo sororum
   Est tibi, sermonis charus & author erit.

NICOLAI VDALLI IN OPERIS COM=
mendationem Tetrastichon.

VT Logice, lingua nos est affata Britanna
    Sic modo Rhetorice uerba Britanna sonat.
Vtraq; nempe soror, patrem cognoscit eundem
Anglia iam natis mater, utramq; fouet.

ROBERTI HILERMII
IN RHETORICEM THO=
mæ Vuilsoni, Epigramma.

ANglia serua diu, & quondam uexata Tyrannis,
    Libera nunc regnat, Rege potita pio:
Et cui iura dedit Roma imperiosa tot annos,
    Legibus ipsa suis uiuit, & imperijs.
Libertas igitur, regniq; antiqua potestas
    Reddita nunc Anglis, quos rigat Oceanus.
Quod licet egregium, & decus immortale parenti
    Conciliet magno: Rexq; Edoarde tibi:
Gloria prisca tamen gentis, uel nomen auitum
    Hoc est: nam fuerant libera sceptra tuis.
At quòd barbaries uestris nunc exulat oris,
    Pulsaq; rusticitas his dominata prius:
Hoc opus, hoc uestrum est, uobis per secula famam
    Quod dabit, & uestrum nomen ad astra feret.
Barbara gens siquidem, gemino sub Principe tali
    Artibus enituit nobilitata bonis:
Moribus & compta est laudandis arte magistra:
    AEditaq; ingenij sunt documenta uirûm.

Viuida

Viuida teſtantur uigilem monimenta laborem,
  Scriptaq́; tot, nulla quæ moritura die.
Exemplum mihi ſit de tot Scriptoribus, unus
  (Namq́; ommes celebres nemo referre queat,)
Vuilſonus, patrio ſub quo ſermone magiſtro,
  Pierides Muſæ perdidicêre loqui.
Cui tamen haud ſatis eſt, quod cum ratione loquantur,
  Ni quoq́; concinné, non putat eſſe ſatis.
Atq́; ob id addubitans, ne operi pars ulla deeſſet,
  Hiſce dedit Muſis, hanc modo Rhetoricem.
O quanta his ſcriptis, linguæ, regniq́; futura eſt
  Maieſtas, & honos : ſi fauor adfuerit.

THOMAS VVILSONVS IN
Anglicam Rhetoricen.

A Nglia ſi doceat, quod Græcia docta : quid obſtat
     Quo minus ex Anglis Anglia, uera ſciat.
Non (quia Græca potes, uel calles uerba Latina)
  Doctus es, aut ſapiens : ſed quia uera uides.
Aurea ſecreto tegitur ſapientia ſenſu.
  Abdita ſenſa teres Anglus? es ergo ſciens.
Sed mea Rhetoricen nequeat cûm lingua polire:
  Cui uacat, hoc unum quod ualet, oro u.lit.

To the right ho-

norable Lorde, John Dudley, Lorde
Lisle, Earle of Warwike, and maister
of the horse to the kynges maiestie: your
assured to commaund Thomas
Wilson.

Hen Pyrrhus Kynge of
the Epirotes made battayle a-
gaynste the Romaynes, & could
neither by force of Armes, nor
yet by anye Policye wynne certayne stronge holdes: he vsed cō-
munely to send one Cineas (a no
ble Oratour, and sometimes scholer to Demosthenes) to perswade with the Capitaynes & people that were in them, that they shoulde yelde vp
the sayde holde or townes without fyght or resi-
staunce. And so it came to passe, that through the
pithye eloquence of this noble Oratoure, diuers
stronge Castels and Fortresses were peaceablye
geuen vp into the handes of Pirrhus, whyche he
shoulde haue founde verye harde and tedious to
wynne by the sworde. And this thinge was not
Pirrhus himselfe ashamed in his commune talke
to the prayse of the sayde Oratoure, openlye to
confesse: allegynge that Cineas throughe the e-
loquence of his tongue, wanne moe Cityes vnto
him, then euer him selfe shoulde els haue bene a-
ble by force to subdue. Good was that Oratour

A.i.   which

whiche coulde do so muche: ✝ wise was that king
which woulde vse suche a meane. For if the worthines of eloquēce may moue vs, what worthier
thing can there be, thē with a word to winne cities ✝ whole coūtries: If profite may perswade,
what greater gayne can we haue, then withoute
blondshed to achiue a conquest: If pleasure may
prouoke vs, what greater delite do we know, thē
to se a whole multitude with the onely talke of a
man rauished ✝ drawen whiche waye him liketh
best to haue them: Boldly then may J aduenture
and without feare steppe forthe to offer that vnto your Lordeshyppe, whiche for the dignitye is
so excellente, and for the vse so necessarye: that no
man oughte to be withoute it, whiche either shall
beare rule ouer manye, or muste haue to do wyth
matters of a Realme . Consideringe therfore
your Lordshyps hyghe estate, ✝ worthy callyng,
J knowe nothyng more sittynge wyth your honoure, then to the gyfte of good reason and vnderstandynge, wherwith we see you notably endued, to ioyne the perfection of Eloquente vtteraunce. And because that aswell by your Lordeshyppes moste tender imbracynge of all suche as
be learned, as also by your right studious exerci-
ses, you do euidently declare, not onely what estimation you haue of all learnynge and excellente
qualities ingenerall, but also what a speciall desyre and affection you beare to eloquence: J therfore commende to youre Lordeshyppes tuition
and patronage, thys traictise of Rhethorique, to
the

The Epistle.

the ende that both ye maye get some furtheraũce
by the same, & J also be discharged of my faithe.
full promyse this laste yere made vnto you.
For where as it pleased you emonge other talke
of learnynge, earnestlye to wysche that ye myghte
one daye see the Preceptes of Rhetorique sette
forthe by me in Englysche, as J hadde erste done
the Rules of Logique: hauynge in my Countrey
thys laste Somer a quiet time of vacation wyth
the ryghte worshypfull sir Edwarde Dymmoke
knyghte: J traueyled so muche as my leasure
myghte serue therunto, not onelye to declare my
good harte to the satisfiynge of youre requeste in
that behalfe, but also throughe that your mocion
to helpe the towardnes of some other, not so well
furnished as your Lordeshyppe is .   For as
touchinge your selfe, by the tyme that perfect experience of manifolde and weyghtye matters of
the commune weale, shall haue encreased the eloquence, whyche alreadye dothe naturallye flowe
in you: J doubt nothing but that you wil so farre
be better then this my boke, that J shal not onelye blowsche to chaïenge you for a Scholer, in
the Arte of Rhetorique, by me rudelye sette forthe: but also be dryuen to sette this simple Traictise to your Lordshyppe to Schole, that it may
learne Rhetorique of youre daylye talke, fyn-
dynge you suche an Oratoure in your speach, as
greate Clarckes do declare what an Oratoure
shoulde be.

A.ii.   Jn

The Epiſtle.

In the meane ſeaſon I ſhall ryghte humblye beſeche your good Lordſhippe ſo to be a Patrone and defendoure of theſe my Laboures to you dedicated: as I ſhal be a continuall peticioner vnto almyghtye God for your preſeruation, and longe continuaunce.

❡ Eloquence first

geuen by God, after loste by man,
and laste repayred by God
agayne.

An (in whom is poured the breathe of lyfe) was made at hys firste beinge an euerliuynge Creature, vnto the likenes of God, endued with reason, and appoynted Lorde ouer all other thinges liuing. But after the fall of our firste father, Sinne so crepte in, that our knowledge was muche darke= ned, and by corruption of this oure fleshe, mans reason and entendement were bothe ouerwhelmed. At what time God beinge sore greued with the folye of one man, pitied of his mere goodnesse, the whole state and posteritie of mankinde. And therfore (wher as throughe the wicked suggestion of our ghostelye enemye, the ioyfull fruition of Goddes glo= rye was altogether loste:) it pleased our heauenly father to repayre mankynde of hys free mercye, and to graunte an e= uerliupnge enheritaunce vnto all suche as woulde by con= stante fayth seeke earnestlye thereafter. Longe it was ere that man knewe himselfe, beinge destitute of Gods grace, so that al thinges wared sauage, the earth vntilled, societye neglected, Goddes will not knowen, man againste manne, one agaynste another, and all agaynste order. Some liued by spoyle, some like brute Beastes grased vpon the ground, some wente naked, some romed lyke woodolses, none did a= nye thing by reason, but most did what they could, by man= hode. None almoste considered the euerliupnge God, but all liued moste communely after their owne luste. By death they thoughte that all thinges ended, by life they loked for none other liuynge. None remembred the true obseruati= on of wedlocke, none tendered the education of their chyl= dren, lawes were not regarded, true dealinge was not once

The Preface.

vſed. ffoz vertue, vpce bare place, foz right & equitie, might
vſed aucthozitie. And therfoze where as man thzough reaſ
ſon might haue vſed ozder, manne thzoughe follpe fell into
errourc. And thus foz lacke of ſkill, and foz wante of grace,
eupll ſo pzcuapled, that the Deupll was mooſte eſtemed, and
GOD either almoſt vnknowen emonge theim all, oz
elles nothinge feared emonge ſo manpe. Therefoze euen
nowe when man was thus paſte all hope of amendemente,
God ſtill tendering his owne wozkemanſhip, ſtirred vp his
fapthfull and elect, to perſwade with reaſon, all men to ſo=
cietpe. And gaue his appoputed miniſters knowlcdge bothe
to ſe the natures of men, and alſo graunted them the gift of
vtteraunce, that they mpghte wpth eaſe wpnne folke at
their will, and frame theim bp reaſon to all good ozder.

And therefoze, where as Menne lpued Bzutpſhlpe
in open feldes, hauing neither houſe to ſhzoude them in, noz
attpze to clothe their backes, noz pet anpe regarde to ſeeke
their beſt auaple: theſe appopnted of God called theim to=
gether bp vtteraunce of ſpeache, and perſwaded with them
what was good, what was badde, and what was gainefull
foz mankpnde. And althoughe at firſte, the rude coulde
hardelie learne, & either foz ſtraungenes of the thing, would
not gladlpe recepue the offer, oz els foz lacke of knowelcdge
could not percepue the goodnes: pet being ſomewhat dzawe
and delighted with the pleaſauutnes of reaſon, & the ſwete=
nes of vtterauce: after a certaine ſpace, thei became thzough
nurture and good aduiſement, of wilde, ſober: of cruel, gen=
tle: of foles, wiſe: and of beaſtes, men. Suche foze hath the
tongue, and ſuch is the power of eloqucnce and reaſon, that
moſt men are fozced euen to pelde in that, whiche moſt ſtan=
deth againſte their will. And therfoze the Poetes do fepne
that Hercules being a man of greate wiſdome, had all men
lincked together bp the eares in a chaine, to dzaw them and
leade them euen as he luſted. ffoz his witte was ſo greate,
his tongue ſo eloquente, & his experience ſuche, that no one
man was able to withſtand his reaſon, but euerpe one was
rather dziuen to do that whiche he woulde, and to wil that
whpch

The Preface.

whiche he did, agreing to his aduile both in word & worke,
in all that euer they were able.

Neither can I lee that menne coulde haue bene broughte
by anye other meanes to lyue together in felowlhyppe of
life, to mayntayne Cities, to deale trulye, and willyngelye
to obeye one another, if menne at the firlte hadde not by Art
and eloquence perlwaded that, which they ful oft found out
by reaſon. for what manne I praye you beinge better able
to maintayne him ſelfe by valeante courage, then by liuing
in baſe ſubiection: would not rather loke to rule like a lord,
then to lyue lyke an vnderlynge: if by reaſon he were not
perlwaded that it behoueth euerye man to lyue in his owne
vocation, and not to ſeke anye hygher rowme, then whereunto he was at the firſt appoynted? who woulde digge and
delue from morne till euening? who woulde trauaile and
toyle with the ſweate of his browes? yea, who woulde for
his kynges pleaſure aduenture and haſarde his life, if witte
hadde not ſo wonne men, that they thought nothing more
nedefull in this world, nor anye thing wherunto they were
more bounden: then here to liue in their dutye, and to traine
their whole lyfe accordynge to their callynge. Therfore
where as menne are in manye thynges weake by Nature,
and ſubiecte to much infirmitye: I thinke in this one point
they paſſe all other Creatures liuynge, that they haue the
gift of ſpeache and reaſon.

And emonge all other, I thinke him moſt worthye fame,
and emongeſt menne to be taken for halfe a God, that therin dothe chiefelye, and aboue all other, excell menne, wherin
men do excell beaſtes. for he that is emonge the reaſonable,
of all moſte reaſonable, and emonge the wittye, of all moſte
wittye, and emonge the eloquente, of all mooſte eloquente:
him thincke I emonge all menne, not onelye to be taken for
a ſinguler manne, but rather to be counted for halfe a God.
for in ſekynge the excellencye hereof, the ſoner he draweth
to perfection, the nygher he commeth to GOD who is
the chiefe wiſdome, and therfore called God, becauſe he is
moſt wiſe, or rather wiſdome it ſelfe.

A.iij.

Nowe

The Preface.

Nowe then seinge that God geueth his heauenlye grace vnto all suche as call vnto him with stretched handes, and humble harte, neuer wantynge to those, that wante not to them selues: I purpose by his grace and especial assistence, to set foorthe preceptes of eloquence, and to shewe what obseruation the wise haue vsed in handeling of their matters, that the vnlearned by seinge the practise of other, may haue some knowledge them selues, and learne by their neyghbours deuise, what is necessarye for them selues in their owne case.

what is Rhetorique.

Þeto?ique is an art to set furthe bp vtteraunce of wo?des, matter at large, o? (as Cicero doeth saie) it is a learned, o? rather an artificiall declaracion of the mynde, in the handelyng of any cause, called in contencion, that maie th?ough reason largelp be discussed.

¶The matter whereupon an O?atour must speake.

ꟶ O?ato? muste be able to speake fullp of all those qu+stions, whiche by lawe and mannes o?dinaunce are enacted, and appopnuted fo? the vse and p?ofite of man, suche as are thought apte fo? the tongue to set fo?ward. Now Astronomie is rather learned by demonstracion, then taught by any greate vtteraunce. A?ithmetique smallp nedeth the vse of eloquence, seepng it maie be had wholp bp noumb?yng onelp. Geometrie rather asketh a good square, then a cleane flowpng tongue, to set out the arte. Therfo?e an O?ato?s p?ofession, is to speake onelp, of all suche matters as maie largelp be exp+unded, fo? mannes behoue, and maie with muche grace be set out, fo? all men to heare them.

Rhetorique oc cupied aboute all lawes, concernyng man.

Questions of two so?tes.

¶Of Questions.

Erp question, o? demaunde in thynges, is of two so?tes. Either it is an infinite question, and without ende, o? els it is definite, and comp?ehended within some ende.

Those questions are called infinite, whiche generallp are p?opounded, withoute the comp?ehension of tyme, place, and person, o? anp suche like: that is to saie, when no certain thyng is named, but onelp woo?des are generallp spoken. As thus, whether it be best to marie, o? to liue single. Whiche is better, a courtiers life, o? a scholers life.

Questions infinite.

Those questions are called definite, whiche set furthe a matter, with the appopntment, and nampng of place, time and persone. As thus. Whether now it be best here in Englande, fo? a P?ieste to Marie, o? to liue single. Whether

Questions definite.

a.i. it

The arte of Rhetorique.

it were mete for the kynges maiestie, that now is, to marie
with a ſtraūger, or to mary with one of his awn ſubiectes.

**Queſtions de-
finite, belong
properly to an
Orator.** Now the definite queſtion (as the whiche concerneth ſome
one perſone) is moſte agreyng to the purpoſe of an Orator
conſideryng particuler matters in the Lawe, are euer de-
bated betwixte certain perſones, the one affirmyng for his
parte, and the other denyyng, as faſt again for his parte.

**Queſtions in-
finite, proper
vnto Logiciās** Thynges generally ſpoken without al circumſtaunces,
are more proper vnto the Logiciā, who talketh of thynges
vniuerſally, without reſpect of perſone, time, or place. And
yet notwithſtandyng, Tullie doeth ſaie, that whoſoeuer
will talke of a particuler matter, muſt remēber that within theſame alſo, is comprehended a generall. As for example. If I ſhall aſke this queſtion, whether it be lawfull for
Willyam Conqueroure to inuade Englande, and wynne
it by force of armour, I muſt alſo conſider this, whether it
be lawfull for any man, to vſurpe power, or it be not lawfull. That if the greater cannot be borne withall, the leſſe
cannot be neither. And in this reſpecte, a generall queſtion
agreeth well to an Orators profeſſion, and ought well to
be knowen, for the better furtheraunce of his matter, notwithſtandyng the particuler queſtiō, is euer called in con-
trouerſie, and the generall onely thereupon conſidered, to
comprehende and compaſſe theſame, as the whiche is more
generall.

¶ The ende of Rethorique.

Three thynges are required of an Orator.

{ To teache.
{ To delight.
{ And to perſwade.

**Orators boūd
to performe
thre thynges.**

Irſt therefore an Orator muſte labour to tell his
tale, that the hearers maie well knowe what he
meaneth, and vnderſtande him wholy, the whiche
he ſhall with eaſe do, if he vtter his mind in plain
**Plain wordes
proper vnto
an Oratour.** wordes, ſuche as are vſually receiued, and tell it orderly,
without goyng aboute the buſſhe. That if he doe not this,
he ſhall neuer do the other. For what manne can be delited

C3

oz pet be perſwaded, with the onely hearyng of thoſe thyn=
ges, whiche he knoweth not what thei meane. The tongue
is ozdeined to expzeſſe the mynde, that one mighte vnder=
ſtande anothers meanyng: Nowe what auaileth to ſpeake,
when none can tell, what the ſpeaker meaneth? Therefoze
Phauozinus the Philoſophier (as Gellius telleth ỹ tale)
did hit a pong man ouer the thumbes, very handſomely foz
vſyng ouer olde, and ouer ſtraunge woozdes. Sirha (ϙ he)
when our old great aunceſters and graundſires wer aliue
thei ſpake plainly in their mothers tongue, ⁊ vſed old lan=
guage, ſuche as was ſpoke then at the buildyng of Rome.
But pou talke me ſuche Latin, as though pou ſpake with
them euen now, that were two oz thze thouſande peres a=
go, and onely becauſe pou would haue no man, to vnder=
ſtand what pou ſaie. Now wer it not better foz the a thou=
ſand fold (thou fooliſhe fellowe) in ſekyng to haue thy de=
ſire, to holde thy peace, and ſpeake nothyng at all? foz then
by that meanes, fewe ſhould knowe what were thy mea=
nyng. But thou ſaieſt, the olde antiquitee doeth like thee
beſt, becauſe it is good, ſobze, ⁊ modeſt. Ah, liue man as thei
did befoze thee, and ſpeake thy mynde now, as menne do at
this daie. And remember that, whiche Ceſar ſaith, beware
as long as thou liueſt, of ſtraunge woozdes, as thou woul=
deſt take hede and eſchewe greate rockes in the Sea.

The next parte that he hath to plaie, is to chere his ge=
ſtes, and to make the take pleaſure, with hearyng of thyn=
ges wittely deuiſed, and pleaſauntly ſet furthe. Therfoze
euery Ozatoz ſhould earneſtly laboure to file his tongue,
that his woozdes maie ſlide with eaſe, and that in his deli=
ueraunce, he maie haue ſuche grace, as the ſound of a lute,
oz any ſuche inſtrument doeth geue. Then his ſentencies
muſt be well framed, and his woozdes aptly vſed, through=
out the whole diſcourſe of his Ozacion.

Thirdly, ſuche quickneſſe of witte muſt be ſhewed, and
ſuche pleaſaunt ſawes ſo well applied, that the eares maie
finde muche delite, whereof I will ſpeake largely, when
I ſhall entreate of mouyng laughter. And aſſuredly no=
thyng is moze nedefull, then to quicken theſe heauie loden

a.if.   wittes

A Philoſophi
ers wittie ſai=
yng to a pong
manne, that
ſoughte to
ſpeake darke
language.

Ozatozs muſte
bſe delightful
woozdes, and
ſayynges.

wittes of ours, and muche to cherishe these our lompishe and vnweldie natures, for excepte menne finde delight, thei will not long abide: delight theim, and wynne them: werie theim, and you lose theim for euer. And that is *Preachers not* the reason, that menne commonly tary the ende of a merie *so diligently* plaie, and cannot abide the halfe hearyng of a sower chec= *heard, as common plaiers.* kyng Sermon. Therefore, euen these auncient preachers, must now and then plaie the fooles in the pulpite, to serue *Preachers must* the tickle eares of their fleetyng audience, or els thei are *sometymes be merie, when thei speake to the people.* like some tymes to preache to the bare walles, for though the spirite bee apte, and our will proue, yet our fleshe is so heauie, and humours so ouerwhelme vs, that wee cannot without refreshyng, long abide to heare any one thyng. Thus we se, that to delight is nedefull, without the whi= che, weightier matters will not be heard at all, and there= fore hym cunne I thanke, that bothe can & will euer, myn= *Delityng* gle swete, emong the sower, be he Preacher, Lawyer, yea, *nedefull.* or Cooke either hardely, when he dresseth a good dishe of *Scurrilitie* meate: now I nede not tell that scurrilitie, or Alehouse ie= *odious.* styng, would bee thought odious, or grosse mirthe would be deamed madnesse: consideryng that euen the meane wit= ted doe knowe that already, and as for other, that haue no witte, thei will neuer learne it, therefore God spede them. Now when these twoo are dooen, he muste perswade, and *Affeccions must* moue the affeccions of his hearers in suche wise, that thei *be mouer.* shalbe forced to yelde vnto his saiyng, wherof(because the matter is large, and maie more aptly bee declared, when I shall speake of Amplificacion)I wil surceace to speake any thyng therof at this tyme.

By what meanes Eloquence is attained.

Firste nedefull it is that he, whiche desireth to ex= cell in this gift of Oratorie, and longeth to proue an eloquent man, must naturally haue a wit, and an aptnesse thereunto: then must he to his boke, & learne to be well stored with knowlege, that he maie be a= ble to minister matter, for all causes necessarie. The which when he hath gotte plentifully, he muste vse muche exer= cise, bothe in writyng, and also in speakyng. For though he haue

haue a wit and learnyng together, yet shal thei bothe litle auaile without much practise. What maketh the Lawyer to haue suche vtteraunce? Practise. What maketh the Prea= cher to speake so roundly? Practise. Yea, what maketh wo= men go so fast awaie with their woordes? Marie practise I warraunt you. Therfore in all faculties, diligent practise, and earnest exercise, are the onely thynges, that make men proue excellent. Many men knowe the arte very well, and be in all poynctes throughly grounded, & acquainted with the preceptes, and yet it is not their hap to proue eloquent And the reason is, that eloquēce it self, came not vp first by the arte, but the arte rather was gathered vpon eloquēce. For wise menne seyng by muche obseruacion, and diligent practise, the compasse of diuerse causes, compiled thereupō preceptes and lessons, worthie to bee knowen and learned of all men. Therefore before arte was inuented, eloquence was vsed, and through practise made parfecte, the whiche in all thynges is a souereigne meane, most highly to excell.

Practise ma= keth all thyn= ges perfect.

Rhetorique firste made by wise men, and not wise men firste made by Rhetorique.

Now before we vse either to write, or speake eloquently we must dedicate our myndes wholly, to folowe the moste wise and learned menne, and seke to fashion, aswell their speache and gesturyng, as their wit or endityng. The whi= che when we earnestly mynde to do, we cannot but in time appere somewhat like theim. For if thei that walke muche in the sōne, and thinke not of it, are yet for the moste part sonne burnt, it cannot be but that thei, whiche wittyngly and willyngly trauaile to counterfecte other, muste nedes take some colour of theim, and be like vnto theim, in some one thyng or other, accordyng to the Prouerbe, by compa= nyng with the wise, a man shall learne wisedome.

Imitacion or folowyng the waies of wise men, is nede= full.

¶To what purpose this arte is set furthe.

TO this purpose and for this vse, is the arte com= piled together, by the learned and wise men, that thosè whiche are ignorant, might iudge of the ler= ned; and labour (when tyme should require) to fo= low their workes accordyngly. Again, the art helpeth well to dispose and order matters of our awne inuencion, the whiche we may folowe, aswell in speakyng, as in writyng

Rhetorique, to what purpose it serueth.

a.iii.   for

The arte of Rhetorique.

Arte, surer guide, then nature.

for though many by nature without art, haue proued wor thie menne, yet is arte a surer guide, then nature, consideryng we se as liuely by the art, what we do, as though we red a thyng in writtyng, wheras natures doynges are not so open to all men. Aga.n, those that haue good wittes, by nature, shall better encrease theim by arte, and the blunte also shalbe whetted through art, that want nature to help them forward.

¶Fiue thynges to be considered in an Oratour.

A   My one that will largely handle any matter, muste fasten his mynde, first of all vpon these fiue especial poynctes that folowe, and learne theim euery one.

Orators must haue fiue thinges to make them perfect.

$\left\{ \begin{array}{l} \text{i. Inuencion of matter.} \\ \text{ij. Disposicion of the same.} \\ \text{iij. Elocucion.} \\ \text{iiij. Memorie.} \\ \text{v. Utteraunce.} \end{array} \right.$

Inuencion, what it is.

HE findyng out of apte matter, called otherwise Inuencion, is a searchyng out of thynges true, or thynges likely, the whiche maie reasonably sette furth a matter, and make it appere probable. The places of Logique, geue good occasion to finde out plentifull matter. And therefore thei that will proue any cause and seke onely to teache thereby the truthe, muste searche out the places of Logique, and no doubte thei shall finde muche plentie. But what auaileth muche treasure and apt matter, if man cánot apply it to his purpose. Therefore in the seconde place is mencioned, the settelyng or orderyng of thynges inuented for this purpose, called in Latine,

Disposicion, what it is.

Dispositio, the whiche is nothyng els, but an apt bestowyng, and orderly placyng of thynges, declaryng where euery argument shalbe sette, and in what maner euery reason shalbe applied, for confirmacion of the purpose.

But yet what helpeth it though we can finde good reasons, and knowe howe to place theim, if we haue not apte wordes, and picked sentences, to commēde the whole matter

ter.Therefore this poynct must nedes folowe, to beautifie
the cause,the whiche beyng called Elocucion, is an appli= *Elocucion,*
yng of apte woordes and sentéces to the matter,founde out *what it is.*
to confirme the cause. When all these are had together, it
auaileth litle,if manne haue no Memorie to contein theim.
The Memorie therefore must be cherished, the whiche is a *Memorie,*
fast holdyng, bothe of matter and woordes couched toge= *what it is.*
ther,to confirme any cause.

Be it now that one haue all these.iiij, yet if he want the
fift,all the other dooe litle profite.For though a manne can
finde out good matter,and good woordes,though he canne
handsomely set them together, and cary them very well a=
waie in his mynde,yet it is to no purpose, if he haue no vt=
teraunce,when he should speake his minde,and shewe men
what he hath to saie.Vtteraunce therefore is a framyng of *Pronunciatió*
the voyce,countenaúce,and gesture,after a comely maner. *what it is.*

Thus we se that euery one of these must go together,to
make a perfecte Oratoure, and that the lacke of one, is an
hynderaunce of the whole,and that aswell all maie be wa=
tyng,as one,if we loke to haue an absolute Oratour.

¶There are.vii.partes in euery Oracion.

⎧ i. The enteraunce or beginnyng.   *Oracions in*
⎪ ij. The Narracion.   *generall,con=*
⎨ iij. The Proposicion.   *sist vpon seuen*
⎪ iiij.The diuisió or seuerall partyng of thynges *partes,*
⎨ v. The Confirmacion.
⎪ vi. The Confutacion.
⎩ vii.The Conclusion.

He Enteraunce or beginnyng, is the former part *Enteraunce,*
of the Oracion, whereby the will of the standers *what it is,*
by,or of the Iudge is sought for, and required to
heare the matter.

The Narració, is a plain and manifest poynctyng of the *Narration.*
matter,and an euident settyng furthe of all thynges, that
belong vnto the same,with a brief rehersall,grounded vpon
some reason.

The

The arte of Rhetorique.

Propoſicion.   The Propoſicion is a pithie ſentence, comprehendyng in a ſmale roume, the ſome of the whole matter.

Diuiſion.   The diuiſion is an openyng of thynges, wherin we agree and reſt vpon, and wherein we ſticke, and ſtande in trauerſe ſhewyng what we haue to ſaie, in our awne behalfe.

Confirmacion.   The Confirmacion, is a declaraciō of our awne reaſons with aſſured and conſtaunt profes.

Confutacion.   The Confutacion, is a diſſolupng or wippng awaie, of all ſuche reaſons as make againſt vs.

Concluſion.   The Concluſion is a clarkely gatheryng of the matter, ſpoken before, and a lappyng vp of it altogether.

Now becauſe in euery one of theſe, greate hede ought to be had, and muche arte muſt be vſed, to content and like all parties: I purpoſe in the ſecond boke to ſet furthe at large euery one of theſe, that bothe we maie knowe in all partes, what to folowe, and what to eſchewe. And firſt when tyme ſhalbe to talke of any matter, I would aduiſe euery man, to conſider the nature of the cauſe ſelf, that the rather he might frame his whole Oracion thereafter.

    Euery matter is conteined in one of theſe. iiii.

Matters i ge-   Ither it is an honeſt thyng, whereof we ſpeake, or
neral, ſtand in   els it is filthy and vile, or els betwixte bothe, and
iiii. poynctes.   doubtfull what to bee called, or els it is ſome triflyng matter, that is of ſmall weight.

Matters i. honeſt.   That is called an honeſt matter, when either wee take in hande ſuche a cauſe, that all menne would maintein, or els gainſaie ſuche a cauſe, that no man can well like.

Matters, ii. filthie.   Then do we hold and defende a filthy matter, whē either wee ſpeake againſt our conſcience in an euill matter, or els withſtande an vpright truthe.

Matters, iii. doubtfull.   The cauſe then is doubtfull, when the matter is half ho- neſt, and halfe vnhoneſt.

Matters, iiii. trifelyng.   Suche are triflyng cauſes, whē there is no weight in thē as if one ſhould phantaſy, to praiſe a Goſe, before any other beaſt liuyng (as I knowe who did) or of fruict to commende nuttes cheſly, as Ouid did, or the feuer quartaine, as Pha- uorinus did, or the Gnatte, as Virgill did, or the battaill of Frogges as Homere did, or diſpraiſe beardes, or commende ſhauen

ſhauen heddes.

¶Good hede to bee taken at the firſte, vpon the
handelyng of any matter in Iudgement.

NOT onely it is neceſſarie to knowe, what maner
of cauſe wee haue taken in hande, when wee firſte
enter vpon any matter, but alſo it is wiſedome to
conſider the tyme, the place, the man for whom we
ſpeake, the man againſt whom we ſpeake, the matter whereof we ſpeake, and the iudges before whom we ſpeake, the rea
ſons that beſt ſerue to further our cauſe, and thoſe reaſons
alſo, that maie ſeme ſomewhat to hynder our cauſe, and in
no wiſe to vſe any ſuche at all, or els warely to mitigate by
proteſtacion, the euill that is in them, and alwaies to vſe
whatſoeuer can bee ſaied, to wynne the chief hearers good
willes, and perſwade theim to our purpoſe. If the cauſe go
by fauour, and that reaſon cannot ſo muche auaile, as good
wil ſhalbe able to do: or els if mouyng affecciõs can do more
good, then bryngyng in of good reaſons, it is meete alwaies
to vſe that waie, whereby we maie by good helpe, get the o-
uer hand. That if mine aduerſaries reaſons, by me beyng cõ
futed, ſerue better to help forward my cauſe, then mine awn
reaſons confirmed, can be able to doe good: I ſhould wholy
beſtowe my tyme, and trauaill to weaken and make ſlender,
all that euer he bryngeth with hym. But if I can with more
eaſe, proue myne awne ſaiynges, either with witneſſes, or
with wordes, then be able to cõfute his with reaſon, I muſt
labour to withdrawe mennes myndes, from myne aduerſaries foundacion, and require the wholy to herken vnto that
whiche I haue to ſaie, beyng of it ſelf ſo iuſt and ſo reaſonable, that none can rightly ſpeake againſt it, and ſhewe theim
that greate pitie it were, for lacke of the onely hearyng, that
a true matter, ſhould want true dealyng. Ouer and beſides
all theſe, there remain twoo leſſons, the which wiſemenne
haue alwaies obſerued, and therefore ought of all men, aſſuredly to be learned. The one is, that if any matter be laied a-
gainſt vs, whiche by reaſon can hardely bee auoyded, or the
whiche is ſo open, that none almoſte can deny, it were wiſedome in confutyng all the other reaſons, to paſſe ouer this

b.j. one

Circũſtaunces
neceſſary in al
cauſes to bee
noted.

Fauoure wyn-
nyng, and af-
feccions mo-
uyng, when
thei are moſte
neceſſarie.

Aduerſaries
reaſons, when
thei ſhuld beſt
be confuted.

Argumentes
who thei ſhuld
chiefly be vſed

Matters, hard
to auoide, ſhuld
alwaies bee
paſt ouer, as
though we ſaw
them not at al

one, as though we sawe it not, and therefore speake neuer a
worde of it.Or els if necessitie shall force a man to saie some

Good to bee bolde in moste daunger, if otherwise wee cannot escape.

what, he may make an outward bragge, as though there wer
no matter in it, euer so speakyng of it, as though he would
stande to the triall, makyng men to beleue, he would fight in
the cause, whe better it were (if necessitie so required) to run
clene awaie. And herein though a man do flie and geue place,
euermore the gladder, the lesse rauyng there is or stirryng in
this matter: yet he flieth wisely, and for this ende, that be=
yng fensed otherwise, & strongly appoynted, he maie take his
aduersary at the best aduauntage, or at the least, werie hym
with muche lingeryng, and make hym with oft suche fliyng,
to forsake his chief defence.

The other lesson is, that whereas we purpose alwaies to
haue the victorie, wee should so speake, that we maie labour

Better not to hurte a good matter by euil speach, then to further it by good talke.

rather not to hynder, or hurt our cause, then to seke meanes
to further it. And yet I speake not this, but that bothe these
are right necessarie, and eu=ry one that will doo good, muste
take peines in theim bothe, but yet notwithstandyng, it is a
fouler faulte a greate deale, for an Orator to be founde hur=
ting his awne cause, then it should turne to his rebuke, if he
had not furthered his whole entent. Therefore not onely is

warenesse in speakyng, and forbearyng to speake.

it wisedome, to speake so muche as is nedefull, but also it is
good reason, to leaue vnspoken so muche as is nedelesse, the
whiche although the wisest can do, and nede no teachyng, yet
these common wittes offende muche nowe and then, in this

The person be fore whom we speake, mustbe well marked.

behalfe. Some man beyng stirred, shall hurt more our cause
then twentie other. Tauntyng wordes before some menne,
will not be borne at all. Sharpe rebukyng of our aduersary
or frumpes geuen before some persones: cannot be sufferd at

Tyme must be obserued.

all. Yea, sometymes a man must not speake all that he kno=
weth, for if he doo, he is like to finde small fauour, although
he haue iuste cause to speake, and maie with reason declare
his mynde at large. And albeit that witlesse folke, can soner
rebuke that, whiche is fondly spoken, then redely praise that
whiche is wisely kept close, yet the necessitie of the matter,
must rather be marked, then the fonde iudgement of the peo
ple esteemed. What a fone saiyng were this? When a lawyer
                                                        shoulu

should take in hande a matter, concernyng life and death,
and another should aske how he hath sped, to hearetel that
the Lawyer, hath not onely cast awaie his cliét, but vndoen
hymself also, in speakyng thynges inconsideratly, as no
doubt it ofté happeneth, that wise men, and those also that
bee none euill men neither, maie vnwares speake thynges,
which afterward thei sore repent, & would cal backe again
with losse of a greate somme. Now what a foly it is, not to
remember the tyme and the men. Or who will speake that
whiche he knoweth will not be liked, if he purpose to finde
fauour at their handes, before whom he speaketh, what má
of reason will praise that before the Iudges, (before whom
he knoweth the determinacion of his cause resteth) whiche
the Iudges self cannot abide to heare spoken at all? Or
doeth not he muche hinder his awne matter, that wtthout
al curtesie or preface made, will largely speake euil of those
men, whom the hearers of his cause, tenderly doo fauour?
Or be it that there be some notable faulte in thyne aduersary, with whiche the Iudges also are infected, were it not
foly for thee, to charge thyne aduersary with the same. Cō-
sideryng the Iudges thereby maie thynke, thou speakest a-
gainst theim also, and so thou maiest perhappes, lose their
fauour in sekyng suche defence, made without all discrecion. And in framing reasons, to confirme the purpose, if any
be spoken plainly false, or els contrary to that, which was
spoken before, dooeth it not muche hynder a good matter?
Therefore in all causes, this good hede ought to bee had,
that alwaies we labour to do some good, in furtheryng of
our cause, or if we cannot so do, at the least that we doo no
harme at all.

⸿There are three kyndes of causes, or Oracions, whiche serue for euery matter

Nothyng can be handled by this arte, but the same Orations, or
is conteined, within one of these .iij. causes. Ei- causes of three
ther the matter consisteth in praise, or dispraise of kyndes.
a thyng, or els in consultyng, whether the cause
be profitable, or vnprofitable, or lastly, whether the matter
be right, or wrong. And yet this one thyng is to be learned

that in euery one of thefe foure caufes, thefe thzee feuerall
endes, maie euerp of them be conteined, in anp one of them.
And therfoze he that fhall haue caufe, to pzaife anp one bo=
dp, fhall haue iufte caufe to fpeake of iuftice, to entreate of
pzofite, and iopntlp to talke of one thpng with another.
But becaufe thefe thzee caufes, are commonlp and foz the
mofte part, feuerallp parted, J will fpeake of them, one af=
ter another, as thei are fette furthe bp wife mennes iudge=
mentes, # particularlp declare their propertics, all in ozder

Ozacion De=
monftratiue.

The Ozacion demonftratiue, ftandeth either in pzaife, oz
difpzaife of fome one man, oz of fome one thpng, oz of fome
one deede doen.

**The kynde Demonftratiue, where=
in chiefly it is occupied.**

Here are diuerfe thpnges, whiche are pzaifed, and
difpzaifed, as menne, Countreis, Citees, Places,
Beaftes, Hilles, Riuers, Houfes, Caftles, dedes
doen bp wozthp menne, and pollicies inuented bp
greate warriers, but mofte commonlp men are pzaifed, foz
diuerfe refpectes, befoze anp of the other thpnges are ta=
ken in hande.

Noble perfo=
nages, howe
thei fhould be
pzaifed.

Nowe in pzaifpng a noble perfonage, and in fettpng
furthe at large his wozthineffe, Quintilian geueth war=
npng, to vfe this thzefolded ozder.

To obferue thpnges.
- Befoze his life.
- In his life.
- After his death.

Befoze a mannes life, are confidered thefe places.

- The Realme.
- The Shire.
- The Toune.
- The Parentes.
- The Aunceftours.

In a mannes life, pzaife mufte be parted thzefolde.
That is to faie, into the giftes of good thpnges of
the mpnde, the bodp, and of fortune. Now the gif=
tes of the bodp, and of fortune, are not pzaife woz=
thp

thy, of their awne nature: but euen as thei are vsed, either to, or fro, so thei are either praised, or displaised. Giftes of the mynde, deserue the whole trumpe and sound commendacion aboue all other, wherein wee maie vse the rehersall of vertues, as thei are in order, and beginnyng at his infancie, tell all his doynges, till his last age.

The places whereof, are these.

- The birthe, and infancie.
- The childhode.
- The striplyng age, or spryng tide
- The mannes state.
- The olde age.
- The tyme of his departure, or deth

Wherunto are referred these.

- Whether the person be a man, or a woman
- The bryngyng vp, ye nurturyng, and the behauour of his life.
- To what study he taketh hymself vnto, what company he vseth, how he liueth.
- Prowesses doen, either abrode, or at home.
- His pollicies & wittie deuises in behoue of the publique wele
- Thynges that haue happened aboute his death.

Now to open al these places more largely, aswell those that are before a mannes life, as suche as are in his life, and after his death, that the reader maie further se the profite, I will do the best I can. The house wherof a noble personage came, declares the state and nature of his auncesters, his alliaunce, and his kynsfolke. So that suche worthy feactes, as thei haue heretofore doen, and al suche honors as thei haue had, for suche their good seruice, redowndes wholy to the encrease and

The house or auncestrie wherof a noble personage cometh

b.iij.   amplifiyng

The arte of Rhetorique.

amplifiyng of his honour, that is now liuyng.

ii. The realme. The Realme, declares the nature of the people. So that some Countrey brengeth more honor with it, then another doth. To be a Frenche manne, descendyng there of a noble house, is more honor then to be an Irishe manne: to bee an Englishe manne borne, is muche more honour, then to be a Scotte, because that by these men, worthy prowesses haue been dooen, and greater affaires by theim attempted, then haue been doen by any other.

iii. The Shire or Toune. The Shire or Toune helpeth somewhat, towardes the encrease of honour: As it is muche better, to bee borne in Paris, then in Picardie, in London, then in Lincolne. For that bothe the aire is better, the people more ciuill, and the wealth muche greater, and the menne for the moste parte more wise.

iiii. The sere or kynde. To bee borne a manchilde, declares a courage, grauitie, and constancie. To be borne a woman, declares weakenes of spirite, neshenes of body, and fikilnesse of mynde.

v. Educacion. Now for the bringing vp of a noble personage, his nurse must be considered, his plaie felowes obserued, his teacher and other his seruauntes, called in remembraunce. Howe euery one of these liued then, with whom thei haue liued afterwardes, and how thei liue now.

vi. Inclinacio of nature. By knowyng what he taketh hymself vnto, and wherin he moste deliteth, I maie commende hym for his learnyng, for his skill in the Frenche, or in the Italian, for his knowlege in Cosmographie: for his skill in the lawes, in the histories of all countreis, and for his gift of endityng. Again, I maie comende hym for plaiyng at weapons, for runnyng vpon a greate horse, for chargyng his staffe at the Tilte, for vautyng, for plaiyng vpon instrumentes, yea, and for paintyng, or drawyng of a platte, as in old tyme noble princes, muche delited therein.

vii Attemptes worthy. Prowesse doen, declare his seruice to the Kyng, and his countrey, either in withstandyng the outwarde enemie, or els in aswagyng the rage of his awne countreymē at home.

viii. His wise counsaill, and good aduise geuen, settes furthe the goodnesse of his witte.

At

At the tyme of his departyng,his sufferaunce of all sick= Tyme of ir.
nesse,may muche commende his worthinesse.As his strong departing this
harte,and cherefull pacience euen to the ende, cannot wāt worlde.
greate praise . The loue of all men towardes hym, and the
lamentyng generally for his lacke,helpe well moste highly
to set furthe his honour.

After a mannes death,are considered his tombe,his cote After depar=
armour set vp,and all suche honours , as are vsed in fune= ture.
ralles. If any one liste to put these preceptes in practise,he
maie doo,as hym liketh best . And surely I do thynke, that
nothyng so muche furthereth knowlege,as daiely exercise,
and enuryng our selfes to do that in dede,whiche we know
in woorde. And because examples geue greate lighte,after
these preceptes are set furthe, I will commende two noble
gentlemen,Henry Duke of Suffolk,and his brother lorde Duke of Suf=
Charles Duke with hym. folke,and lord
Charles.

C An example of commendyng a noble personage.

Etter or more wisely can none do,then thei which
neuer bestowe praise , but vpon those that best de=
serue praise, rather myndyng discretly , what thei
ought to dooe,then vainly deuisyng what thei best
can doo,sekyng rather to praise menne,suche as are founde
worthy , then curiously findyng meanes to praise matters,
suche as neuer wer in any.For thei which speake otherwise
then truthe is,mynd not the commendacion of the persone,
but the settyng furthe of their awne learnyng.As Gorg= Gorgias.
as in Plato,praisyng vnrighteousnes, Heliogabalus D= Heliogabalus
ratours,commendyng whoredome,Phauorinus the Phi= Phauorinus.
losophier,extollyng the feuer Quartaine , thought not to
speake as the cause required , but would so muche saie as
their wit would geue,not weighyng the state of the cause,
but myndyng the vant of their brain,lookyng how muche
could be said,not passyng how litle should be saied.But I
bothe knowyng the might of Gods hand,for suche as loue
fables,and the shame that in yearth redoundeth to euil re=
porters , will not commende that or those , whiche neede
no good praise,but will commende them,that no man iust=
ly cau dispraise , nor yet any one is well able worthely to
praise.

p;aife.Their towardnes was suche,& their giftes so great,
that I know none whiche loue learnyng,but hath sorowed
the lacke of their beeyng, and I knowe that the onely na;
myng of theim, will stirre honest hartes, to speake well of
them.I will speake of twoo brethren,that lately departed,

Henry duke of the one Henry Duke of Suffolke, and the other Lorde
Suffolke, and Charles his brother, whom God thinkyng meter for hea;
lorde Charles uen,then to liue here vpon pearth, toke from vs in his an;
his brother. ger,for the betteryng of our doynges , and amendement of
our euill liuyng . These twoo gentlemen were borne in
noble England, bothe by father and mother,of an high pa;
rentage.The father called Duke Charles, by mariage be;
yng brother,to the worthy kyng of famous memorie, Hery
theight,was in suche fauour,and did suche seruice,that all
Englande at this houre,doeth finde his lacke,and Fraunce
yet doth fele,that suche a duke there was,whom in his life
tyme,the godly,loued: the euil,feared:the wise men,hono;
red for his wit,and the simple,vsed alwaies for their coun;
saill.Their mother,of birthe noble,and witte great, of na;
ture getle,and mercifull to the poore,and to the godly,and
especially to the learned, an earnest good patronesse, and
moste helpyng Lady aboue all other. In their youthe their
father died,the eldest of the beyng not past .ix. yeres of age.
After whose death,their mother knowyng,that welth with
out wit,is like a sworde in a naked mannes haud,& assured;
ly certain,that knowlege wouldconfirme iudgemet,proui;
ded so for their bringyng vp,in al vertue and learnyng,that
ij.like were not to be had,within this realme again. When
thei bega bothe,to ware somewhat in yeres,beyng in their
primetide,& spryng of their age,thelder waityng of the kyn;
ges maiestie that now is,was generally well estemed , and
sucheh ope was conceiued of his towardnes,both for lear;
nyng,and al other thinges,that fewe wer like vnto hym in
al the courte.The other kepyng his boke,emong the Cam;
brige men,profited(as thei all well knowe)bothe in vertue
and learnyng , to their greate admiracion. For the Greke,
the Latine,and the Italian, I knowe he could dooe more,
then would be thought true by my report. I leaue to speke
of

of his skill in pleasaunt instrumentes, neither will I vt=
ter his aptnes in Musike,& his toward nature, to all exer=
cises of the body.But his elder brother in this tyme (besi=
des his other giftes of the mynde, whiche passed all other,
and were almoste incredible) folowyng his fathers nature
was so delited with ridyng, and runnyng in armour vpon
horsebacke,and was so comely for that feacte,and could do
so well in chargyng his staffe,beyng but.xiiij.yeres of age,
that menne of warre, euen at this houre, mone muche the
want of suche a worthy gentleman. Yea, the Frenche men
that first wondered at his learnyng, when he was there e=
mong theim,and made a notable Oracion in Latine: were
muche more astonied whē thei saw his comely ridyng,and
litle thought to finde these twoo ornamentes, iopned bothe
in one,his peres especially beyng so tender,and his practise
of so small tyme. Afterward commyng from the courte,as
one that was desierous to be emong the learned, he laie in
Cambrige together with his brother, where thei bothe so
profited,and so gently vsed themselfes, that all Camb= ge
did reuerence,bothe hym and his brother, as two iewell=s
sent frō God.Thelders nature was suche,that he thought
hymself best, when he was emong the wisest, and yet con=
tempned none, but thankefully vsed all, gentle in behauior
without childishenes,stoute of stomacke without al pride,
bold with all warenesse,and frendly with good aduisemēt.
The yonger beeyng not so ripe in yeres, was not so graue
in looke,rather chereful,then sad:rather quicke,then aun=
cient : but yet if his brother were sette a side , not one that
went beyonde hym.A childe that by his awne inclinacion,
so muche yelded to his ruler, as fewe by chastement haue
doen the like,pleasaunt of speeche, prompte of witte , sti=
ryng by nature,hault without hate,kynde without crafte,
liberall of harte,gentle in behauiour,forward in all thyn=
ges, gredy of learnyng, and lothe to take a fople , in any
open assembly.Thei bothe in al attemptes,sought to haue
the victory,and in exercise of witte,not onely the one with
the other,did ofte stande in contencion,but also thei bothe
would matche with the best,and thought themselfes moste

c.i.   happie,

The arte of Rhetorique.

happie, when thei might haue any iust occasion, to put their wittes in triall. And now when this grene fruicte began to war: ripe, and all menne longed to haue tast, of suche their greate forwardnesse: God preuentyng mannes expectacion, toke theim bothe aboute one houre, and in so shorte tyme, that first thei wer knowen to be dedde, or any abrode could tell thei wer: sicke. I neede not to reherse, what bothe thei spake, before their departure (consyderyng, I haue seuerally written, bothe in Latine and in Englishe, of thesame matter) neither will I heape here so muche together as I can, because I should rather renewe greate sorowe to many, then do moste men any great good, who loued them so well generally, that fewe for a greate space after, spake of these twoo gentle menne, but thei shewed teares, with the onely vtteraunce of their wordes, and some through ouer muche sorowyng, wer fain to forbeare speakyng. God graūt vs al so to liue, that the good men of this world, map be alwaies lothe to forsake vs, and God maie still be glad to haue vs, as no doubt these twoo children so died, as all men should wishe to liue, and so thei liued bothe, as al should wishe to die. Seyng therfore these two wer suche, bothe for birthe, nature, and all other giftes of grace, that the like are hardely founde behynde theim: let vs so speake of theim, that our good report maie warne vs, to folowe their godly natures, and that lastly, wee maie enioye that enheritaunce, whereunto God hath prepared the and vs (that feare him) from the beginnyng. Amen.

The partes of an Oracion, made in praise of a manne.
{
The Entraunce.
The Narracion.
Sometymes the confutacion.
The Conclusion.

If any one shall haue iust cause, to dispraise an euill man, he shall sone do it, if he can praise a good man. For (as Aristotle doeth saie) of contraries, there is one and thesame doctrine, and therfore he that can do the one, shall sone be able to do the other,

D.2

31

¶Of an Ozacion demonstra=
tiue, foz some deede doen.

The kynd demonstratiue of some thyng doen is this,
when a man is commended oz disprailed, foz any acte a deede,
committed in his life.

Ozacion De=
monstratiue of
a deede.

¶The places to confirme this cause, when any
one is commended, are fixe in nomber.

The places of
Cofirmacion.

- j. It is honest.
- ij. It is possible.
- iij. Easie to be doen,
- iiij. hard to be doen.
- v. Possible to be doen,
- vi. Impossible to be doen.

Seuen circumstaunces, whiche are to bee considered in
diuerse matters.

The circum=
staunces.

- j. Who did the deede.
- ij. What was doen.
- iij. Where it was doen.
- iiij. What helpe had he to it.
- v. Wherefoze he did it.
- vi. How he did it.
- vij. At what tyme he did it.

¶The circumstaunces in meter.

Who, what, and where, by what helpe, and by whole:
Why, how, and when, do many thynges disclose.

These places helpe wonderfully, to set out any mat=
ter, and to amplifie it to the vttermoste, not onely in
praisyng, oz disprailyng, but also in all other causes
where any aduisement is to bee vsed. Yet this one
thyng is to bee learned, that it shall not bee necessarie, to vse
theim altogether, euen as thei stande in ozder: but rather as
tyme and place shall best require, thei maie bee vsed in any
parte of the Ozacion, euen as it shall please hym that hath
the vsyng of them.

Again, if any manne bee disposed, to rebuke any offence, he
maie vse the places contrary vnto theim that are aboue re=
hersed, and apply these circumstaunces euen as thei are, to

c.ij.   the

The arte of Rhetorique.

the profe of his purpose.

¶An example of commendyng kyng Dauid, for killyng greate Goliah, gathered and made by obseruacion of circumstaunces.

Dauid comended for killing Goliah.

GOD beyng the author of mankynde, powryng into hym the breath of life, and framyng hym of claie in suche a comely wise, as we al now se, hath from the beginnyng, been so carefull ouer his electe and chosen, that in al daungers, he is euer redy to assist his people, kepyng theim harmelesse, when thei were often paste all mannes hope. And emong all other his fatherly goodnesse, it

who: Dauid against Goliah.

pleased hym to shewe his power, in his chosen seruaūt Dauid, that all mighte learne to knowe his mighte, and reken with themselfes, that though man geue the stroke, yet God it is that geueth the ouerhande. For wheras Dauid was of small stature, weake of body, poore of birthe, and base in the sight of the worlde! pnges, God called hym firste to matche with an huge monster, a litle body, againste a mightie Gyaunte, an abiecte Israelite, against a moste valiaunt Philistine, with whom no Israelite durst encounter. These Philistines mynded the murder and ouerthrowe, of all the Israelites, trustyng in their awne strength so muche, that thei feared no perill, but made an accompte, that all was theirs before hande. Now when bothe these armies were in sight, the Philistines vpon an hill of the one side, and the Israelites vpon an hill, of the other side, a vale beyng betwixte theim bothe, there marched out of the campe, a base borne Philistine, called Goliah of Geth, a manne of sixe cubites high. This souldiour, when through the bignes and stature of his body, and also with greate bragges, & terrible threateninges, he had wonderfully abashed the whole armie of the Israelites, so that no man durst aduenture vpon hym, God to the ende he mighte del uer Israell, and shewe that in mannes helpe, with all his armour, litle auaile to get victory, without his especiall grace: and again, to the ende he might set vp Dauid, and make hym honourable emong the Israelites, did then call out Dauid, the sonne of Ephrateus, of Bethleem Juda, whose name was Isai, who keepyng
but

but a child in peres, did kill out of hande, by Goddes might 　*what:*
and power, Goliah the moste terrible enemie of all other, 　*Dauid killed*
that bare hate againſt the children of Iſraell. When this 　*Goliah.*
mightie felowe was ſlain, aboute the bale of Terebinthus, 　*where:*
betwixt both tharmies, the Iſraelites reioyſed, that befoꝛe 　*About the bale*
quaked, and wondered at hym then, whom thei would ſcant 　*of Terebithus*
knowe befoꝛe, & no doubt this ꝺede was not onely wonder:
full, but alſo right godly. foꝛ in battaill to kill an enemie,
is thoughte right woꝛthy, oꝛ to aduenture vpon a rebell,
(though the ſucceſſe folowe not) is generally commended:
yea, to put one to the woꝛſe, oꝛ to make hym flie the grou̅d,
is called manly, but what ſhall we ſaie of Dauid, that not
onely had the better hande, not onely bette his enemie, but
killed ſtreight his enemie, yea, and not an enemy, of the co̅:
mon ſtature of men, but a mightie Gyaunt, not a man, but 　*Dauids enter:*
a monſter, yea, a deuill in hart, and a beaſt in body? Can a: 　*pꝛiſe, honeſt*
ny be coumpted moꝛe honeſt, then ſuche as ſeke to ſaue their 　*and godly.*
coũtrey, by haſardyng their carcaſſes, and ſhedyng of their
bloude? Can loue ſhewe it ſelf greater, then by yeldyng of 　*By what helo*
life, foꝛ the health of an armie? It had been muche, if half a 　*and by whoſe?*
doſen had diſpatched, ſuche a terrible Gyaunte, but now, 　*Alone, & with:*
when Dauid without helpe, beyng not yet a manne, but a 　*out the help of*
boye in peres, ſlewe hym hande to hande, what iuſte pꝛaiſe 　*any manne li:*
dooeth he deſerue? If we pꝛaiſe other, that haue ſlain euill 　*uyng.*
men, and compte them haulte, that haue killed their mat: 　*Dauids enter:*
ches, what ſhall we ſaie of Dauid, that beyng wonderful: 　*pꝛiſe, pꝛaiſe*
ly ouermatched, made his partie good, and gotte the gole of 　*woꝛthy.*
a monſter? Lette other pꝛaiſe Hercules, that thinke beſt of
hym: let Ceſar, Alexander, and Hanniball, bee bꝛuted foꝛ
warriers: Dauid in my iudgement, bothe did moꝛe manly,
then all the other wer able, & ſerued his countrey in grea:
ter daunger, then euer any one of theim did. And ſhall wee
not call ſuche a noble capitain, a good man of warre? De:
ſerueth not his manhode and ſtoute attempte, wonderfull
pꝛaiſe? If vertue could ſpeake, would ſhe not ſone confeſſe
that Dauid had her in full poſſeſſion? And therfoꝛe if well
doynges, by right maie chalenge woꝛthy bꝛute, Dauid wil
be knowen, and neuer can want due pꝛaiſe, foꝛ ſuche an ho:
　　　　　　　　C.iij.　　　　　neſt

nest deede. And what man wil not faie, but that Dauid did mynde nothyng els herein, but the faufegarde of his countrey, thinkyng it better for himfelf to die, and his countrey to liue, then hymfelf to liue, and his countrey to die. What gain got Dauid, by the death of Goliah, or what could he hope, by the death of fuche a monfter, but onely that the loue whiche he bare to the Ifraelites, forced hym to hafard his

Dauides enterprife, profitable to hymfelf and his countrey.

awne life: Thinkyng that if the Philiftines fhould preuail the Ifraelites wer like to perifhe, euery mothers fonne of theim? Therefore he haffardyng this attempte, confidered with hymfelf, the faufegard of the Ifraelites, the mainteinaunce of iuftice, his duetie towardes God, his obedience

Dauides enterprife, appered eafy to hymfelf

to his prince, and his loue to his countrey. And no doubte, God made this enterprife appere full eafie, before Dauid could haue the harte, to matche hymfelf with fuche a one. For though his harte might quake, beeyng voyde of Gods helpe, yet affuredly he wanted no ftomacke, when God did fet hym on. Let tirauntes rage, let hell ftand open, let Sathan fhewe his mighte, if God bee with vs, who can bee againft vs? Though this Goliah appered fo ftrong, that .x. Dauides were not able, to ftande in his hande: yet .x. Goliaths were all ouer weake for Dauid alone. Man cannot iudge, neither can reafon comprehende, the mightie power of God. When Pharao with all his armie, thoughte fully to deftroye the children of Ifraell, in the redde fea, did not God preferue Mofes, and deftroye Pharao? What is man and all his power that he can make, in the handes of God, vnto whom all creatures, bothe in heauen and in pearth, are fubiecte at his commaundement? Therefore it was no maftery for Dauid, beyng affifted with God, afwel to matche with the whole armp, as to ouerthrowe this one man. But

Dauides enterprife, accompted of his frendes, harde and impoffible.

what did the Ifraelites, when thei fawe Dauid take vpon hym, fuche a bolde enterprife? Some faied he was rafhe, or ther mocked hym to fcorne, & his brethren called hym foole. For thought thei, what a madde felowe is he, beeyng but a lad in yeres, to matche with fuche a monfter in body? How can it be poffible otherwife, but that he fhalbe torne in peces, euen at his firfte commyng? For if the Philiftine maie
ones

ones hit hym, he is goen though he had tenne mennes lifes. Now what should he meane, so vnegally to matche himself except he were, wery of his life, oz els were not well in his wittes? yea, and to geue his enemies, all the aduauntage that could bee, he came vnarmed, and whereas the Phili= stine, had very strõg armour. bothe to defende hymself, and a strong weapon to fight withall, Dauid came with a slyng onely, as though he would kill crowes, whereat, not onely the Philistine laughed, ⁊ disdained his folie, but also bothe the armies thought he was but a dedde man, befoze he gaue one stroke. And in deede, by all reason and deuise of manne there was none other waie, but deathe with hym, out of hande. Dauid notwithstandyng, beeyng kyndeled in harte with Gods might, was strong enough foz him, in his awne opinion, and fozced nothyng, though all other were muche against hym. And therefoze made no moze a dooe, but beyng redy to reuenge in Goddes name, suche greate blasphemie, as the Philistine then did vtter, marched towardes his ene= mie, and with castyng a stone out of a slyng, he ouerthzewe the Philistine at the first. The whiche when he had dooen, out with his swozde, and chopt of his hedde, carieng it with his armoure, to the Campe of the Israelites: whereat the Philistines wer greatly astonied, and the Israelites much pzaised God, that had geuen suche grace, to suche a one, to compasse suche a deede. And the rather this manly acte, is highly to be pzaised, because he subdued this houge enemi⸗, when Saul firste reigned kyng ouer Israell, and was soze assaied with the greate armie of the Philistines. Lette vs therefoze that be now liuyng, when this acte oz suche like, come into our myndes: remember what God is, of how in= finite power he is, and let vs pzaise God in them, by whom he hath wzought suche wonders, to the strengthenyng of our faithe, and constaunt kepyng of our pzofession, made to hym, by euery one of vs, in our Baptisme.

How⸗
with a slyng.

⸿ Examinyng of the circumstaunces

j. Who did the deede?

D Auid beeyng an Israelite, did this deede, beeyng the sonne of Isai, of the Tribe of Juda, a boye in yeres,

This

The arte of Rhetorique.

This circumstaunce was vsed, not onely in the narracion, but also when I spake of the honestie and godlinesse, whiche Dauid vsed, when he slewe Goliah.

ij. what was doen?

He slewe Goliah, the strongest Giaunt emong the Philistines. This circumstaunce I vsed also, when I spake of the honestie, in killyng Goliah.

iij. where was it doen?

Aboute the vale of Terebinthus.

iiij. what helpe had he to it?

He had no help of any man, but went himself alone. And wheras Saul offred him harnes, he cast it away, & trusting onely in God, toke him to his sling, with. iiij. or. v. smal stones in his hand, the whiche wer thought nothyng in manes sight, able either to do litle good, or els nothing at al. This circumstaunce I vsed, when I spake of the easenesse & possibilite, that was in Dauid, to kill Goliah, by Goddes help.

v. wherefore did he it?

He aduentured his life, for the loue of his countrey, for the maintenaunce of iustice, for thaduauncement of Gods true glory, and for the quietnesse of all Israell, neither seekyng fame, nor yet lokyng for any gain. I vsed this circumstaunce, when I shewed what profite he sought, in aduenturyng this deede.

vi. How did he it?

Marie he put a stone in his slyng, and when he had cast it at the Philistine, Goliah fel doune straight. I vsed this circumstaunce, when I spake of the impossibilitie of the thing.

vij. what tyme did he it?

This deede was doen, when Saul reigned, first kyng ouer the Israelites, at what tyme the Philistines, came against the Israelites. Thus by the circumstaunces of thynges, a right worthy cause, maie be plentifully enlarged.

⟨ Of the Oracion demonstratiue, where thynges are sette furthe, and matters commended.

℘ He kynde demonstratiue of thynges, is a meane wherby we do praise, or dispraise thynges, as vertue, vice, tounes, cittees, castles, woddes, waters, hilles, and mountaines.

The

Of Rhetorique.   *Fol.*13.

¶ Places to confirme thynges are.iiii.

	i.	Thynges honeſt.
Places of confirmacion.	ij.	Profitable.
	iij.	Eaſie to be doen.
	iiij	Harde to be doen.

Any learned, will haue recourſe to the places of Logique in ſtede of theſe. iiij. places, when they take in hand to commende any ſuche matter. The whiche places if they make them ſerue rather to commende the matter, then onely to teache men the truth of it, it were wel done & Oratourlike. for ſeyng a man wholly beſtoweth his wit to plaie the Oratour, he ſhoulde chefely ſeke to compaſſe that whiche he entēdeth, & not do that onely which he but half mynded. for by plaine teachyng, the Logi= cian ſhewes hymſelfe, by large amplification and beautifi= yng of his cauſe, the Rhetorician is alwaies knowne.

¶ The places of Logique are theſe.

	Definition.
	Cauſes.
	Partes.
	Effectes.
	Thynges adioynyng.
	Contraries.

Do not ſe otherwiſe but that theſe places of Logi= que are confounded with thother.iiij. of confirma= cion, or rather I thinke theſe of Logique muſt firſt be mynded ere thother can well be had. For what is he that can cal a thyng honeſt & by reaſon proue it, except he firſt knowe what the thyng is, the whiche he can not bet= ter doe, then by definyng the nature of the thyng. Againe how ſhal I know whether myne attempte be eaſie, or hard, if I know not the efficient cauſe, or be aſſured how it maie be doen. In affirmyng it to be poſſible, I ſhall not better knowe it, then by ſearchyng thende, and learnyng by Lo= gique what is the final cauſe of euery thyng.

Logique muſt be learned for confirmacion of cauſes.

               D.i.   An

The Arte

❡ An example in commendacion of Justice,
or true dealyng.

SO many as loke to liue in peaceable quietnesse, be
yng mynded rather to folowe reason, than to be
led by wilfull affection:desire iustice in al thynges
without the which no countrie is able long to cō=
tinue. Then may I be bolde to commende that, whiche all
men wishe & fewe can haue, whiche all men loue, & none can
want:not doubtyng but as I am occupied in a good thyng,
so al good men wil heare me with a good wil. But woulde
God I were so wel able to perswade all men to Iustice, as
al men know the necessarie vse therof:and then vndoubted=
ly I woulde be muche boulder, and force some by violence,
whiche by faire wordes can not be entreated. And yet what
nedes any perswasion for that thyng, whiche by nature is
so nedeful, & by experience so profitable, that looke what we
want, without iustice we get not, loke what we haue, with=
out iustice we kepe not. God graūt his grace so to worke in
the hartes of al men, that they may aswel practise well do=
yng in their owne lyfe, as they would that other should fo=
lowe iustice in their lyfe:I for my part wil bestow some la=
bor to set forth the goodnes of vpright dealing that al other
men the rather may do therafter. That if through my wor=
des, God shal worke with any man, than may I thynke my
self in happy case; & reioyce much in the trauaile of my wit.
And how can it be otherwyse, but that al men shalbe forced
inwardly to allowe that, whiche in outwarde acte many do
not folowe: seyng God poured first this law of nature into
mans hart, & graūted it as a meane wherby we might know
his wil, & (as I might saie) talke with hun, groundyng stil
his doinges vpō this poinct, that mā should do as he would
be done vnto, the whiche is nothyng elles, but to lyue vp=
rightly, without any wil to hurte his neighbour. And ther=
fore hauyng this light of Goddes wil opened vnto vs tho=
rowe his mere goodnesse, we ought euermore to referre al
our actions vnto this ende, both in geuyng iudgement, and
deuisyng lawes necessarie for mans lyfe. And here vpon it
is that when men desire the lawe for trial of a matter, they

meane

Justice com=
mended.

Justice natu=
rally in euery
one of vs.

Of Rhetorique. *Fol.14.*

meane nothyng elles but to hȝue iuſtice,the whiche iuſtice
is a vertue that yeldeth to euery man, his owne: to the e=
uer liuyng God,loue aboue al thynges: to the Kyng, obe=
dience:to the inferiour,good counſel: to the poore mã,mer=
cie:to the hateful and wicked,ſufferaunce:to it ſelf,truthe:
and to al men,perfite peace,and charitie. Now what can be
moȝe ſaid in pȝaiſe of this vertue,oȝ what thyng can be like
pȝaiſed? Are not al thynges in good caſe,when al men haue
their owne? And what other thyng doeth iuſtice,but ſeketh
meanes to contente al parties? Then how greatly are they
to be pȝaiſed,that meane truely in al their dopnges,and not
onely,do no harme to any,but ſeke meanes to helpe al. The
ſunne is not ſo wonderful to the woȝld (ſaith Ariſtotel) as
the iuſt dealyng of a gouernour is merueilous to al mē. No
the yerth yeldeth not moȝe gaine to al creatures,than doth
the iuſtice of a Magiſtrate to his whole Realme. foȝ,by a
lawe,we liue,and take the fruites of the yearth,but where
no law is,noȝ iuſtice vſed:there,nothyng cã be had,though
al thynges be at hande: foȝ, in hauyng the thyng, we ſhall
lacke the vſe,and liuyng in great plentie, we ſhal ſtande in
great nede. The meane therfoȝe that maketh men to enioye
their owne,is iuſtice, the whiche beyng ones taken away,
all other thynges are loſt with it, neither can any one ſaue
that he hath,noȝ yet get that he wanteth. Therfoȝe if woȝng
doyng ſhoulde be boȝne withal,and not rather puniſhed by
death,what man coulde lyue in reſte? Who coulde be ſuer
either of his lyfe,oȝ of his liuyng one whole day together?
Now becauſe euery man deſiereth the pȝeſeruation of hym
ſelfe,euery man ſhould in lyke caſe deſire the ſauegarde of
his neighbour. foȝ if J ſhoulde wholly mynde myne own
caſe,and folowe gaine without reſpect to the hinderaunce
of myne euen Chȝiſtian:why ſhould not other vſe theſame
libertie,and ſo euery man foȝ hymſelfe,and the deuil foȝ vs
al,catche that catche may? The whiche cuſtome if all men
folowed,the earth woulde ſoone be voide foȝ want of men,
one ſhoulde be ſo gredie to eate vp an other. foȝ in ſekyng
to lyue,we ſhoulde loſe our lyues, ȝ in gapyng after good=
des,we ſhoulde ſoone go naked. Therefoȝe to repȝeſſe this

D.ij.   rage

Right margin notes:

Juſtice what
it is,and howe
laigely it er=
tendeth.

Ariſtotel.

Wȝong dea=
lyng deſerueth
death.

rage,and with holſome deuiſes to traine men in an order,
God hath lightened man with knowledge,that in al thyn=
ges he may ſe what is right, and what is wrong,and vpon
good aduiſement deale iuſtly with al men. God hath crea=
ted al thynges for mans vſe, and ordeined man for mannes
ſake,that one man might helpe another. For thoughe ſome

Iuſtice neceſ=
ſarie for almſ.

one haue giftes more plentifully then the comune ſorte,yet
no man can liue alone without helpe of other.Therfore we
ſhoulde ſtriue one to helpe another by iuſte dealyng, ſome
this way,& ſome that way,as euery one ſhal haue nede,and
as we ſhalbe alwaies beſt able,wherein the lawe of nature
is fulfilled,and Goddes commaundemēt folowed.We loue
them here in pearth that geue vs faire wordes, and we can
be content to ſpeake wel of them,that ſpeake wel of vs:and
ſhall we not loue them, and take them alſo for honeſt men,

From the leſſe
to the greater.

whiche are contented from tyme to tyme to yelde euery mā
his owne, and rather woulde dye then conſent to euill do=
yng?If one be ientle in outwarde behauiour, we lyke hym
wel,and ſhal we not eſteeme hym that is vpright in his out=
ward liuyng? and like as we deſire that other ſhould be to
vs,ought not we to bee likewyſe affected towardes them?
Euen emong brute beaſtes nature hath appoincted a law, &

Young Sto==
kes.

ſhal we men lyue without a lawe? The Storke beyng not
able to feede her ſelfe for age, is fedde of her youngones,
wherin is declared a natural loue,and ſhal we ſo lyue,that
one ſhal not loue another? Man ſhoulde be vnto man as a
God,& ſhal man be vnto man as a Deuil?Hath God crea=

Vnnaturalnes
in man towar=
des God.

ted vs , and made vs to his owne likeneſſe , endewyng vs
with al the riches of the pearth,that we might be obedient
to his wil,and ſhal we neither loue him,nor like his?How
can we ſay that we loue God,if there be no charitie in vs?
Do I loue hym,whoſe mynde I wil not folowe,although
it be right honeſt?If you loue me(ſaith Chriſte)folow my

Ihon.xiiii.
Marth.xix,
Marc.x.

commaundementes.Chriſtes will is ſuche that we ſhoulde
loue God aboue al thinges,and our neighbour as our ſelf.
Then if we do not iuſtice(wherin loue doeth conſiſt) we do
neither loue man,nor yet loue God. The Wyſe man ſaith:

Prouer.xvi.

The begynnyng of a good lyfe,is to do iuſtice.Yea,the bleſ=
ſyng

ȝyng of the Lorde is vpon the heade of the iuste. Heauen is Prouer.iiii.
theirs (saith Dauid) that do iustly frō tyme to tyme. What Psal.xcvi.
els then shal we do that haue any hope of the general resur=
rection, but do the will of God, and lyue iustly all the daies
of our life? Let euery man, but consider with hymself what Profite of
iustice.
case he shal finde therby, ⁊ I doubt not but euery one depe=
ly waiyng the same, wil in hart confesse that iustice maketh
plentie, and that not one man coulde long holde his owne, if
lawes were not made to restraine mans will. We trauaile
now, Wynter ⁊ Sommer, we watche, and take thought for
maintenaunce of wife ⁊ children, assuredly purposyng (that Sauegarde had
by iustice.
though God shal take vs immediatly) to leaue honestly for
our familie. Now to what ende were all our gatheryng to=
gether, if iust dealyng were set a side, if lawes bare no rule,
if what the wicked list, that they may, and what they may, Gradation.
that they can, ⁊ what they can, that they dare, ⁊ what they The necessitie
of iustice.
dare, the same they do, ⁊ whatsoeuer they do, no man of po=
wer is agreued therwith? What maketh wicked mē (which
els woulde not) acknowlege the Kyng as their souereigne
lorde, but the power of a lawe, ⁊ the practise of iustice for e=
uil doers? Could a Prynce mainteine his state royal, if law
and right had not prouided that euery man shoulde haue his
owne? Would seruauntes obey their masters, the sonne his
father, the tenaunt his landlorde, the citezen his maiour, or
Shirife: if orders were not set ⁊ iust dealyng appoincted for
al states of men? Therfore the true meanyng folke in all a=
ges geue thē selues some to this occupacion, ⁊ some to that,
sekyng therin nothing els, but to mainteine a poore life, and
to kepe them selues true men both to God and the worlde.
What maketh men to perfozme their bargaines, to stand to
their promises, ⁊ yelde their debtes, but an order of a lawe Where iustice
is executed,
vice is exiled.
grounded vpō iustice? Where right beareth rule, there craft
is coumpted vice. The lyar is muche hated, where truth is
wel estemed. The wicked theues are haged, where good men
are regarded. None can holde vp their heades, or dare showe
their faces in a well ruled commune weale, that are not
thought honest, or at the least haue some honest way to lyue.
The Egiptians therfore hauyng a worthy and a wel gouer=

ued

¶ Ægiptians
what ozder
they vſed to
baniſhe ydel-
neſſe.ned publike weale, prouided that none ſhoulde lyue idly,
but that euery one monethly ſhould geue an accompte how
he ſpente his tyme, and had his name regeſtrede in a Booke
foz the ſame purpoſe. But Lozde, if this lawe were vſed in
England, how many would come behynde hande with their
reckenynges at the audite daie. I feare me there doynges
woulde be ſuche, that it would be long ere they gotte there
quietus eſt. Therfoze the wourſe is our ſtate, the leſſe that
this euil is loked vnto. And ſuerly, if in other thynges we
ſhoulde be as negligent, this Realme could not long ſtand.
But thankes be to God, we hang theim a pace that offende
a lawe, and therfoze we put it to their choiſe, whether they
wil be idle and ſo fal to ſtealyng, oz no: they knowe their rewarde, go to it, when they will. But if therewithall ſome
good ozder were taken foz education of pouthe, and ſettyng
loiterers on wozke (as thankes be to God the Citie is moſt
Godly bent that way) all would ſoone be well without all
doubt. The wyſe and diſcrete perſons in al ages ſought all
meanes poſſible to haue an ozder in all thynges, & loued by
Iuſtice eaſy to
be obſerued, if
wil be not wā-
tyng.iuſtice to directe al their doynges, wherby appereth both an
apt wil in ſuche men, & a natural ſtirryng by Godes power
to make al men good. Therfoze, if we doe not well, we muſt
blame our ſelues, that lacke a wil, and do not cal to God foz
grace. Foz though it appere hard to do wel, becauſe no man
can get perfection without continaunce: yet aſſuredly to an
humble mynde that calleth to God, and to a willyng harte
that faine would do his beſt, nothing can be hard. God hath
ſet al thinges to ſale foz labouz, and kepeth open ſhop, come
who will. Therefoze in all ages whereas we ſee the feweſt
good. we muſt wel thinke, the moſt did lacke good wil to aſke, oz ſeke foz the ſame. Lozde, what loue had that wozthie
Prince Seleucus to maintein iuſtice, & to haue good lawes
kepte, of whome ſuche a wondzefull thyng is wzitten.
Foz whereas he eſtabliſhed moſte holſome lawes foz ſauegarde of the Locrenſiãs, and his owne ſonne thereupon taken in adultrie, ſhould loſe bothe his iyes accozdyng to the
lawe then made, and yet notwithſtandyng, the whole Citie
thought to remitte the neceſſitie of his puniſhement foz the
honour

honour of his father, Seleucus woulde none of that in any water.lib.vi.
wyse. Yet at last through importunitie, beyng ouercome, he
caused first one of his owne iyes to be pluckte out, & next after, one of his sonnes iyes, leauyng onely the vse of sight to
hymself & his sonne. Thus through equitie of the lawe, he
vsed the dew meane of chastisement, showyng hymself by a
wonderful temperature both a merciful father, & a iust lawe
maker. Nowe happy are thei ỹ thus obserue a law, thinking
losse of body, lesse hurt to the man, then sparyng of punishe=
mēt, mete for the soule. For God wil not faile thē that haue
suche a desire to folowe his wil, but for his promise sake, he
wil rewarde them for euer. And now, seeyng that iustice na=
turally is geuē to al men without the whiche we could not
liue, beyng warned also by God alwaies to doe vprightly,
perceauyng againe the commodities that redounde vnto vs
by liuyng vnder a lawe, & the sauegard wherin we stand ha=
uyng iustice to assiste vs: I trust that not onely all men wil
cōmende iustice in worde, but also wil liue iustly in dede, the
which that we may do, God graunt vs of his grace, Amen.

¶ An Oration deliberatiue.

AN Oration deliberatiue, is a meane, wherby we do   Oration deli-
perswade, or disswade, entreate, or rebuke, exhorte, or   beratiue.
dehorte, commende, or cōforte any man, In this kynd
of Oration we doe not purpose wholly to praise any
body, nor yet to determine any matter in cōtrouersie, but the
whole compasse of this cause is, either to aduise our neigh:
bour to that thyng, whiche we thynke most nedeful for hym
or els to cal him backe frō that folie, which hindereth muche
his estimacion. As for exāple, if I would counseil my frende
to trauaile beyond the Seas for knowlege of the tongues, &
experience in forein countries: I might resorte to this kinde
of Oration, & finde matter to cōfirme my cause plentifully.
And the reasons which are commonly vsed to enlarge suche
matters, are these that folowe.

{ The thyng is honest.   { Saufe.
{ Profitable.   { Easie.
{ Pleasaunt,   { Harde.

It is

The Arte

{ Lawful and meete.
{ Praise worthie.
{ Necessarie.

honestie comprehendeth al vertues.

NOw in speakyng of honestie, I may by deuision of the vertues make a large walke. Againe loke what lawes, what customes, what worthie dedes, or saynges haue bene vsed heretofore, all these might serue wel for the confirmacion of this matter. laſtly where honeſtie is called in, to eſtabliſh a cauſe: there is nature and God hym ſelfe preſent from whome commeth al goodneſſe.

Profite howe largely it extendeth.

In the ſeconde place where I ſpake of profite, this is to be learned, that vnder the ſame is comprehended the gettyng of gaine, and the eſchewyng of harme. Againe, concernyng

Profite beareth the name of goodnes, whiche is three folded.

profite (which alſo beareth the name of goodneſſe) it parte-ly perteineth to the bodie, as beautie, ſtrength, and healthe, partely to the mynde, as the encreaſe of witte, the gettyng of experience, and heaping together of muche learnyng: and partely to fortune (as Philoſophers take it) wherby bothe wealth, honor, and frendes are gotten. Thus he that diui-deth profite, can not want matter. Thirdely in declaryng it

Pleaſures, largely ſette out.

is pleaſaunt, I might heape together the varietie of plea-ſures, whiche comme by trauaile, firſte the ſwetneſſe of the tongue, the holſomneſſe of the aper in other countries, the goodly wittes of the ſentlemen, the ſtraunge and auncient buildynges, the wonderful monumentes, the great learned Clerckes in al faculties, with diuerſe other like, and almoſt infinite pleaſures.

eaſineſſe of trauaile.

The eaſines of trauaile may thus beperſwaded, if we ſhew that freepaſſage is by wholſō lawes appointed, for al ſtraū-gers, & waie fairers. And ſeyng this life is none other thyng but a trauaile, & we as pilgrymes wander frō place to place, muche fondeneſſe it were to thinke that hard, which nature hath made eaſie, yea & pleaſaunt alſo. None are more healthful, none more luſty, none more mery, none more ſtrōg of bo-dy, thē ſuche as haue trauailed countries. Mary vnto them

Trauaile vnto whome it is harde.

that had rather ſleape al day, then wake on houre, choſyng for honeſt labour ſleuthful ydleneſſe: thinking this life to be none other thyng but a continual reſtyng place, vnto ſuche

pardie

pardy,it shall seme painfull to abide any labour.To learne
Logique, to learne the Lawe, to some it semeth so harde,
that nothyng can enter into their heddes, and the reason is,
that thei want a will, and an earnest mynde to do their en=
deuour. For vnto a willyng harte, nothyng can bee harde,
lade lode on suche a mannes backe, and his good harte maie **Good wil ma**
soner make his backe to ake, then his good will, can graunt **kes great bur**
to yelde and refuse the weighte.And now where the sweete **deines light.**
hath his sower ioyned with hym, it shalbee wisedome to
speake somewhat of it, to mitigate the sowernesse thereof,
as muche as maie be possible.

That is lawfull and praise worthy, whiche lawes doee **Lawfull.**
graunt, good men do allowe,experience commendeth, and
men in all ages haue moste vsed.

A thyng is necessary twoo maner of waies.first, when **Necessary two**
either we must do some one thyng,or els do wor c.As if one **waies taken.**
should threaten a woman,to kill her,if she would not lie w
him,wherin appereth a forcible necessitie.As touchyng tra=
uaile we might saie,either a man must be ignoraunt,of ma=
ny good thinges,and want greate experience,or els he must
trauaill.Now to be ignoraunt,is a greate shame, therefore
to trauaill is moste nedefull,if we will auoyde shame.The
other kynde ef necessitie is,when we perswade men to beare
those crosses patiently, whiche God doeth sende vs, consi=
deryng will we,or nill we,nedes must we abide them.

⸿To aduise one,to study the lawes of Englande.

Gain,when we se our frende,enclined to any kynde
of learnyng, wee muste counsaill hym to take that
waie still,and by reason perswade hym, that it wer
the metest waie for hym,to dooe his countrey moste
good.As if he geue his mynde, to the Lawes of the realme, **Lawes of**
and finde an aptnes thereunto,we maie aduise hym,to con= **Englande.**
tinue in his good entent,and by reason perswade hym,that
it were moste mete for him so to do.And first we might shew
hym,that the study is honest and godly, consideryng it one=
ly foloweth Justice,and is grounded wholy vpon naturall
reason.Wherein we mighte take a large scope, if we would
fully speake of all thynges,that are comprehended vnder ho=
c.i. nestie.

The arte of Rhetorique.

nestie. For he that will knowe what honestie is, muste haue an vnderstandyng, of all the vertues together. And because the knowlege of theim is moste necessary, I will briefly set them furth. There are foure especial and chief vertues, vnder whom all other are comprehended.

(margin: Vertues especiall and chief foure in nõber)

- Prudence, or wisedome.
- Justice.
- Manhode.
- Temperaunce.

(margin: Prudence what it is?)

Prudence or wisedome (for I will here take them bothe for one) is a vertue that is occupied euermore, in searchyng out the truthe. Nowe wee all loue knowlege,& haue a desire to passe other therin, and thinke it shame to be ignoraunt: and by studyng the Lawe, the truth is gotten out, by knowyng the truth, wisedome is attained. Wherefore, in perswadyng one to studie the Lawe, you maie sh we hym that he shall get wisedome thereby. Under this vertue are comprehended.

(margin: Partes of Prudence.)

- Memorie.
- Understandyng.
- Foresight.

The memorie calleth to accompte those thynges, that wer doen heretofore, and by a former remembraūce, getteth an after witte, and learneth to auoyde deceipt.

Understandyng seeth thynges presently dooen, and perceiueth what is in them, waiyng and debatyng them, vntill his mynde be fully contented.

Foresight, is a gatheryng by coniectures, what shall happen, and an euident perceiuyng of thynges to come, before thei do come.

Justice.

(margin: Justice, what it is.)

Justice is a vertue, gathered by long space, geuyng euery one his awne, mindyng in all thynges, the cõmon profite of our countrey, whereunto man is moste bounde, and oweth his full obedience.

Now, nature firste taught manne, to take this waie, and woulde euery one so to do vnto another, as he would be doen
vnto

vnto hymnself. for whereas Rain watereth all in like, the Sonne shineth indifferentlp ouer all, the fruict of the perth encreaseth egually, God warneth vs to bestowe our good wil after the same sort, doping as duetie bpndeth vs, and as necessitie shall b: st require. Yea, God graunteth his giftes diuerslp emong men, because he would man should knowe, and fele, that man is borne for man, and that one hath nede of another. And therefore, though nature hath not stirred some, yet through the experiece that man hath, concernyng his commoditie: manp haue turned the lawe of nature, into an ordinarp custome, and folowed the same, as though thei were bounde to it bp a Lawe. Afterwarde, the wisedome of Princes, and the feare of Goddes threate, whiche was vt: tered bp his woorde, forced men bp a lawe, bothe to allowe thinges cōfirmed bp nature, and to beare with old custome or els thei should not onelp suffer in the bodp, temporal pu: nishement, but also lose their soules for euer. Nature is a righte, that phantasie hath not framed, but God hath graf: fed, & geuen man power therunto, wherof these are deriued.

(margin: Nature, what it is.)

> Religion and acknowlegpng of God.
> Naturall loue to our children, and other.
> Thankfulnesse to all men.
> Stoutnesse bothe to withstande and reuenge.
> Reuerence to the superiour.
> Assured and constaunt truthe in thpnges.

R Eligion is an humble worshippng of God, acknow
legpng hpm to be the creatour of creatures, and the onelp geuer of al good thpnges.

(margin: Religion.)

Naturall loue is an inward good will, that we beare to our parentes, wife, children, or anp other that bee nighe of kpnne vnto vs, stirred thereunto not onelp bp our flethe, thinkpng that like as we wold loue our selfes, so we should loue theim but also bp a likenesse of mpnde: and therefore generallp we loue all, because all bee like vnto vs, but pet we loue them moste, that bothe in bodp and mpnd, be moste like vnto vs. And hereby it cometh that often we are libe: ral, & bestowe our goodes vpon the nedp, rememberpng that

(margin: Naturall loue.)

thei are all one flefhe with vs,and fhould not wante,when we haue it, without our greate rebuke, and token of our mofte vnkynde dealyng.

Thankfulnes. Thankefulneffe is a requityng of loue,for loue,and wil, for will,fhewyng to our frendes,the like goodneffe that we finde in them,yea,ftriuyng to paffe theim in kyndeneffe,lofyng neither tyme nor tide,to do them good.

Stouteneffe. Stoutnes to withftand & reuenge euil, is then vfed whe either we are like to haue harme,and do withftand it,orels whe we haue fuffred euill for the truthfake,& therupon do reuenge it,or rather punifhe the euill,whiche is in the man

Reuerence. Reuerence,is an humbleneffe in outward behauor, whe we do our dutie tothem,that are our betters,or vnto fuche as are called to ferue the kyng,in fome greate vocacion.

Affured and conftant truth Affured and conftant truthe is,when we doo beleue that thofe thynges,whiche are or haue been , or hereafter are as aboute to be,cannot otherwife be,by any meanes poffible.

Right by cuftome. That is right by cuftome,whiche long tyme hath confirmed,beyng partly grounded vpon nature,and partly vpon reafon,as where we are taught by nature,to knowe the euer liuyng God,and to worfhip him in fpirite,we turnyng natures light,into blynde cuftome,without Goddes will, **Cuftome with our natures grounde,vngodly.** haue vfed at lengthe to beleue, that he was really with vs here in pearthe , and worfhipped hym not in fpirite, but in Copes,in Candleftickes,in Belles,in Tapers,and in Cenfers,in Croffes,in Banners,in fhauen Crounes and long gounes,and many good morowes els, deuifed onely by the phantafie of manne,without the expreffe will of God.The whiche childifhe topes, tyme hath fe long confirmed , that the truthe is fcant able to trie theim out, our hartes bee fo harde,and our wittes be fo farre to feke.

Again wher we fe by nature,that euery one fhould deale truely , cuftome encreafeth natures will , and maketh by aunctent demeane ; thynges to bee iuftly obferued , whiche nature hath appoynted.

As {
Bargainyng.
Commons,or equalitee.
Iudgement geuen.

Argainyng is, whn twoo haue agreed, for the sale of some one thyng, the one will make his felowe to stande to the bargain, though it be to his neighbors vndoyng, restyng vpon this poyncte, that a bargain is a bargain, and must stand without all excepciō, although nature requireth to haue thynges dooen by conscience, and would that bargainyng should bee builded vpon Iustice, whereby an vpright dealyng, and a charitable loue is vtte= red emongest all men.

Communes or equalitee, is whē the people by long time haue a ground, or any suche thyng emong theim, the whiche some of them will kepe still, for custome sake, and not suffer it to be fensed, and so turned to pasture, though thei mighte gain ten tymes the value: but suche stubburnesse in kepyng of Commons for custome sake, is not standyng with Iu= stice, because it is holden againt all right. *Commons.*

Iudgement geuen, is when a matter is confirmed by a Parlamente, or a Lawe, determined by a Iudge, vnto the whiche many hed strong men, wil stande to dye for it, with= out sufferaunce of any alteracion, not remembryng the cir= cumstaunce of thynges, and that tyme altereth good actes. *Iudgement geuen.*

That is righte by a Lawe, when the truthe is vttered in writyng, and commaunded to bee kepte, euen as it is seite furthe vnto them. *Right by Lawe.*

¶ Fortitude or manhode.

Ortitude is a considerate hassardyng vpon daun= ger, and a willyng harte to take paines in behalfe of the right. Now when can stoutnes be better v= sed, then in iust maintenaunce of the lawe, and cō= staunt tryeng of the truthe? Of this vertue there are foure braunches. *Manhode.*

> Honourablenesse.
> Stoutenesse.
> Sufferaunce.
> Continuaunce.

Onorablenesse, is a noble orderyng of weightie mat= ters, with a lustie harte, and a liberall vsyng of his wealthe, to the encrease of honour. *Honorablenes*

c.iii   Stoutnesse

The arte of Rhetorique.

Stoutenesse. Stoutnesse is an assured trust in hymself, when he impugneth the compasse of moste weightie matters, and a couragious defendyng of his cause.

Sufferaunce. Sufferaunce is a willyng and a long bearyng of trouble and takyng of paines, for the mainteinaunce of vertue, and the wealthe of his countrey.

Continuaunce Continuaunce is a stedfast and constant abidyng, in a purposed and well aduised matter, not yeldyng to any manne in querell of the right.

Temperaunce.

Temperaunce. Temperaunce is a measuryng of affeccions, accordyng to the will of reason, and a subduyng of luste vnto the Square of honestie. Yea, and what one thyng doth soner mitigate the immoderate passions of our nature, then the perfect knowlege of right and wrong and the iuste execucion appoynted by a lawe, for asswagyng the wilfull? Of this vertue there are three partes.

> Sobrietie.
> Jentlenesse.
> Modestie.

Sobrietie. Sobrietie is a bridelyng by discrecion the wilfulnesse of desire.

Jentlenesse. Jentlenesse is a caulmyng of heate, when wee begin to rage, and a lowly behauior in all our body

Modestie. Modestie is an honest shamefastnesse, whereby we kepe a constant loke, and appere sober in all our outward doynges. Now euen as we should desire the vse of all these vertues, so should we eschewe not onely the contraries herunto, but also auoyde all suche euilles, as by any meanes doe withdrawe vs from well doyng.

It is profitable.

A fter we haue perswaded our frend, that the Lawe is honest, drawyng our argumentes fro the heape of vertues, we must go further with hym, & bryng hym in good beleue, that it is very gainfull. For many one seke not **Hope of rewarde maketh men take paines.** the knowlege of learnyng for the goodnesse sake, but rather take paines for the gain, which thei se doth arise by it. Take awaie the hope of lucre, and you shall se fewe take any paines;

nes: No,not in the vineparD of the loꝛDe. Foꝛ although none
ſhoulD folowe any traDe of life,foꝛ the gain ſake,but euē as
he ſeeth it is moſte neceſſary,foꝛ thaDuauncement of GoDs
gloꝛy,ꝯ not paſſe in what eſtimacion thinges are haD in this
woꝛlDe:yet becauſe we are all ſo weake of wit, in our tēder
yeres,that we cannot weigh without ſelfes what is beſt,ꝯ
our boDy ſo neſhe,that it loꝛeth euer to bee cheriſhed, wee
taꝛe that,whiche is moſte gainfull foꝛ vs, and foꝛſake that
altogether,whiche we oughte moſte to folowe. So that foꝛ
lacke of honeſt meaues,and foꝛ want of gooD oꝛDer, the beſt
waie is not vſeD,neither is GoDDes honoꝛ in our firſt yeres
remembꝛeD. I haD rather(ſaiDe one)make my chilD a cobler
then a pꝛeacher , a taukerD bearer,then a ſcholer. Foꝛ what
ſhall my ſonne ſeke foꝛ learnyng,when he ſhall neuer gette
therby any liuyng? Set my ſonne to that,wherby he maie
get ſomewhat? Do ye not ſe how euery one catcheth ꝯ pul-
leth fꝛō the churche what thei can? I feare me one Day thei
will plucke Doune churche and all. Call you this the Goſ-
pell,when men ſeke onely to pꝛouiDe foꝛ their belies,ꝯ care
not a grote though their ſoules go to helle? A patrone of a
benefice wil haue a pooꝛe yngrame ſoule,to beare the name
of a perſone foꝛ.xx.marke,oꝛ.x.li:and the patrone hymſelf,
wil take vp foꝛ his ſnapſhare,as gooD as an.c.marke. Thus
GoD is robbeD,learnyng Decaied, England Diſhonoꝛed, and
honꝛtie not regarDeD. Thold Romaines not yet knowyng
Chꝛiſt,and yet beyng leD by a reuerēt feare towarDes GoD,
maDe this lawe.Sacrum ſacroue commendatū qui clepſe;
rit,rapſeritue,parricida eſt He that ſhall cloſely ſteale, oꝛ
foꝛcibly take awaie that thyng, whiche is holy,oꝛ geuen to
the holy place:is a murDerer of his coūtrey. But what haue
I ſaiD,I haue a greater matter in hand,then wherof I was
a ware,my penne hath run ouer farre, when my leaſure ſerueth not, noꝛ yet my witte is able to talke this caſe in ſuche
wiſe,as it ſhoulD bee,and as the largeneſſe therof requireth.
Therefoꝛe to my lawyer again,whom I Doubte not to perſwaDe,but that he ſhall haue the Deuill and all,if he learne a
paſe , and Dooe as ſome haue Dooen befoꝛe hym . Therefoꝛe
I will ſhewe howe largely this pꝛofite extenDeth , that

The Romay-
nes lawes foꝛ
Churche Di-
gnities.

I

The arte of Rhetorique.

I may haue him the foner, to take this matter in hand. The lawe therefore not onely bryngeth muche gain with it, but alfo auaunceth men bothe to worſhippe, renoume, and ho nour. All men ſhall ſeke his fauour, for his learnyng fake: the beſt ſhall like his cōpany, for his callyng: and his welth with his ſkill ſhalbe ſuche, that none ſhalbe able to wooꝛke hym any wꝛong. Some conſider pꝛofite, by theſe circum ſtaunces, folowyng.

> To whom.
> When.
> Where.
> Wherefore.

Either can I vſe a better oꝛder, then theſe circum ſtaunces miniſter vnto me. To whom therefore is the Lawe pꝛofitable? Marie to them that bee beſt learned, that haue redy wittes, and will take pai nes. When is the lawe pꝛofitable? Aſſuredly both now and euermoꝛe, but eſpecially in this age, where all men go to gether by the eares for this matter, and that matter. Suche alteracion hath been heretofoꝛe, that hereafter nedes muſte enſue muche altercacion. And where is all this a do? Euen in litle Englande, oꝛ in Weſtminſter hall, where neuer yet wanted buſines, noꝛ yet euer ſhall. Wherefoꝛe is the lawe pꝛofitable? Undoubtedly becauſe no manne could hold his awne, if there were not an oꝛder to ſtaie vs, and a Lawe to reſtrain vs. And I pꝛaie you who getteth the money? The Lawyers no doubt. And were not lande ſometymes cheaper bought, then got by the triall of a lawe? Do not men com

monly for trifles fall out? Some for loppyng of a tree, ſpe des al that euer thei haue, another for a Goſe, that graſeth vpon his ground, tries the lawe ſo hard, that he pꝛoues him ſelf a Gander. Now when men bee ſo mad, is it not eaſie to

gette money emong theim. Undoubtedly the lawyer neuer dieth a begger. And no maruaill. For an. C. begges for hym, and makes awaie all that thei haue, to get that of hym, the whiche the oftener he beſtoweth, the moꝛe ſtill he getteth. So that he gaineth alwaies, aſwell by encreaſe of lernyng as by ſtoꝛyng his purſe with money, wheras the other get a warme

warme fonne often tymes, and a flappe with a fore taile for
al that euer thei haue fpent.And why woulde they? Tufhe,
if it were to do againe, thei would do it:therfore the lawyer
can neuer want a liupng,til the pearth want men, and al be
voyde.

❧ The lawe eafie to many,and
harde to fome.

Doubt not, but my lawyer is perfwaded that the
law isprofitable:now muft I beare him in had that
it is an eafie matter to become a lawier.the whiche
if I fhalbe able to proue, I doubt not, but he will
proue a good lawier, & that right fhortly.the law is grounded
vpon reafon. And what hardeneffe is it for a man by reafon
to fynde out reafon. That can not be ftraung vnto him, the
grounde wherof, is graffed in his breft. What, though the
lawe be in a ftraunge tongue,the wordes may be gotte with
out any paine, when the matter felfe is compaft with eafe.
Tufhe, a litle lawe will make a greate fhowe, and therfore
though it be muche to becomme excellent, yet it is eafie, to
get a taift.And furely for getting of money,a litle wil do as
muche good oftentymes, as a greate deale. There is not a
word in the law,but it is a grote in þ lawiers purfe. I haue
knowne diuerfe that by familiar talkyng, & moutyng together haue comme to right good learning without any great
booke fkil,or muche beating of their braine by any clofe ftu
die,or fecrete mufyng in their chaber.But where fome fay
the lawe is very harde,and difcourage young men from the
ftudie therof, it is to be vnderftande of fuche as wil take no
paines at al, nor yet mynde the knowlege therof.For what
is not hard to man,when he wanteth wil to do his beft.As
good flepe,and faie it is harde:as wake,and take no paines.

The lawe. 〉 Godly.
        Jufte.
        Neceffarie.
        Pleafaunt.

What nedeth me to proue the lawe to be Godly,iuft,
or neceffarie, feeyng it is grounded vpon Goddes

54

The Arte of Rhetorique.

wil, and all lawes are made for the maintenaunce of iustice. If we will not beleue that it is necessarie, let vs haue rebelles againe to disturbe the Realme. Our nature is so fonde that we knowe not the necessitie of a thyng, til wee fynde some lacke of the same. Bowes are not estemed as they haue bene emong vs Englishmen, but if we were ones well beaten by our enemies wee shoulde soone knowe the wante, and with feelyng the smarte lament muche our folie. Take awaie the lawe, and take awaie our lifes, for nothyng mainteineth our wealthe, our health, & the sauegard of our bodies, but the lawe of a Realme, wherby the wicked are condempned, and the godly are defended.

Lawes maintaine lyfe.

¶ An Epistle to perswade a young ientleman to Mariage, deuised by Erasmus in the behalfe of his frende.

Albeit you are wyse enough of your selfe throughe that singulare wisedome of yours (most louyng Cosyn) and litle needes the aduise of other, yet either for that olde fryndshippe whiche hath bene betwixt vs, and continued with our age euen from our cradles, or for suche your greate good turnes showed at all tymes towardes me, or elles for that faste kynred and alliaunce whiche is betwixt vs: I thought my selfe thus muche to owe vnto you if I woulde be suche a one in deede, as you euer haue taken me, that is to saie a man bothe frendly and thankeful, to tell you freely (whatsoeuer I iudged so apperteine either to the sauegarde, or worshippe of you, or any of yours) and willyngly to warne you of the same. We are better seen oftentymes in other mens matters, than we are in our owne. I haue felte often your aduise in myne owne affaires, and I haue founde it to be as fortunate vnto me, as it was frendly. Nowe if you wil likewyse in your awne matters folowe my counsail, I truste it shal so come to passe that neither I shal repent me for that I haue geuen you counsail, nor yet you shal forthynk pour self, that you haue obeyed, and folowed myne aduise. There was at supper with me the twelfe daie of Aprill when I laie in the

country

The Arte of Rhetorique.   *Fol.22.*

countrie, Antonius Baldus, a man (as you knowe) that
moſt earneſtly tendꝛeth your welfare, and one that hath
bene alwaies of great acquaintaunce and familiaritie with
your ſonne in lawe: A heauie feaſt we had, and ful of much
mournyng. He tolde me greatly to bothe our heauineſſe,
that your mother that moſte godly woman, was departed
this lyfe, ⁊ your ſiſter beyng ouercome with ſoꝛow ⁊ heaui=
neſſe, had made her ſelfe a Nunne, ſo that in you onely re=
maineth the hope of iſſue and maintenaunce of your ſtocke.
whereupon your frendes with one conſent haue offerde
you in Mariage a ientlewoman of a good houſe, and muche
wealthe, fayre of bodie, very well bꝛought vp, and ſuche
a one as loueth you with all her harte. But you (either foꝛ
your late ſoꝛowes whiche you haue in freſhe remembꝛaunce
oꝛ elles foꝛ Religion ſake)haue ſo purpoſed to lyue a ſyngle
lyfe, that neither can you foꝛ loue of your ſtocke, neither
foꝛ deſier of iſſue, noꝛ yet foꝛ any entreatie that your fren=
des can make, either by pꝛayeng, oꝛ by weppyng: be bꝛought
to chaunge your mynde.

And yet notwithſtandyng all this (if you wil folowe my
counſaill) you ſhalbe of an other mynde, and leauyng to
lyue ſyngle whiche bothe is barren, and ſmally agreepng
with the ſtate of mannes nature, you ſhall geue your ſelfe
wholy to moſte holy wedlocke. And foꝛ this parte I will
neither wiſhe that the loue of your frpndes, (whiche elles
ought to ouercome your nature) noꝛ yet myne auctho=
ritie that I haue ouer you, ſhoulde doe me any good at all
to compaſſe this my requeſte, if I ſhall not pꝛoue vnto
you by moſte plaine reaſons, that it will be bothe muche
moꝛe honeſt, moꝛe pꝛofitable, and alſo moꝛe pleaſaunt foꝛ
you, to marie, than to lyue otherwyſe. Yea, what will you
ſaie, if I pꝛoue it alſo to be neceſſarie foꝛ you at this tyme
to Marie.   And firſte of all, if honeſtie maie moue you in
this matter (the whiche emong all good men ought to bee
of muche weighte,) what is moꝛe honeſt then Matrimo=
nie, the whiche CHRISTE hym ſelfe did make honeſt,
when not onely he, voucheſaufed to bee at a Mariage
with his Mother, but alſo did conſecrate the Mariage

F.ij.   feaſt

feaſte with the firſt miracle that euer he did vpon pearthe? What is moze holie then Matrimonie whiche the creatour of all thynges did inſtitute, did faſten, and make holie, and nature it ſelfe did eſtabliſhe? What is moze praiſe woz- thie than that thyng, the whiche whoſoeuer ſhall diſ- praiſe, is condempned ſtreight foz an Heretique? Matrimo- nie is euen as honourable, as the name of an Heretique, is thought ſhamefull. What is moze right, oz meete, than to geue that vnto the poſteritie, the whiche we haue receiued of our aunceſters? What is moze inconſiderate than vnder the deſire of holineſſe to eſcew that as vnholie, which God hym ſelfe the fountaine and father of al holineſſe, woulde haue to be counted as moſte holie? What is moze vnmanly than that man ſhoulde go againſt the lawes of mankynde? What is moze vnthankfull than to deny that vnto younge- lynges, the whiche (if thou haddeſt not receyued of thine el- ders) thou couldeſt not haue bene the man liuyng, able to haue denied it vnto theim. That if you woulde knowe who was the firſt founder of Mariage, you ſhal vnderſtande that it came vp not by Licurgus, noz yet by Moſes, noz yet by Solon, but it was firſt ozdeined, & inſtituted by the chief founder of all thynges, commended by the ſame, made ho- nourable and made holie by theſame. Foz at the firſte when he made man of the pearthe, he did percepue that his lyfe ſhoulde be miſerable and vnſauerie, excepte he ioyned Eue as mate vnto hym. Wherupon he did not make the wyfe v- pon the ſame claie wherof he made man, but he made her of Adams ribbes, to the ende we might plainely vnderſtande that nothyng ought to be moze deare vnto vs thē our wyfe, nothyng moze nigh vnto vs, nothyng ſurer ioyned, and (as a man woulde ſaie) faſter glewed together. The ſelfe ſame GOD after the generall floude, beyng reconciled to man- kynde is ſaied to proclaime this lawe firſte of all, not that men ſhoulde lyue ſingle, but that they ſhoulde encreaſe, be multiplied, and fill the pearth. But howe I praie you could this thyng be, ſauyng by mariage and lawful compyng toge- ther? And firſt leaſt we ſhoulde allege here either the liber- tie of Moyſes lawe, oz els the neceſſitie of that tyme: What

other

Praiſe woz- thie to marie.

Right and meete to marie.

Mariage firſt made by God.

After mā was made, the wo- man was ioy- ned vnto hym.

Matrimonie renewed after the floude.

other meanyng els hath that commune and commēdable re= ¶Natures
pozte of Chziste in the Gospell, foz this cause (saieth he) worke allowed
shall man leaue father and mother and cleaue to his wyfe. worde.

And what is moze holie than the reuerence and loue due vn=
to parentes? and yet the truthe promised in Matrimonie is
pzeferred befoze it, and by whose meanes? Mary by GOD
hym self, at what time? Fozsouth not onely emōg the Iues,
but also emong the Chzistians. Men fozsake father and mo=
ther and takes themselfes wholie to their wyfes. The sonne
beyng past one and twentie yeres, is free and at his libertie.
Yea the sonne beyng abdicated, becommeth no sonne. But
it is death onely that parteth maried folke, if yet death doe
part them. Now if the other Sacramentes (whereunto the
Churche of Chziste chiefely leaneth) bee reuerently vsed,
who doeth not see that this Sacramente shoulde haue the
most reuerence of al, the whiche was instituted of GOD,
and that firste and befoze all other. As foz the other they
were instituted vpon yearthe, this was ozdeined in Para=
dise: the other were geuen foz a remedie, this was appoinc=
ted foz the felowshippe of felicitie: the other were applied
to mannes nature after the fall, this onely was geuen when
man was in moste perfite state. If we counte those lawes
good that moztall men haue enacted, shall not the lawe of
Matrimonie be moste holie, whiche wee haue receyued of
him, by whome we haue receiued lyfe, the whiche lawe was
then together enacted whē man was first created? And last=
ly to strengthen this lawe with an example and deede doen Mariage beau
Chziste beyng an young man (as the Stozie repozteth) was tified by a mi=
called to a Mariage, and came thither willyngly with his racle.
mother, and not onely was he there pzesent, but also he did
honest the feaste with a wonderfull meruaile begynnyng
first in none other place to worke his wounders, and to doe
his miracles. Why then I pzaie you (will one saie) howe
happeneth it that Chzist foзbare Mariage? as though good
Seir there are not many thynges in Chziste at the whiche
we oughte rather to meruaile, than seeke to folowe. he was
boзne and had no father, he came into this woзlde without
his mothers painefull trauaile, he came out of the graue
f.iij.   when

The Arte of Rhetorique.

when it was cloſed vp, whꜳt is not in hym aboue nature?
Let theſe thynges be pꝛopꝛe vnto hym. Let vs thaꞏ lyue
within the boundes of nature, reuerence thoſe thynges
that are aboue nature, and folowe ſuche thynges as are
within our reache ſuche as we are able to compaſſe. But
yet (you ſaie) he woulde bee boꝛne of a Uirgine: Of a
Uirgine (I graunt) but yet of a maried Uirgine. A Uirꝛ
gyne beyng a mother did moſte become G O D, and beyng
maried ſhe did ſhowe what was beſte foꝛ vs to doe. Uirꝛ
ginitie did become her, who beyng vndefiled, bꝛought hym
foꝛthe by heauenly inſpiration thꜳt was vndefiled. And
yet Joſeph beyng her houſbande dothe commende vnto vs
the lawe of chaiſte wedlocke. Yea, howe coulde he better
ſette out the ſocietie in wedlocke, than that willyng to deꞏ
clare the ſecrete ſocietie of his diuinꞏ nꜳture with the boꞏ
die and ſoule of man, whiche is wonderfull euen to the
heauenly Aungelles, and to ſhowe his vnſpeakable and eꞏ
uer abidyng loue towarde his Churche:he doeth call hym
ſelfe the Bꝛydegꝛome, and her the Bꝛyde. Greate is the
Sacrament of Matrimonie (ſaith Paule) betwixt Chꝛiſte
and his Churche. If there had bene vnder heauen any hoꞏ
lier yoke, if there had bene any moꝛe religiouſe couenaunt
than is Matrimonie, without doubte the example thereof
had bene vſed. But what lyke thyng doe you reade in all
Scripture of the ſyngle lyfe? The Apoſtle S. Paul in the
thirteen Chapi. of his Epiſtle to the Hebꝛues calleth Maꞏ
trimonie honourable emong all men, and a bedde vndefilꞏd,
and yet the ſyngle lyfe is not ſo muche as ones named in
the ſame place. Nay they are not boꝛne withall that lyue
ſyngle, except they make ſome recompence with doyng ſome
greater thyng. foꝛ elles, if a man folowyng the lawe of
nature, doe labour to gette childꝛen, he is euer to be pꝛeferꞏ
red befoꝛe hym that lyueth ſtill vnmaried, foꝛ none other
ende, but becauſe he woulde bee out of trouble, and lyue
moꝛe free. Wee doe reade that ſuche as are in very deede
chaiſte of their body, and lyue a Uirgines lyfe, haue bene
pꝛaiſed, but the ſyngle lyfe was neuer pꝛaiſed of it ſelfe.
Nowe againe the lawe of Moſes accurſeth the barreneſſe
of maried

*Mariage hoꞏ
noꝛable.*

of maried folke, and wee doe reade that some were excom=
municated for the same purpose, and banished from the aul=
tar. And wherefore I praie you? Marie Sir because that
they like vnprofitable persones, and liuyng onely to them
selues, did not encrease the worlde with any issue. In
Deuteronomie it was the chiefest token of Goddes bles= Deut. vi.
synges vnto the Israelites that none shoulde be barren a=
mong them, neither man, nor yet woman. And Lya is Lia.
thought to bee out of Goddes fauour, because she coulde
not bryng furth children. Yea, and in the Psalme of Dauid
an hundreth twentie and eight, it is counted one of the chie=
fest partes of blesse to bee a frutefull woman, Thy wyfe
(sayeth the Psalme) shalbe plentifull lyke a vine, and thy
children lyke the braunches of Olyues, rounde about thy
Table. Then if the lawe do condempne, and vtterly dissa=
lowe barren Matrimonie, it hath alwaies muche more con=
dempned the syngle lyfe of Bacchelaures. Yf the fault of
nature hath not escaped blame, the will of man can neuer
wante rebuke. Yf they are accursed that woulde haue chil=
dren, and can gette none, what deserue they whiche neuer
trauaile to escape barreinesse?

The Hebrues had suche a reuerence to maried folke, Hebrues lawe
that he whiche had maried a wyfe, the same yeare shoulde for maried
not be forced to go on warrefaire. A Citie is lyke to fall folke.
in ruine, excepte there be watchemen to defende it with
armour. But assured destruction muste here needes folowe
excepte men throughe the benefite of Mariage supplie is=
sue, the whiche through mortalitie doe from tyme to tyme
decaie.

Ouer & besides this the Romaines did laie a penaltie v=
pon their backe that liued a syngle lyfe, yea they would not Plutarchus
suffer them to beare any office in the comure weale. But they iu the lyfe of
that had encreased the worlde with issue, had a reward by co Cato.
imune assent, as men that had deserued well of their coun=
trie. The olde foren lawes did appoincte penalties for suche
as liued syngle, the whiche although they were qualified by
Constantius the Emperour in the fauor of Christes religio,
yet these lawes do declare howe litle it is for the commune
                                            weales

weales aduauncement,(that either a Citie ſhould be leſſened
for loue of ſole life,or els that the countrie ſhoulde be filled
ful of baſtardes.And beſides this, the Emperour Auguſtus
being a ſore puniſher of euil behauiour,examined a ſouldior
becauſe he did not marie his wife accordyng to the lawes,
the whiche ſouldiour had hardely eſcaped iudgement, if he
had not gotte. iij. children by her. And in this point doe the
lawes of al Emperours ſeeme fauourable to maried folke,
that they abrogate ſuche vowes as were proclaimed to be
kept and brought in by Miſcella,and woulde that after the
penaltie were remitted, ſuche couenauntes, beyng made a
gainſt al right and conſcience,ſhoulde alſo be taken of none
effect,and as voide in the lawe.Ouer and beſides this,Vl
pianus doth declare that the matter of Dowries was euer
more and in al places the chiefeſt aboue al other,the whiche
ſhould neuer haue bene ſo,excepte there came to the comune
weale ſome eſpecial profite by mariage. Mariage hath euer
bene reuerenced,but frutefulneſſe of body hath bene muche
more.for ſo ſone as one gotte the name of a father,there diſ
cended not onely vnto him enheirtaunce of lande,but al be
queſtes,and gooddes of ſuche his frendes as dyed inteſtate.
The whiche thyng appereth plaine by the Satyre Poete.

Through me thou art made,an heire to haue lande,

Thou haſt al bequeſtes one with another,

All gooddes and cattel are come to thy hande

Yea gooddes inteſtate,thou ſhalt haue euer.

Now he that had.iij.children, was more fauoured,for he
was exempted from al outward ambaſſages.Againe he that
had fyue childen was diſcharged and free from all perſonal
office, as to haue the gouernaunce, or patronage of younge
ientlemē,the whiche in thoſe daies was a great charge & ful
of paines without any profit at al.He that had.xiij.children
was free by the Emperour Iulianus law,not onely frō be
yng a mā at Armes,or Captaine ouer horſemen:but alſo frō
al other offices in the comune weale.And the wiſe foundsers
of all lawes geue good reaſon why ſuche fauor was ſhewed
to maried folke.For what is more bleſſeful thā to liue euer?

Now

Now where as nature hath denied this, Matrimony doth
geue it by a certaine sleyght, so muche as maye be. who
dothe not desire to be bruted, and liue through fame emõg
men hereafter? Now there is no buildinge of pillers, no e-
rectinge of Arches, no blasinge of Armes, that dothe more
sette forthe a mannes name, then doth the encrease of chil-
dre. Albinus obteined his purpose of the Emperour Adria,
for none other desert of his, but ẙ he had begote an house-
full of children. And therfore the Emperoure (to the hin-
deraũce of his treasure) suffred the children to enter who-
lye vpon their fathers possession, forasmuche as he knewe
well that his realme was more strengthened with encrease
of children, then with store of money. Againe, all other lawes are neither agreynge fo: all Countryes, nor yet v-
sed at all times. Licurgus made a lawe, that they whiche
maried not, shoulde be kepte in Somer from the sighte of
stage playes, and other wonderfull shewes, and in winter
they shoulde go naked aboute the market place, and accur-
singe theim selues, they shoulde confesse openly that they
hadde iustlye deserued suche punishment, because they did
not liue accordinge to the lawes. And without any more
a doe, will ye knowe how much our olde Auncesters heretofore estemed Matrimonie? weye well, and consider the
punishment for breaking of wedlocke. The Grekes heretofore thought it mete to punishe the breache of Matrimonie
with battaile that continued ten yeres. Yea, moreouer not
onely by the Romaine lawe, but also by the Hebrues and
straũgers, aduouterous persons wer punished with death.
If a thiefe payde .iiij. times the value of that which he toke
awaye, he was deliuered, but an aduouterers offence, was
punished with the swoorde. Emonge the Hebrues, the people stoned the aduouterers to death, with their owne handes, because they had broken that, without which the wo-:
lde could not continue. And yet they thought not this sore
law sufficient inough, but graunted further to runne him
thorowe withoute lawe, that was taken in aduoutrye, as
who shoulde saye, they graunted that to the griefe of maried folke, the whiche they woulde hardlye graunte to hym

G.i.   that

Licurgus law
against vnma-
ried folke.

Punish-mates
appoynted for
breaking of
wedlocke.

The Grecians
reuengement
for aduoutrye.

The Hebrues
stoned Aduou-
terers.

Lawful for the
maried man a-
mong the He-
brues to kyll
the aduouterer

that ſtode in his owne defence foʒ ſaufegarde of his life, as though he offended moʒe haynouſly that toke a mans wife, then he did that toke away a mannes lyfe. Aſſuredly wed= locke muſte neades ſeme to be a mooſte holye thinge, conſi= deringe that beinge once bʒoken, it muſte neades be purged with mannes bloude, the reuenger wherof is not foʒced to abide either lawe oʒ iudge, the whiche libertie is not graũ= ted anye to vſe vpon him that hathe killed either his father oʒ his mother. But what do we with theſe Lawes wʒit= ten? This is the lawe of Nature, not wʒitten in the Ta= bles of Bʒaſſe, but firmelye pʒynted in oure myndes, the whiche Lawe, whoſoeuer dothe not obeye, he is not woʒ= thye to be called a manne, muche leſſe ſhall he be counted a Citezen. foʒ if to liue well (as the Stoikes wittelye do diſpute) is to folowe the courſe of Nature, what thin=

Matrimonie naturall

ge is ſo agreynge with Nature as Matrimonye? foʒ there is noʒhinge ſo naturall not onelye vnto mankinde, but al= ſo vnto all other liuinge creatures, as it is foʒ euerye one of theim to kepe their owne kinde from decaye, and thʒou= ghe encreaſe of iſſue, to make the whole kinde immoʒtall. The whiche thinge (all menne knowe) can neuer be dooen, withoute wedlocke and carnall copulation. It were a fowle thinge, that bʒute beaſtes ſhoulde obeye the lawe of Nature, and menne like Gyauntes ſhoulde fighte againſt Nature. whoſe woʒke if we woulde narowly loke vpon, we ſhall percepue that in all thinges here vpon earthe, the woulde there ſhoulde be a certaine ſpice of mariage. I wil not ſpeake nowe of Trees, wherin (as Plinie mooſte cer= tainelye wʒiteth) there is founde Mariage with ſome ma=

Mariage e= monge trees.

nifeſte difference of bothe kyndes, that excepte the houſ= bande Tree do leane with his boughes euen as thoughe he ſhoulde deſire copulation vpon the womenne Trees gro= wynge rounde aboute him: they woulde elles altogether ware barraine. The ſame Plinie alſo dothe repoʒt that certaine aucthoures do thincke there is bothe male and fe=

Mariage e= mong pʒeci= ous ſtones.

male in all thinges that the Earthe yeldeth. I will not ſpeake of pʒecious ſtones, wherein the ſame aucthoure af= firmeth, and yet not he onelye neither, that there is bothe

male

male and female emonge theim. And I praye you hath not GOD so knitte all thinges together with certaine lyn=ckes, that one euer semeth to haue neade of another? what saye you of the skye or firmamente, that is euer stirrynge with continuall mouinge? Dothe it not playe the parte of a husbande, while it puffeth vp the Earthe, the mother of all thinges, and maketh it fruitefull with castinge seede (as a manne woulde saye) vpon it. But I thincke t ouer tedious to runne ouer all thinges. And to what ende are these thinges spoken? Marye sir, because we might vnder=stande that throughe Mariage, all thing:s are, and do styll continue, and withoute the same all thinges do decaye, and come to noughte. The olde auncient and moste wise Po=etes do feyne (who hadde euer a desire vnder the coloure of fables to set forthe the preceptes of Philosophie) that the Gi=auntes whiche had snakes fete, and were borne of th earth, builded greate hilles that mounted vp to heauen, minding therebey to be at vtter defiaunce with God and all his aun=gelles. And what meaneth this fable? Marye it sheweth vnto vs, that certaine fierce and sauage menne, suche as were vnknowen, coulde not abide wedlocke for anye wor=ldes good, and therefore they were stricken downe heade=longe with lighteninge, that is to saye: they were vtterlye destroyed, when they soughte to eschue that, whereby the weale and saulfegarde of all mankinde onelye dothe con=siste. Nowe againe, the same Poetes do declare that Or=pheus the musician and minstrell, did styrre and make softe with his pleasaunte melodye the mooste harde rockes and stones. And what is their meaninge herein? Assuredlye nothinge elles, but that a wise and well spoken manne, did call backe harde harted menne, suche as liued abroade like Beastes, from open whoredome, and broughte them to lyue after the mooste holpe lawes of Matrimonye. Thus we se plainelye, that suche a one as hathe no minde of Mariage, semeth to be no manne, but rather a Stone, an enemye to Nature, a rebel to God him selfe, seking throughe his owne folye, his last ende and destruction.

G.ij.   well,

Marginal notes:

Mariage be=twene the fir=mament and the earth.

The fable of Giauntes that fought against Nature.

Orpheus.

Well, let vs go on ſtill(ſeynge we are fallen into fables that are not fables altogeth‑r)when the ſame Oꝛpheus in the middes of Hell, foꝛced Pluto him ſelfe and all the deuilles there, to graunte him leaue to carye awaye his wife Euridice, what other thinge do we thinke that the Poets meant, but only to ſet foꝛthe vnto vs the loue in wedlocke

The moſt wic‑ked can not choſe but alow mariage.
the whiche euen amonge the Deuilles was compted good and Godlye.

And this alſo makes wel foꝛ the purpoſe, that in olde time they made Jupiter Gamelius, the God of mariage, & Juno Lucina ladye midwif‑, to helpe ſuche women as labou‑ red in child bedde, beynge fondlye deceiued, and ſuperſtici‑ ouſlie erring in naming of the Gods, and yet not miſſinge the trueth, in declaring that Matrimonie is an holy thin‑ ge, and mete foꝛ the woꝛthines therof, that the Goddes in heauen ſhoulde haue care ouer it. Emonge diuers coun‑ tries, and diuers menne, there haue bene diuers lawes and cuſtomes vſed. Yet was there neuer anye countrey ſo ſa‑ uage, none ſo farre from all humanitie, where the name of wedlocke was not counted holpe, and hadde in great reue‑

All nacions e‑uer eſtemed mariage.
rence. This the Thꝛacian, this the Sarmate, this the Indi‑ an, this the Grecian, this the Latine, yea, this the Bꝛittain that dwelleth in the furtheſte parte of all the woꝛlde, oꝛ if there be anye that dwell beyonde them haue euer counted to be moſte holpe. And why foꝛ? Marye becauſe that thinge muſt neades be commune to all, whiche the commune mo‑ ther vnto all, hath graffed in vs all, and hath ſo thoꝛowlye graffed the ſame in vs, that not onely ſtockedoues and Pi‑ gions, but alſo the moſt wilde beaſtes haue a natural felin‑ ge of this thinge. Foꝛ the Lyons are gentle againſt the Li‑ oneſſe. The Tygers fight foꝛ ſafegard of their yong whel‑ pes. The Aſſe runnes thꝛough the hote fyꝛe(which is made to kepe her awaie)foꝛ ſafegarde of her iſſue. And this they call the lawe of Nature, the whiche as it is of moſt ſtren‑ gthe and foꝛce, ſo it ſpꝛeadeth abꝛoade moſt largely. Ther‑ foꝛe as he is counted no good gardener, that being content with thinges pꝛeſent, doth diligentlye pꝛopne his old trees, and hath no regard either to pynpe oꝛ graffe yong ſettes: be

cauſe

caufe the felfe fame Oʒcharde (thoughe it be neuer fo well
trimmed) mufte nedes decape in time, and all the trees dpe
within fewe peres: So he is not to be counted halfe a diʒ
ligent citizen, that beinge contente with the pʒefent multiʒ
tude, hathe no regarde to encreafe the number. Therefoʒe
there is no one man that euer hath bene counted a woʒthp
Citezen, who hath not laboured to get childʒe, and fought
to bʒing them vp in Godlines.

Emonge the Hebʒues and the Perfians he was moft The Hebʒues and Perfians
commended, that had moft wiues, as thoughe the countrep had a number
were moft beholding to him, that encreafed the fame with of wiues
the greateft number of childʒen. Do pou feke to be compted
moʒe holte then Abʒaham him felfe? well, he fhould neuer Abʒaham.
haue bene compted the father of manpe Macions, and that
thʒough Gods furtheraunce, if he had foʒboʒne the compaʒ
npe of his wife. Do pou loke to be reckened moʒe deuoute
then Jacob? He doubteth nothinge to raunfome Rachel Jacob.
from her greate bondage. will pou be taken foʒ wifer then
Salomon? And pet J pʒape pou what a number of wiues Salomon.
kept he in one houfe? will pou be compted moʒe chafte the
Socrates, who is repoʒted to beare at heme with ʒantippe Socrates
that verpe fhʒewe, and pet not fo muche therefoʒe (as he
is wonte to iefte accoʒdinge to his olde maner) becaufe he
might learne pacience at home, but alfo becaufe he mighte
not feme to come behinde with his dutpe in dopng the wil
of nature. Foʒ he bepnge a manne, fuche a one (as Appolʒ
lo iudged him bp his Oʒacle to be wife) did well percepue
that he was gote foʒ this caufe, boʒne foʒ this caufe, and
therfoʒe bounde to pelde fo muche vnto nature. Foʒ if the
olde auncient Philofophers haue faide wel, if our diuines
haue pʒoued the thinge not without reafon, if it be vfed eʒ
uerpe where foʒ a commune pʒouerbe, and almoft in euerpe
mans mouthe, that neither God noʒ pet Nature, did euer
make anp thinge in vapne: whp did he geue vs fuch memʒ
bʒes, how happeneth we haue fuche lufte, and fuche power
to get iffue, if the fingle lpfe and none other be altogether
pʒapfe woʒthpe? If one fhoulde beftowe vpon pou a verpe
good thinge, as a bowe, a coate, oʒ a fwoʒde, al men would

G.iii.　　　thinke

The arte of Rhetorique.

thincke you were not worthye to haue the thinge, if either you coulde not, o: you woulde not vse it, and occupie it. And where as all other thinges are o:deyned vpon suche greate considerations, it is not like that Nature slepte o: fo:gate her selfe when she made this one thinge. And nowe here will some saye, that this fowle and filthye desire, and styrringe vnto lufte, came neuer in by Nature, but through Sinne: fo: whose wo:des J passe not a strawe, seinge their saipnges are as false, as God is true. Fo: J p:ay you was not Mat:imonye insticuted (whose wo:ke can not be done wittboute these membres) before there was anye Synne. And againe, whence haue all other b:ute beastes their p:o: uocations? of Nature, o: of Sinne? A man woulde thinke they hadde theim of Nature. But shall J tell you at a wo:de, wee make that filthye by oure owne Jmagination, whiche of the owne nature is good and Godlye. O: elles if we will examine matters, (not acco:dinge to the opini: on of menne, but weye them as they are ef their owne Na: ture) howe chaunceth it that we thincke it lesse filthye, to eate, to chewe, to digest, to emptye the bodye, and to slepe, then it is to vse carnall copulation, such as is lawfull, and permitted. Naye sir (you will saye,) we muste folowe ver: tue, rather then Nature. A gentle dishe. As thoughe anye thinge can be called vertue that is contrary vnto Nature. Assuredly there is nothinge that can be perfectlye gote, ei: ther throughe laboure, o: throughe learning, if man gro: unde not his doynges altogether vpon Nature.

But you will liue an Apostles life, suche as some of them did that liued single, and exho:ted other to the same kinde of life. Tushe, let them folowe the Apostles that are Apostles in deede, whose office seynge it is bothe to teache and b:inge vp the people in Goddes doctrine, they are not able to discharge their dutyes bothe to their flocke, and to their wife and familye. Althoughe it is well knowen that some of the Apostles had wiues. But beit that Bishoppes liue single, o: graunt we them to haue no wiues. What do you folowe the p:ofession of the Apostles, beynge one that

is

is fartheſt in life from their Vocation, beinge bothe a tem=
po2all manne, and one that liueth of poure owne. They
hadde this Pardon graunted them to be cleane voyde from
Mariage, to the ende they mighte be at leaſure to get vnto
Ch2iſte a mo2e plentifull number of his child2en. Let this
be the o2der of P2ieſtes and Monkes, who belike haue en=
tred into the Religion and rule of the Eſſens, (ſuche as
amonge the Jewes lothed Mariage) but poure callinge is
an other waye. Naye, but (you will ſaye) Ch2iſte him ſelfe
hath compted theim bleſſed, whiche haue gelded theim ſel=
ues fo2 the Kingdome of GOD. Sir, J am contente to
admitte the aucth02itie, but thus J erpounde the meaning.
Firſte, J thincke that this doctrine of Ch2iſte did chieflye
belonge vnto that time, when it behoued theim chieflye to
be voyde of all cares and buſines of this wo2lde. They
were fayne to trauaple into all places, fo2 the perſecutou=
res were euer readye to laye handes on theim. But nowe
the wo2lde is ſo, that a manne can finde in no place the vp=
rightnes of behauioure leſſe ſtayred, then emonge maried
folke. Let the ſwarmes of Monkes and Nunnes ſette fo2=
the their o2der neuer ſo muche, let theim boaſte and b2agge
their bealies full, of their Ceremonies and church ſeruice,
wherin they chieflye paſſe all other: yet is wedloche (be=
ynge well and trulye kepte) a mooſte holye kinde of life.
Againe, would to God they were gelded in very dede, what
ſoeuer they be, that coloure their noughtye liuinge wyth
ſuch a toye name of geldinge, liuing in muche mo2e filthye
luſte vnder the cloke and p2etence of chaſtitie. Neither can
J repo2te fo2 verye ſhame, into howe filthye offences they
do often fall, that will not vſe that remedye whiche Na=
ture hath graunted vnto manne. And laſt of all, where do
you reade that euer Ch2iſte commaunded anye manne to
liue ſingle, and yet he dothe openlye fo2bidde diuo2cement.
Then he dothe not wo2ſte of all (in my Judgemente) fo2
the commune weale of Mankinde, that graunteth libertye
vnto P2ieſtes: yea, and Monkes alſo (if neade be) to marỹ, P2ieſtes ma=
and to take them to their wiues, namely ſeing there is ſuche riage.

G.iiij.   an vn=

an vnreaſonable number euerye where, emonge whom I
praye you how many be there that liue chaſte. How muche
better were it to turne their concubines into wyues, that
where as they haue them now to their greate ſhame wyth
an vnquiet conſcience, they mighte haue the other openlye
with good report, and get children, and alſo bringe them vp
godlye, of whom they them ſelues not onelye mighte not be
aſhamed, but alſo might be counted honeſt men for them.

And I thinke the biſhoppes officers woulde haue procured
this matter longe agoe, if they had not founde greater gai
nes by prieſtes lemmans, then they were like to haue by prie
ſtes wiues. But virginitie forſothe is an heauenlye thing,
it is an Aungels life. I aunſwer, wedlocke is a manly thin
ge, ſuche as is mete for man. And I talke now as man vnto
man, I graunte you, that virginitie is a thinge praiſe wor
thy, but ſo farre I am content to ſpeake in praiſe of it, if it be
not ſo praiſed, as though the iuſt ſhuld altogether folow it,
for if men commenly ſhould begin to like it, what thing could
be inuented more perilous to a commune weale then virgi
nitie. ſ owe be it that other deſerue greate praiſe for their
maydenheade, you notwithſtandinge can not wante greate
rebuke. ſeynge it lieth in your handes to kepe that houſe fro
decaye wherof you lineallye deſcended, and to continue ſtill
the name of your auunceſters, who deſerue moſte worthely to
be knowen for euer. And laſte of all, he deſerueth as muche
praiſe, as they whiche kepe their maydenhode: that kepes
him ſelfe true to his wife, and marieth rather for encreaſe
of children, then to ſatiſfy his luſte ſfor if a brother be com
maunded to ſtirre vp ſede to his brother that dieth without
iſſue, will you ſuffer the hope of all youre ſtocke to decaye,
namely ſeinge there is none other of your name and ſtocke,
but your ſelfe alone, to continue the poſteritie. I know wel
inoughe, that the auncient fathers haue ſet forthe in greate
volumes, the praiſe of virginitie, emonge whom, Hierom
dothe ſo take on, and prayſeth it ſo much aboue the ſtarres,
that he fell in maner to depraue Matrimonie, and therfor
was required of Godly Biſhoppes to cal ba ke his wordes
that he had ſpoken. But let vs beare with ſuche heate for
that

Virginitie.

Hieroms prai
ſe vpon virgi
nitie.

that tyme sake,J would wiſhe nowe,that thei, whiche ex=
hozt yong folke euery where,and without reſpect(ſuche as
yet knowe not thēſelfes)to liue a ſingle life,and to pzofeſſe
virginitie:that thei would beſtowe theſame labour, in ſet=
tyng furth the deſcripcion of chaſt and pure wedlocke.And
yet thoſe bodies that are in ſuche great loue with virgini=
tie , are well contented that menne ſhould fight againſt the
Turkes,whiche in nomber are infinitely greater then wee
are. And now if theſe menne thinke right in this behalfe,it
muſt nedes be thought right good and godly,to labour ear=
neſtly foz chilozen gettyng , and to ſubſtitute youthe from
tyme to tyme,foz the maintenaunce of warre. Except par=
auenture thei thīnke that Gunnes,Billes,Pikes,and na=
uies,ſhould be pzouided foz battaill, and that men ſtand in
no ſtede at all with them.Thei alſo allowe it well,that we
ſhould kill miſcreaunt and Heathen parentes, that the ra=
ther their chilozen not knowyng of it, might bee Baptized
and made Chziſtians.Nowe if this bee righte and lawfull,
how muche moze ſentleneſſe were it to haue chilozen Ba=
ptized,beyng boznt in lawfull mariage.There is no nacion
ſo ſauage,noz yet ſo hard harted,within the whole wozlde,
but theſame abhozreth murderyng of infauntes , and newe
boznt babes.Kynges alſo and hedde rulers , dooe likewiſe
puniſhe moſte ſtreightly, all ſuche as ſeke meanes to be de=
liuered befoze their tyme , oz vſe Phiſicke to waxe barren,
and neuer to beare chilozē.What is the reaſon?Marie thei
compt ſmall difference betwixt hym, that killeth the child,
ſo ſone as it beginneth to quicken: and thother, that ſeketh
all meanes poſſible,neuer to haue any child at all. The ſelf
ſame thyng that either withereth and dzieth awaie in thy
body, oz els putrifieth within thee,and ſo hurteth greatly
thy healthe, yea,that ſelf ſame, whiche falleth from thee in
thy ſlepe,would haue been a manne, if thou thy ſelf haddeſt
been a man.The Hebzues abhozre that man,and wiſhe him *Hebzues.*
Goddes curſſe,that(beyng commaunded to marie with the
wife of his dedde bzother)did caſt his ſeede vpon the groūd
leaſt any iſſue ſhould bee had, and he was euer thought vn=
wozthy to liue here vpon yerth, that would not ſuffer that

h.i.   child

that chilo to liue, whiche was quicke in the mothers wōbe. But I praie pou how litle do thei swarue from this offence whiche bpno themselfes to liue barren, all the daies of their life: Doo thei not seme to kill as many men, as were like to haue been bozne, if thei hao beſtowed their endeuors to haue got chilozen: Now I praie pou, if a man hao lande that wer very fatte and fertile, and ſuffered theſame foz lacke of ma: nerpng, foz euer to ware barren, ſhould he not, oz wer he not woztbp to be puniſhed bp the lawes, confiderpng it is foz the cōmon wpales behoue, that euery man ſhould wel and truly huſbande his awne. If that mā be puniſhed, who litle heeth the maintenaunce of his Tillage, the whiche although it be neuer ſo wel manered, pet it peldeth nothpng els but wheat barlep, beanes, and peaſon: what puniſhement is he woztbp to ſuffer, that refuſeth to Plough that lande, whiche bepng tilled, peldeth chilore. And foz ploughpng land, it is nothpng els, but painfull toplpng from tpme to tpme, but in gettpng chilozen, there is pleaſure, whiche bepng ozdeined, as a redp reward foz paines takpng, aſketh a ſhozt trauaill foz all the tillage. Therfoze if the wozkpng of nature, if honeſtie, if ver tue, if inwarde zeale, if Godlineſſe, if duetie maie moue pou, whp can pou not abide that, whiche God hath ozdeined, na: ture hath eſtabliſhed, reaſon doeth counſaill, Gods wozde and mannes wozde do cōmende, all Lawes do commaunde, the conſent of all nacions doeth allowe, whereunto alſo the example of all good men, doth exhozt pou. That if euery ho: neſt man ſhould deſire many thpnges, that are moſte painful foz none other cauſe, but onelp foz that thei are honeſte, no doubt but matrimonie ought aboue all other, moſte of all to be deſired, as the whiche wee maie doubte, whether it haue moze honeſtie in it, oz bzpng moze delite and pleaſure with it. foz what can bee moze pleaſaunt, then to liue with her, with whom not onelp pou ſhalbe iopned, in felowſhip of faithful: nes, and moſte hartie good will, but alſo pou ſhalbe coupled together moſte aſſuredlp, with the cōpanp of bothe pour bo: dies: If we compt that great pleaſure, whiche we receiue of the good will of our frendes and acquaintaunce, how plea: ſaunt a thpng is it aboue all other, to haue one, with whom

pou

pou maie bꝛeake the botome of pour harte,with whõ pe maie
talke as frelp,as with pour self,into whofe tꝛuſte,pou maie
fauſlp cõmit pour felf,fuche ꝛone as thinketh al pour gooꝰes
to be her chaꝛge.Now wꝫat an heauenlp b'iſſe (trow pou)is
the companie of man and wife together, fepng thꝛt in all the
woꝛlde,there can nothpng be found,either of greater weight
and woꝛthineſſe,oꝛ els of moꝛe ſtrengthe and aſſuraunce.Foꝛ
with frendes,we iopne onelp with them in good will,& faith
fulneſſe of mpnde,but with a wife,we are matched together,
bothe in harte and mpnde, in bodp and foule, fealed together
with the bõnde and league of an holp Sacrament,& partpng
all the gooꝰes we haue,indifferentlp betwiꝛt vs.Again whẽ
other are matched together in frendſhip, do we not fee what
diſſemblpng thei vfe, whꝫt falſhode thei pꝛactife, and what
deceiptfull partes thei plaie? Pea,euen thofe whõ we thinke
to be our moſt aſſured frenꝰes,as fwallowes flie awaie whẽ
fommer is paſt,fo thei hide their hedꝰes,whẽ foꝛtune gpnnes
to faile.And oft tpmes when we get a newe frend,we ſtreight
foꝛfake our old.We heare tell of berp fewe,that haue conti꞉
nued frendes,euen till their laſt ende.Whereas the faithful꞉
neſſe of a wife,is not ſtained with deceipte, noꝛ duſked with
anp diſſẽblpng,noꝛ pet parted with anp chãuge of the woꝛld
but diſſeuered at laſt bp death onelp,no not bp death neither.
She foꝛfakes and fettes lighte bp father and mother, fiſter &
bꝛother foꝛ pour fake,and foꝛ pour loue onelp.She onlp paſ꞉
feth bpon pou,fhe puttes her truſt in pou,and leaueth wholp
bpon pou, pea, fhe defires to die with pou . Haue pou anp
woꝛldlp fubſtance? Pou haue one that will maintain it,pou
haue one that will encreafe it.Haue pou none ? Pou haue a
wife that will get it . If pou liue in pꝛofperitee,pour iope is
doubled:if the woꝛlde go not wͭ pou, pou haue a wife to put
pou in good comfoꝛt,to be at pour commaundemẽt,& redp to
ferue pour defire, & to wifhe that fuche euill as hath happe꞉
ned vnto pou,miꝫht chaũce vnto her felf.And do pou thinke
that anp pleafure in al the woꝛld,is able to be cõpared with
fuche a goodlp felowfhip & familier liupng together? If pou
kepe home,pour wife is at hand to kepe pour cõpanp,the ra꞉
ther that pou might fele no werines of liuing al alone,if pou

riue furth,pou haue a wife to bid pou fare well with a kiffe
longpng muche for pou,bepng from home,and glad to bidde
pou well come at pour next returne. A fwete mate in pour
pouthe,a thankfull comforte in pour age. Euerp focietie or
companipng together, is delitefull and wifched for bp nature of all menne,forafmuche as nature hath ordeined vs to
be,fociable,frendlp,and loupng together. Jowe howe can
this felowfhtp of manne and wife, be otherwife then moste
pleafaut, where all thpnges are common together betwixt
them bothe. Jow I thinke he is moste worthp,to bee defpi-
fed aboue all other, that is borne, as a man would faie for
hpmfelf,that liueth to hpmfelf,that feketh for himfelf,that
fpareth for himfelf,maketh cost onelp vpon himfelf,that loueth no man,and no man loueth hpm. Would not a manne
thinke that fuche a monster,were mete to be caste out of all

Timon a dead- mennes companie(with Tpmon that careth for no manne)
ly hater of all into the middest of the fea. Jeither do I here vtter vnto pou
companie. thofe pleafures of the bodp,the which,wheras nature hath
made to be moste pleafaunt vnto man, pet thefe greate wit-
ted men,rather hide them,and diffemble them(I cannot tel
how)then vtterlp contempne them. And pet what is he that
is fo fower of witte,and fo drowppng of braine (I will not
faie)blockheDded,or infenfate,that is not moued with fuche
pleafure,namelp if he maie haue his defire, without offence
either of God or man, and without hpnderaunce of his estimacion. Truelp I would take fuche a one, not to be a man,
but rather to bee a verp stone. Although this pleafure of the
bodp,is the least parte of all thofe good thpnges,that are in
wedlocke. But bee it that pou paffe not vpon this pleafure,
and thinke it vnworthp for man to vfe it, although in deede
we deferue not the name of manne without it, but compte it
emong the least and vttermoste profites, that wedlocke
hath: Jow I praie pou, what can be more hartelp defired,
then chaft loue,what can bee more holp, what can bee more
honest? And emong all thefe pleafures, pou get vnto pou a
iolp fort of kinffolke, in whom pou maie take muche delite.
Pou haue other parentes, other brethren, fisterne, and nephewes. Jature in deede can geue pou but one father,& one
mother

mother : By mariage you get vnto you another father, and
another mother, who cannot chuse, but loue you with all
their hartes, as the whiche haue put into your handes, their
awne fleshe and bloud. Now again, what a ioye shal this be
vnto you, when your moste faire wife, shall make you a fa=
ther, in bringyng furthe a faire childe vnto you, where you
shall haue a pretie litle boye, runnyng vp and doune youre
house, suche a one as shall expresse your looke, and your wi=
ues looke, suche a one as shall call you dad, with his swete
lispyng wordes. Now last of all, when you are thus lynked
in loue, the same shalbee so fastened and bounde together, as
though it wer with the Adamant stone, that death it self cã
neuer be able to vndo it. Thrise happie are thei (ꝙ Horace)
yea, more then thrise happie are thei, whom these sure ban=
des dooe holde, neither though thei are by euill reporters,
full ofte sette a sonder, shall loue be vnlosed betwixt theim
two, till death them bothe depart. You haue them that shal
comforte you, in your latter daies, that shall close vp your
iyes, when God shall call you, that shall bury you, and ful=
fill all thynges belongyng to your ffunerall, by whom you
shall seme, to bee newe borne. ffor so long as thei shall liue,
you shall nede neuer bee thought ded your self. The goodes
and landes that you haue gotte, go not to other heires, then
to your awne. So that vnto suche as haue fulfilled all thyn
ges, that belong vnto mannes life, death it self cannot seme
bitter. Old age cometh vpon vs all, will we, or nill we, and
this waie nature prouided for vs, that we should waxe yong
again in our children, and nephewes. ffor, what man can be
greued, that he is old, when he seeth his awne countenaũce
whiche he had beyng a childe, to appere liuely in his sonne?
Death is ordeined for all mankynd, and yet by this meanes
onely, nature by her prouidence, mynдeth vnto vs a certain
immortalitie, while she encreaseth one thyng vpon another
euen as a yong graffe buddeth out, when the old tree is cut
doune. Neither can he seme to dye, that, when God calleth
hym, leaueth a yong child behinde hym. But I knowe well
enough, what you saie to your self, al this while of my lõg
talke. Mariage is an happie thyng, if all thynges hap well,

what and if one haue a curſte wife ? what if ſhe be lighte?
what if his childꝛen bee vngracious? Thus I ſee you will
remember all ſuche men, as by mariage haue been vndoen.
Well, go to it, tell as many as you can, & ſpare not: you ſhal
finde all theſe were the faultes of the perſones, and not the
faultes of Mariage. Foꝛ beleue me, none haue euill wifes,
but ſuche as are euill me. And as foꝛ you ſir, you may chuſe
a good wife, if ye liſt. But what if ſhe be croked, and marde
altogether, foꝛ lacke of good oꝛderyng. A good honeſt wife,
maie be made an euill woman, by a naughtie huſbande, and
an euill wife, hath been made a good woman, by an honeſt
man. We crie out of wifes vntruly, and accuſe them with?
out cauſe. There is no man (if you wil beleue me) that euer
had an euil wife, but thꝛough his awne default. Now again
an honeſt father, bꝛyngeth furthe honeſt childꝛen, like vnto
hymſelf. Although euen theſe childꝛen, how ſo euer thei are
boꝛne, commonly become ſuche men, as their educacion and
bringyng vp is. And as foꝛ ielouſy you ſhal not nede to feare
that fault at all. Foꝛ none be troubled with ſuche a diſeaſe,
but thoſe onely that are fooliſhe louers. Chaſte, godly, and
lawfull loue, neuer knew what ielouſie ment. What meane
you to call to your mynde, and remember ſuche ſoꝛe trage?
dies and doulefull dealynges, as haue been betwixt manne
and wife. Suche a woman beyng naughte of her body, hath
cauſed her huſbande to loſe his hedde, another hath poyſo?
ned her goodmā, the thirde with her churliſhe dealyng (whi?
che her huſbande could not beare) hath been his outer vn?
doyng, & bꝛought hym to his ende. But I pꝛaie you ſir, why
doo you not rather thinke vpon Coꝛnelia, wife vnto Tbe?
rius Gracchus? Why do ye not mynde that moſte woꝛthy
wife, of that moſt vnwoꝛthy man Alceſtes? Why remembꝛe
ye not Julia Pompeyes wife, oꝛ Poꝛcia Bꝛutus wife? And
why not Artemiſia, a womā moſte woꝛthie, euer to bee re?
membꝛed ? Why not Hipſicratea, wife vnto Mithꝛidates
kyng of Pontus? Why do ye not call to remembꝛaunce the
ientle nature of Tertia Aemilia? Why doo ye not conſider
the faithfulneſſe of Turia? Why cometh not Lucretia and
Lentula to your remēbꝛaūce? and why not Arria? why not
thouſandes

Euill wifes
happen to euil
men onely.

Jelouſie vn?
knowen to
wiſe men.

Coꝛnelia.

Alceſtes wife.
Julia.
Poꝛtia.
Artemiſia.
Hipācratea.
tertia Aemilia
Turia.
Lucretia.
Lentula.
Arria.

thousandes other, whose chastite of life, and faithfulnes to=
wardes their husbandes could not bee chaunged, no not by
death. A good woman (you will saie) is a rare birde, & hard
to be founde in all the worlde. Well then sir, imagine your
self worthy to haue a rare wife, suche as fewe men haue. A
good woman (saith the wiseman) is a good porcion. Be you Prouer.r.
bold to hope for such a one, as is worthy your maners. The
chifest poynate standeth in this, what maner of woman you
chuse, how you vse her, and how you order your self towar=
des her. But libertee (you will saie) is muche more plea=
saunt: for, who soeuer is maried, wereth fetters vpon his
legges, or rather carieth a clogge, the whiche he can neuer
shake of, till death part their yoke. To this I answere, I cã
not see what pleasure a man shall haue to liue alone. For if
libertie be delitefull, I would thinke you should get a mate
vnto you, with whõ you should parte stakes, and make her
priuey of all your ioyes. Neither can I see any thyng more
free, then is the seruitude of these twoo, where the one is so
muche beholdyng and bounde to thother, that neither of the
bothe wold be louse, though thei might. You are bound vnto
him, whõ you receiue into your frendship: But in mariage
neither partie findeth fault, that their libertie is take awaie
from them. Yet ones again your are sore afraied, least when
your childrẽ are taken awaie by death, you fal to mourning
for wãt of issue. Well sir, if you feare lacke of issue, you must
marie a wife for the self same purpose, the which onely shal
be a meane, that you shall not want issue. But what do you
serche so diligently, naie so carefully, al the incõmodities of
matrimonie, as though single life had neuer any incõmodi=
tie ioyned w it at al. As though there wer any kinde of life
in al the world, that is not subiect to al euils that may hap=
pẽ. He must neds go out of this world, ŷ lokes to liue wout
felyng of any grief. And in cõparison of ŷ life which ŷ sain=
ctes of god shal haue in heauẽ, this life of mã is to be cõpted
a deth, & not a life. But if you cõsider thinges within the cõ=
passe of mankynde, there is nothyng either more saufe, more
quiet, more pleasaunt, more to be desired, or more happy, then
is the maried mãnes life. How many do you se, that hauyng
                                        ones

ones felt the fwetnesse of wedlocke, doeth not desire eftso=
nes to enter into thesame? My frende Mauricius, whō you
knowe to be a very wise man, did not he, the nexte monethe
after his wife died (whom he loued derely) get hym streight
a newe wife ? Not that he was impacient of his luste, and
could not forbeare any longer, but he said plainly, it was no
life for hym, to bee without a wife, whiche should bee with
hym as his yoke felowe, and companion in all thynges. And
is not this the fourthe wife, that our frende Iouius hath
maried? And yet he so loued the other, whē thei wer on liue
that none was able to comforte hym in his heauinesse : and
now he hastened so muche (when one was ded) to fill vp and
supply the voyde roume of his chamber, as though he had
loued the other very litle. But what do we talke so muche
of the honestie and pleasure herein, seyng that not onely pro
fite doeth aduise vs, but also nede doeth earnestly force vs,
Necessitee
enforceth
mariage.
Xerxes. to seke mariage. Let it bee forbidden, that man and woman
shall not come together, & within fewe yeres, all mankynds
must nedes decaye for euer. When Xerxes kyng of the Per=
sians, behelde from an high place, that greate armie of his,
suche as almoste was incredible, some said he could not for=
beare weppyng, considerying of so many thousandes, there
was not one like to bee a liue, within seuentie yeres after.
Now why should not we consider thesame of all mankynd,
whiche he meant onely of his armie. Take awaie mariage,
and howe many shall remain after a hundreth yeres, of so
many realmes, countrees, kyngdomes, citees, and all other
assemblies that be of men, throughout the whole world? on
now, praise we a gods name the single life aboue the nocke,
the whiche is like for euer to vndooe all mankynde. What
plague, what infection can either heauen or hell, sende more
harmefull vnto mankynd? What greater euill is to be fea=
red by any floud? What could be loked for, more sorowfull,
although the flame of Phaeton should set the world on fire
again? And yet by suche sore tempestes, many thynges haue
been saued harmelesse, but by the single life of man, there cā
be nothyng left at all. We se what a sorte of diseases, what
diuersitee of misshappes doo night and daie lye in waite to
lessen

leſſen the ſmal number of mankynde. Howe many doeth the
plague deſtroie, how many do the Seas ſwallowe, how ma=
ny doeth battaile ſnatche vp? For I will not ſpeake of the
daily dyeng that is in al places. Deathe taketh her flight e=
uery where rounde about, ſhe runneth ouer theim, ſhe cat=
cheth theim vp, ſhe haſteneth aſmuche as ſhe can poſſible to
deſtroie al mankynde, & now do we ſo highly commend ſyngle
lyfe and eſchewe Mariage? Except happely we like the pro=
feſſion of the Eſſens (of whome Ioſephus ſpeaketh that
they wil neither haue wyfe, nor ſeruauntes) or the Dulopo=
litans, called otherwyſe the Raſcalles and Slaues of Ci=
ties, the whiche companie of theim is alwaie encreaſed and
continued by a ſorte of vagabounde peaſauntes that conti=
nue, and be from time to time ſtil together. Do we loke that
ſome Iuppiter ſhoulde geue vs that ſame gifte, the whiche
he is reported to haue geuen vnto Bees that wee ſhoulde
haue iſſue without procreacion, and gather with our
mouthes out of flowers, the ſeede of our poſteritie? Or elles
do we deſier, that lyke as the Poetes feyne Minerua to be
borne out of Iuppiters head: in lyke ſorte there ſhould chil=
dren leape out of our heades? Or laſt of al doe we looke ac=
cordyng as the olde fables haue been, that men ſhoulde be
borne out of the perth, out of rockes, out of ſtockes, ſtones, &
olde trees. Many thynges breede out of the pearth without
mans labour at all. Young ſhrubbes growe and ſhoute vp
vnder the ſhadowe of their groundſyre trees. But nature
woulde haue man to vſe this one waie of encreaſyng iſſue,
that through labour of bothe the houſband and wyfe, man=
kynd might ſtil be kept from deſtruction. But I promiſe you
if all men tooke after you, and ſtill forbare to marie: I can
not ſee but that theſe thynges whiche you wonder at, and e=
ſteme ſo muche, could not haue been at al. Do you yet eſteme
this ſyngle lyfe ſo greatly? Doe you praiſe ſo muche virgi=
nitie aboue al other? Why man, there will be neither ſyngle
men, nor virgines a lyue, if men leaue to marie, and mynde
not procreation. why do you thẽ preferre virginitie ſo muche
why ſet it you ſo hye, if it be the vndoyng of all the whole
worlde? It hath been muche commended, but it was for that

Eſſens ha=
ted Mariage.

Ioſephus rbiii
cap.lib.ii.

i.i.   tyme

The Arte of Rhetorique.

tyme,and in a fewe. God woulde haue men to fee as though
it were a paterne, o2 rather a picture of that heauenly habi⸝
tacion, where neither any fhalbe maried, no2 yet any fhall
geue theirs to Mariage.But when thynges be geuen fo2 an
example, a fewe may fuffife, a nomber were to no purpofe.
fo2 euen as al groundes though they be very frutefull, are
not therefo2e turned into tillage fo2 mans vfe and commo⸝
ditie, but parte lyeth fallowe, and is neuer mannered, parte
is kepte and cherifed to lyke the eye and fo2 mans pleafure:
and yet in al this plentie of thynges, where fo great ſto2e of
lande is, nature fuffereth very litle to waxe barren: But
nowe if none fhould be tilled,and plowe men went to plaie,
who feeth not but that wee fhoulde al ſterue, and bee faine
fho2tely to eate aco2nes : Euen fo, it is p2aife wo2thie if a
fewe liue fyngle,but if al fhould feke to lyue fyngle,fo ma⸝
ny as be in this wo2lde, it were to great an inconuentence.
Now again be it that other deferue wo2thie p2aife that feke
to liue a virgines life, yet it muſt nedes be a great faulte in
you. Other fhalbe thought to feke a purenefte of lyfe, you
fhalbe coumpted a parricide,o2 a murcherer of your ſtocke:
that whereas you may by honeſt mariage encreafe your po⸝
ſteritie:you fuffer it to decaie fo2 euer,th2ough your wilful
fingle lyfe.A man may hauyng a houfe'ful of child2en, com⸝
mende one to God to lyue a virgine al his lyfe. The plowe
man offereth to God the tenthes of his owne, and not his
whole croppe al together: But you Sir, muſte remember
that there is none lefte aliue of al your ſtocke,but your felf
alone . And nowe it mattereth nothyng whether you kill,
o2 refufe to faue that creature,which you onely might faue
and that with eafe.But you wil folow the erample of your
fiſter,and lyue fyngle as fhe doth.And yet me thynketh you
fhoulde chefely euen fo2 this felfe fame caufe, be afraied to
lyue fingle.fo2 whereas there was hope of iſſue heretofo2e
in you bothe,nowe ye fee there is no hope left but in you o2
nely.Be it that your fiſter may be bo2ne withal,becaufe fhe
is a woman, and becaufe of her yeares, fo2 fhe beyng but a
girle and ouercome with fo2ow fo2 loſſe of her mother toke
the w2ong way, fhe caſt her felfe doune headlong, and be⸝
                                                    came

came a Nunne at the earneſt ſute either of foliſhe women,
oz elles of doultiſhe Munkes : but you beyng muche elder,
muſt euermoze remember that you are a man. She woulde
nedes dye together with her aunceſters, you muſte labour
that your aunceſters ſhal not dye at all. Your ſiſter woulde
not doe her dutie, but ſhzanke away: thynke you nowe with
your ſelfe that you haue, iſ offices to diſcharge. The daugh‐
ters of Lothe neuer ſtuck at the matter to haue a doe with
their dzonken father, thinkyng it better with wicked whoze
dome and inceſte to pzouide foz their poſteritie, than to ſuf‐
fer their ſtocke to dte foz euer, and wil not you with honeſt,
Godly, and chaiſt Mariage (whiche ſhalbe without trou‐
ble and turne to your greate pleaſure) haue a regarde to
your poſteritie moſt like elles foz euer to decaie? Therfoze,
let them on Goddes name folow the purpoſe of chaiſt Hip‐
politus, let them lyue a ſyngle life, that either can bee ma‐
ried men, and yet can gette no childzen, oz els ſuche, whoſe
ſtocke may be continued by meanes of other their kynſfolke
oz at the leaſt whoſe kyndzed is ſuche that it were better
foz the commune weale, they were all deade, than that any
of that name ſhoulde be a lyue, oz elles ſuche men, as the e‐
uerliuyng God of his moſte eſpeciall goodnes hath choſen
out of the whole wozlde to erecute ſome heauenly office,
wherof there is a marueilouſe ſmal nomber. But whereas
you accozdyng to the repozte of a Phiſicion that neither is
vnlearned, noz yet is any lyar, are lyke to haue many chil‐
dzen hereafter, ſeeyng alſo you are a man of greate landes,
and reuenues by your aunceſters, the houſe whereof you
came, beyng bothe right honourable and right auncient, ſo
that you coulde not ſuffer it to periſhe without youre
great offence, and greate harme to the commune weale: a‐
gaine ſeeyng you are of luſtie yeares, and very comely foz
your perſonage, and may haue a maide to your wyfe ſuche
a one as none of your countrie hath knowen any to bee
moze abſolute foz all thynges, commyng of as noble a
houſe as any of theim, a chaiſte one, a ſobze one, a God‐
lie one, an ercellent fayze one, hauyng with her a won‐
derfull Dowzie : ſeeyng alſo youre frendes deſpze you,

l.ij.　　your

pour kynſſolke wepe to wynne pou, pour Cofyns and alï-
aunce are earneſt in hande with pou, pour countrie calles
and cries vpon pou:the aſſhes of your aunceſters from their
graues make hartp ſute vnto pou,do pou pet holde backe,do
pou ſtil mynde to lpue a ſpngle lpfe? Pf a thpng were aſked
pou that were not halfe honeſt,oʒ the whiche pou could not
wel compaſſe,pet at the inſtaunce of pour frendes,oʒ foʒ the
loue of pour kynſfolke, pou woulde be ouercome, and pelde
to their requeſtes:Then howe muche moʒe reaſonable were
it that the weppng teares of pour frendes, the hartie good
wil of pour countrie, the deare loue of pour elders might
wynne that thpng at pour handes, vnto the whiche bothe
the lawe of God and man doth exhoʒte pou,nature pʒicketh
pou foʒwarde,reaſon leadeth pou, honeſtie allureth pou, ſo
manp commodities cal pou, and laſt of all, neceſſitie it ſelfe
doeth conſtraine pou.But here an ende of al reaſonpng.ffoʒ
J truſt pou haue now and a good while ago chaunged pour
mpnde thoʒowe mpne aduiſe, and taken pour ſelfe to better
counſell.

¶ Of Exhoʒtation.

<small>Exhoʒtyng.</small>

The places of exhoʒtpng and dehoʒtpng,are the ſame
whiche wee vſe in perſwadpng and diſſuadpng, ſa-
ypng that he whiche vſeth perſwaſiou, ſeeketh bp
argumētes to compaſſe his deuiſe:he that laboures
to exhoʒte, doeth ſtirre affections.

Eraſmus ſheweth theſe to be the moſt eſpeciall places
that do perteine vnto exhoʒtation.

> Pʒaiſe,oʒ Commendacion.
> Expectation of al men.
> Hope of victoʒie.
> Hope of renowme.
> ffeare of ſhame.
> Greatneſſe of rewarde.
> Reherſall of examples, in all ages, and
> eſpeciallp of thpnges lately doen.

<small>Pʒaiſyng a
deede.</small>

Pʒaiſyng is either of the man, oʒ of ſome deede doen.
We ſhall exhoʒte men to doe the thpng,if we ſhowe
them

them that is a worthy attempte, a Godly enterprise, & suche
as fewe men hetherto haue aduentured.

In praisyng a man, we shal exhorte hym to go forwarde, Praisyng a
man, the ra-
ther to encou-
rage hym.
consideryng it agreeth with his wounted manhode, and that
hetherto he hath not slacked to hasarde boldely vpon the
best and worthiest deedes, requiryng hym to make this ende
aunswereable to his mooste worthie begynnynges, that he
maye ende with honour, whiche hath so long continued
in suche renowme. ffor it were a foule shame to lose honour
through folie, whiche hath been gotte through virtue, and
to appere more slacke in kepyng it, than he semed carefull at
the first to atteine it.

Againe whose name is renowmed, his doynges from time
to tyme wil be thought more wonderfull, and greater promises wil men make vnto them selues of suche mens aduentures in any commune affaires, than of others, whose vertues are not yet knowne. A notable Master of fence is marueilouse to beholde, and men looke earnestly to see hym doe
some wonder, howe muche more will they looke when they
heare tel that a noble Captaine, & an aduenturouse Prince
shal take vpon hym the defence, and sauegarde of his countrie against the raggyng attemptes of his enemies? Therfore
a noble man can not but go forwarde with most earnest wil, Expectacion
of al men.
seyng al men haue suche hope in hym, and count hym to bee
their onely comforte, their fortresse, and defense. And the rather to encourage suche right worthie, we may put them in
good hope to compasse their attempte, yf wee showe them Hope of victorie.
that God is an assured guide vnto all those, that in an honest quarell aduenture them selues, and showe their manly
stomake. Sathan hym selfe the greatest aduersarie that man
hath, yeldeth lyke a captiue, when G O D dothe take our
parte, muche sooner shal al other be subiecte vnto hym, and
crye Peccaui, for if God be with hym, what matereth who
be against hym?

Nowe when victorie is got, what honour doeth ensewe?
here openeth a large fielde to speake of renowme, fame, and
endles honour. In all ages the worthiest men haue alwaies Fame foloweth worthy
feactes,
aduentured their carcases for the sauegarde of their coun-

J.iii.   trie.

trie, thynkyng it better to dye with honoz, than to liue with shame. Againe the ruine of our Realme shoulde put vs to moze shame, than the losse of our bodies should turne vs to smarte. Foz our honestie beyng stained, the paine is endles, but our bodies beyng gozed, either the wounde maie sone be healed, oz elles our paine beyng sone ended, the glozy endureth foz euer.

Lastly he that helpeth the nedelesse, defendeth his poore neighbours, & in the fauour of his countrie, bestoweth his lyfe: wil not God besides al these, place hym where he shall lyue foz euer, especially seeyng he hath doen all these enterprises in faith and foz Christes sake?

Nowe in al ages to recken suche as haue bene right soueraine, and victoriouse, what name gotte the worthie Scipio that withstood the rage of Annibal? what Brute hath Cesar foz his most worthie conquestes? what triumphe of glozy doth sounde in al mennes eares vpon the onely namyng of mightie Alexander, and his father Kyng Philippe? And now to come home, what head can expresse the renowmed Henry the fifte Kyng of Englande of that name after the conquest? What witte can sette out the wonderful wysedom of Henry the seuenth, and his greate forsight to espie mischiefe like to ensewe, and his politique deuises to escape daungers to subdewe rebelles, and maintayne peace?

¶ Of mouyng pitie, and stirryng men to shewe mercie.

Lkewise we may exhorte men to take pitie of the fatherlesse, the widowe, and the oppressed innocent, if we set befoze their iyes the lamentable afflictions the tyrannouse wronges, and the miserable calamities, whiche these poore wretches do susteine. Foz if fleshe and bloude moue vs to loue our children, our wyfes, and our kynsfolke: muche moze shoulde the spirite of God and Christes goodnes towardes man stirre vs to loue our neighbours moste entirely. These exhortacions the preachers of God may most aptely vse, when they open his Gospell to the

the people,and haue iuſt cauſe to ſpeake of ſuche matters.

¶Of Commendyng.

Ꙇ N commendyng a man, wee vſe the reporte of his ☞The maner of
witte,honeſtie,faithfull ſeruice, painefull labour, commendyng.
and carefull nature to do his maiſters will, or any
ſuche lyke, as in the Epiſtles of Tullie there are
examples infinite.

¶Of Comfortyng.

Ꙏ OW after al theſe,the weake woulo be comforted ☞The maner of
and the ſorowfull woulde bee cheriſed that there comfortyng.
grief might bee aſwaged, and the paſſions of man
brought vnder the obedience of reaſon. The vſe
hereof is great,aſwell in priuate troubles, as in commune
miſeries.As in loſſe of gooddes, in lacke of frendes, in ſick=
nes,in darthe, ϟ in death.In all whiche loſſes,the wyſe vſe
ſo to comforte the weake, that they geue them not iuſt cauſe
euen at the firſte to refuſe all comforte. And therefore they Comfortyng
vſe two waies of chereſhyng the troubled mindes.The one two waies
is when wee ſhowe that in ſome caſes and for ſome cauſes vſed.
either they ſhoulde not lament at all, or elles bee ſory very
litle:the other is when we graunt that they haue iuſt cauſe
to bee ſadde, and therfore wee are ſad alſo in their behalfe,
and woulde remedie the matter,if it coulde be,and thus en=
teryng into felowſhippe of ſorowe, wee ſeeke by litle and
litle to mitigate their grief. For all extreme heauineſſe,and
vehement ſorowes, cannot abyde comforte,but rather ſeeke
a mourner that woulde take parte with theim.

Therefore muche wareneſſe ought to be vſed,when wee
happen vpon ſuche exceedyng ſorowfull, leaſte wee rather
purchace hatred,than aſwage grief.

Thoſe harmes ſhoulde bee moderatly borne, whiche
muſte needes happen to euery one, that haue chaunced
to any one. As deathe, whiche ſpareth none, neither
Kyng, nor Cayſer, neither poore, nor riche. Therefore
to bee impacient for the loſſe of our frendes, is to fall
out

out with God,becaufe he made vs men,and not Aungelles. But the Godly (I trufte) will alwaies remitte thozder of thynges to the wil of God,and fozce their paffions to obey neceffitie. When God lately vifited this Realme with the fweatyng difeafe, and receiued the two wozthie ientlemen Henry Duke of Suffolke,& his bzother Lozde Charles: I leeyng my Ladies grace their mother takyng their deathe moft greauouflie could not otherwife foz the duetie whiche I then did,and euer fhall owe vnto her,but comfozte her in that her heauineffe, the whiche vndoubtedly at that tyme muche weakened her bodie. And becaufe it may ferue foz an example of comfozte, I haue been boulde to fet it fozthe as it foloweth hereafter.

Sweatyng difeafe.

¶An example of comfozte.

Hough myne enterpzife maie be thought foz lifhe,and my doynges very flender in bufiyng my bzaine to teache the expert, to gyue coun= fel to other whenI lacke it my felf,and wher as moze neede were foz me to be taught of oz ther, to take vpon me to teache my betters, yet dutie byn= dyng me to doe my befte,and emong a nomber though I can doe leafte, yet good will fettyng me fozthe with the foze= meft:I cannot choufe but wzite what I am able,and fpeake what I can poffible foz the better comfoztyng of your grace in this your great heauines, and foze vifitacion fent from GOD, as a warnyng to vs all. The Phifician then de= ferueth mofte thanke, when he pzactifeth his knowlege in tyme of neceffitie, and then traueileth mofte painefullie, when he feeleth his paciente to be in mofte daunger. The fouldiour at that tyme,and at no tyme fo muche is thought moft truftie,when he fhoweth at a nede his faithfull harte, and in tyme of extreme daunger doeth vfe, and beftowe his mofte earneft labour. In the wealthe of this wozlde what valiaunt man can wante affiftence? What mightie Pzince can miffe any helpe to compaffe his defire?who lac= keth men that lacketh no monie? But when God ftriketh the mightie with his ftrong hand,and difplaceth thofe that
were

were hyghelye placed, what one manne dothe once looke backe for the better easemente of his deare Brother, and Godlye comfortynge his euen Chziſtian, in the chieſe of all his ſorowe. All menne communelye moze reioyce in the Sunne riſynge, then they doe in the Sunne ſettinge. The hope of Lucre and expectation of pziuate gayne, maketh manye one to bear oute a countenaunce of fauoure, whoſe herte is inwardelye fretted wyth deadlye rancoure. But ſuche frendes, euen as pzoſperitye doithe getts theim, ſo aduerſitye dothe trye theim. God is the ſearcher of euery mannes thought, vnto whoſe iudgemente I referre the aſ= ſuraunce of my good wyll.

And thoughe I can do little, and therfore deſerue as lit= tle thancke, as I loke foz pzayſe (whyche is none at all) yet will I endeuoure carreſtlye at all tymes, as well foz mine owne diſcharge, to declare my duty, as at this pzeſent to ſay ſomewhat foz the better eaſemente of poure grace, in thys poure heauines. The paſſions of the mynde haue diuers ef= fectes, and therfoze wozke ſtraungelye, accozdynge to theyz properties. foz like as ioye comfozteth the harte, nouriſheth bloude, and quickeneth the whole bodye: ſo heauineſſe and care hinder digeſtion, engender euyll humoures, waſte the principall partes, and wyth time conſume the whole bodye. foz the better knowledge thereof, and foz a liu:lye ſpght of the ſame, wee neade not to ſeeke farre foz anye exampl=, but euen to come ſtrapghte vnto poure grace, whoſe bodye as I vnderſtande crediblye, and partelye ſee my ſelfe, is ſooze ap= papzed within ſhozte tyme, poure mynde ſo troubled, & poure harte ſo heauye, that you hate in a maner all lyght, you lyke not the ſighte of anye thynge that myght be your comfozte, but altogether ſtricken in a dumpe, you ſeke to be ſolitarye, deteſtinge all ioye, and delityng in ſozowe, wiſhynge wyth harte (if it wore Goddes will) to make poure laſt ende. In whyche poure heauineſſe, as I deſire to be a comfoztoure of poure grace, ſo I c in noz blame poure naturall ſozowe, if that nowe after declaration of the ſame, pou woulde mo= deraie all poure griefe hereafter, and call backe poure penſiſe nes, to the pzeſcripte ozder of reaſon. R.I.

Paſſions woz che diuerſlye

　　　　　　　　　　　R.I.　　　　And

And firſte, foz the better remedye of euerye diſeaſe, and troubled paſſion, it is beſte to knowe the principall cauſe, and chiefe occaſion of the ſame. Poure grace hadde two ſonnes, howe noble, howe wittye, howe learned, and how Godlye, manye thouſandes better knowe it, then anye one is able well to tell it. God at his pleaſure hath taken them bothe to his mercy, and placed them with him, which were ſurelye ouer good to tarye here with vs. They bothe dyed as your grace knoweth verye younge, whiche by courſe of Nature, and by mannes eſtimation, mighte haue liued muche longer. They bothe were together in one houſe, lodged in two ſeuerall chambers, and almoſte at one time bothe ſickened, and both departed. They died bothe dukes, bothe well learned, bothe wiſe, and bothe right Godlye. They bothe befoze gaue ſtraunge tokens of death to come. The elder ſittinge at Supper, and verye merye, ſaide ſou⸗ dainlye to that ryghte honeſte Matrone, and Godly aged gentilwoman, that moſt faythful & longe aſſured ſeruaunt of yours, whoſe life God graunte longe to continue: Oh Lozde, where ſhall we ſupye to mozowe at night, whereu⸗ pon ſhe beinge troubled, and yet ſaipnge comfoztablye, I truſte my lozde, either here, oz elles where at ſome of your frendes houſes: Naye (quod he) we ſhall neuer ſuppe toge⸗ ther againe in this wozlde, be you well aſſured, and with that ſeinge the gentilwoman diſcoinfozted, turned it vnto mirthe, and paſſed the reſte of his Supper with much ioye, and the ſame night after. xij. of the clocke, beynge the. xiiij. of Julye ſickened, and ſo was taken the nexte moзning a⸗ boute. vij. of the clocke, to the mercye of God, in the yeare of our Lozde. M. D. Li. When the elder was gone, the younger woulde not tarye, but tolde befoze (hauinge no knowledge therof by anye bodye liuinge) of his bzothers Deathe, to the greate wonderinge of all that were there, declaringe what it was to loſe ſo deare a frende, but com⸗ foztinge him ſelfe in that paſſion, ſaide: well, my bzother is gone, but it maketh no matter, foz I will go ſtraight af⸗ ter him, and ſo did within the ſpace of halfe an houre, as your grace can beſt tell, whiche was there pzeſente. Nowe

I

The arte of Rhetorique. Fol. 38.

I renue thefe wordes to youre graces knowledge, (that you might the more ftedfaftlie confider their time to be then appointed of GOD to forfake this euill worlde, and to liue with Abraham, Ifaac, and Iacob, in the Kingedome of heauen. But wherfore did God take two fuche awaye, and at that time? Surelye to tell the principall caufe, we maye by all likenes affirme, that they were taken awaye from vs for our wretched finnes, and moofte vile naughtines of life, that therby we beinge warned, might be as readie for God, as they nowe prefentlie were, and amend our liues in time, whom God will call, what time we knowe not. Then as I can fee, we haue fmall caufe to lament the lacke of them, whiche are in fuche bleffed ftate, but rather to amende our owne liuinge, to forthinke vs of oure offences, and to wifhe of GOD to purge oure hartes, from all filthines and vngodlie dealinge, that we maie be (as they nowe be) bleffed with God for euer. Notwithftandinge the worckes of God are vnfearcheable, without the compaffe of mannes braine precifelye to comprehende the verie caufe, fauinge that this perfwafion oughte furelye to be grounded in vs, euermore to thinke that God is offended with finne, and that he punifheth offences to the thirde and fourthe generation of all them that breake his commaundementes, beinge iufte in all his worckes, and doinge all thinges for the befte. And therfore when God plagueth in fuche forte. I would wifh that our faithe might alwaies be ftaied vpon the admiration of Goddes glorie, througheoute all his doinges, in whom is none euil, neither yet was there euer any guile found. And I doubt not but your grace is thus affected, and vnfaynedlye confeffinge your owne offences, taketh this fcourge to come from God as a iufte punifhmente of Sinne, for the amendemente not onelye of your owne felfe, but alfo for the amendemente of all other in generall. The lamentable voyce of the poore (whiche is the mouthe of God) througheout the whole Realme declares full well the wickednes of this life, and fhowes plainelye that this euill is more generallye felte, then anye man is able by worde, or by writinge at full to fet forthe.

when

The caufe why God taketh awai the mofte worthieft.

88

The arte of Rhetorique.

When God therfore that is Lord, not onelye of the riche
but also of the poore, ieeth his grounde spoyled frome the
holesome profite of manye, to the vapne pleasure of a fewe,
and the ea:the made priuate to suffise the luste of vnsacia;
ble couetousnesse, and that those whiche be his true mem;
bres cannot liue for the intollerable oppression, the soore
enhaunsynge, and the moost wicked grasing of those thro;
ughout the whole Realme, whiche otherwise myght well
lyue wi.h the onelye value and summe of their landes and
perelye reuenues: he striketh in his anger the innocentes
and tēder ponglinges, to plague vs with the lacke of them,
whose innocencye and Godlines of life mighte haue bene a
iuste example for vs to amende our moost euill doynges.
In whiche wonderfull woorcke of God, when he receiued
these two moost noble pympes, and his chyldren elected to
the euerlastinge Kingedome, I can not but magnifye his
moost glorious name, from time to tyme, that hath so gra;
ciouslye preserued these two worthy gentilmenne from the
daunger of further euil, and moost vile wretchednes, moost
like righte shortelye to ensue, excepte wee all repente, and
forthincke vs of oure former euill liupnge. And pet I spea;
ke not this, as thoughe I knewe anye cryme to be more
in pou, then in anye other: but I tell it to the shame of all
those vniuersallye within this Realme, that are gyltye of
suche offences, whose inward consciences condempne their
owne doinges, and their open deedes beare witnes againste
their euil nature. For it is not one house that shal feele the
fall of these two prynces, neither hath God taken them for
one priuate personnes offence: but for the wickednes of the
whole Realme, whyche is lyke to feele the smarte, excepte
God be merciful vnto vs. But now that they be gone, tho;
ughe the fleshe be frayle, weake, & tender, and muste neades
smart, being woūded or cut: pet I doubt not but pour grace
lackinge two suche porcions of pour owne fleshe, and ha;
uing theim (as a manne woulde saye) cutte awaye frome

*When necessi;
tie ruleth, so;
row is nedeles* poure owne bodye, will suffer the smarte with a good sto;
make, and remembre that sorowe is but an euil remedye to
heale a sore. For if pour hande were detrenched, or poure
                                                        bodie

bodie maimed with some soddaine stroake, what profite
were it for you to wepe vpon your wounde, and when the
harme is done, to lamente still the sore? seinge that with
wepinge it will not be lesse, and maye yet throughe weping
full sone be made more. For the sore is encreased, when sor:
rowe is added, and the paine is made double, whiche before
was but single. A constante christian shoulde beare all mi:
serie, and with pacience abide the force of necessitie, shew:
inge with sufferaunce the strengthe of his faithe, and espe:
ciallie when the chaunge is from euyll to good, from woe
to weale, what solye is it to sorowe that, for the whiche
they iove that are departed? They haue taken nowe their
rest, that liued here in trauaile: they haue forsaken their bo:
dies, wherin they were bounde, to receiue the spirite, wher:
by they are free. They haue chosen for sickenes, healthe: for
earth, heauen: for life transitorie, life immortall: and for
manne, God: then the whiche, what can they haue more?
Or howe is it possible they can be better? Undoubtedly
if euer they were happpe, they are nowe moste happie: if e:
uer they were well, they are nowe in beste case, beynge de:
liuered frome this presente euyll worlde, and erempted
from Sathan, to lyue for euer with Christe our Sauioure.

Then what meane we that not onelye lamente the want
of other, but also desire to tarye here oure selues, hopinge
for a shorte, vayne, and therewith a paynefull pleasure, and
refusynge to enioye that continuall, perfecte, and heauen:
lye enheritaunce, the whiche so soone shal happen vnto vs,
as Nature dissolueth this Earthlye bodye. Truthe it is
wee are more fleshelye then spirituall, soner fealynge the
ache of our bodye, then the griefe of oure Soule: more stu:
dious with care to be healthfull in carkasse, then sekynge
with prayer to be pure in Spirite. And therfore if oure
frendes be stayned with synne, wee dooe not, or we wyll
not espye their sore, we counte theim faulteles, when they
are mooste wicked: neither sekinge the redresse of their e:
uyll doynge, nor yet once amendynge the faultes of oure
owne liuynge.

R.iij. But

The folye of
such as sorow
the want of
their frendes.

But when oure frende departeth this worlde, and then forsaketh vs when Spune forsaketh him : wee begynne to shewe oure fleshelpe natures, we wepe, and we wayle, and with longe sorowe withoute discretion declare our wante of Goddes grace, and all goodnes. For wheras we see that as some be borne, some do dye also, menne, women, and chil; dren, and not one houre certaine to vs of all oure life, yet we neuer mourne, we neuer to epe, neither markynge the deathe of suche as we knowe, nor regardynge the euyll lyfe of those whom we loue. But when suche departe as were eith r nighest of oure kynred, or elles moost oure frendes, then wee lamente withoute all comforte, not the spunes of their Soules, but the chaunge of their bodyes, leauinge to doe that whiche we shoulde, and doynge that onelye why; che we shoulde not do at all. wherin not onelye we declare muche wante of Faythe, but also we shewe greate lacke of wytte. For as the other are gone before, either to heauen or elles to hell : so shall oure frendes and kinsfolke folowe af; ter. We are all made of one metall, and ordeyned to dye, so maupe as l'us . Therfore what folye is it in vs, or rather what fleshelpe madnesse immoderatelye to wayle their death wh in God hathe ordeyned to make their ende, excepte wee lamente the lacke of oure owne liuinge ? For euen as well we myght at theyr firste byrthe bewayle theyr Natiuitye, consideryng they must nedes dye, because they are borne to lyue. And whatsoeuer hath a beginnynge, the same hath al; so an endynge, and the ende is not at oure will whiche de; sire continuaunce of life, but at hys wyll whyche gaue the begynnynge of lyfe. Nowe then, seynge God hath ordeyned all to dye, accordynge to his appointed wil, what meane they that woulde haue theirs to lyue ? Shall God alter his fyrst purpose for the onelye satisfyinge of oure folyshe pleasure? And where God hathe mynded that the whole worlde shall decaye, shall anye man desyre that anye one house may stand? In my mynde, there can be no greater comforte to anye one liuynge for the lacke of his frende, then to thinke that thys happened to him, whyche all other eyther haue felte, or elles shall feele hereafter: And that God the rather made Deathe

Deathe com;
mune to all.

com;

commune to all, that the vniuersall plague and egalnes to
all, myght abate the fiercenes of deathe, and comfore vs in
the crueltie of the same, considerynge no one man hath an
ende, but that all shall haue the lyke, and dye we muste es
uerpe mothers sonne of vs, at one time or other. But you
will saye: my chyldren might haue liued longer, they dyed
younge. Sure it is by mannes estimation they myght haue
liued longer, but had it bene best for them thincke you to
haue continued styll in this wretched worlde, where Uyce
bareath rule, and Uertue is subdued, where G O D is
neglected, his lawes not obserued, his worde abused, and
his Prophetes that preache the iudgemente of God almost
euery where contemned. If your children were aliue, & by
thaduice of some wicked person were brought to a brothell
house, where entisinge harlottes liued, and so were in dau=
ger to commit that fowle sinne of whoredome, and so, ledde
from one wickednes to another: I am assured your grace
woulde call them backe with laboure, and would with ex=
hortations induce theim to the feare of God. and vtter de=
testation of al synne, as you haue ful often heretofore done,
rather fearing euil to come, then knowing any open faulte
to be in either of them. Nowe then, seynge God hath done
the same for you him selfe, that you woulde haue done for
them if they hadde liued, that is, in deliuerynce them bothe
from this present euil worlde, whiche I counte none other
then a brothel house, and a life of al noughtines: you ought
to thanke God highlye, that he hath taken awaye your two
sonnes, euen in their youthe, beynge innocentes bothe for
their liuynge, and of such expectation for their towardnes,
that almoste it were not possible for them hereafter o satis=
fye the hope in their age, whyche all menne presentlye hadde
conceyued of their youthe. It is thought, and in dede it is
no lesse thē a great poynct of happines to dye happyly. Now
when coulde youre two noble gentilmen haue dyed better
then when they were at the best, mooste Godlye in manye
thynges, offendinge in fewe, beloued of the hoe esse, and ha=
ted of none, (if euer they were hated) but of suche as hate
the best. As in deede, noble vertue neuer wanted cankarde

Euil, to liue emonge the euil.

To dye hap= pelye is great happines.

                    R.iiij.   Enuye

The arte of Rhetorique.

enuy to folow her. And confidering that this life is fo wretched, that the beste are euer most hated, & the vilest alwayes
most estemed, and pou; .ii. fonnes of the other fide beynge in
that ftate of honestie, & trained in that pathe of Godlines (as
I am able to b: a liuely witnes, none hath ben like thefe ma
ny peres, oz at the left, none better brought vp) what thinke
you of god, did he enuye them, oz els did he prouidently foz
fee vnto them bothe, when he toke them bothe from vs. At
Obisd.iiii. furedly whom god loueth best, thofe he taketh foneft, accoz-
dinge to the faying of Salomon: The righteous man (meaninge Enoch and other the chofen of God) is fodainely taken away, to the entente that wickednes fhoulde not alter
his vnderftandinge, and that hypocrifie fhould not begile
his foul. Foz the craftie bewitching of lies, make good thin
ges darke, the vnftedfaftnes alfo and wickednes of volup-
tuoufe defire, turne afide the vnderftanding of the fimple.
And thoughe the righteous was fone gone, yet fulfilled he
much time, foz his foule pleafed God, and therfoze hafted he
to take him away from amonge the wicked. Pea, the good
men of god in al ages, haue euer had an earneft defire to be
Pfal. lrrriiii. diffolued. My foule (quod Dauid) hath an earneft defire to
enter into the courtes of the lozd. Pea, like as the herte de-
Pfal.rlii. fireth the water brookes, fo longeth my foule after the O
God. My foule is a thyzft foz God: yea, euen fo: the liuing
God, when fhall I come to appeare befoze the prefence of
God? Paule and al the Apoftles wifhed and longed foz the
daye of the Lozd, and thought euery daye a thoufand yere,
till their foules were parted from their bodies. Then what
fhould we waile them which are in that place where we al
fhuld wifh to be, and feke fo to liue. that we might be ready
whe it fhal pleafe god of his goodnes to cal vs to his mercy
Let vs be ficke foz our owne finnes, & liue here on earth, &
reiopce in their moft happy paffage that are gone to heaue.
They haue not left vs, but gone befoze vs to enherite with
Chrift, their kingdom prepared. And what fhuld this greue
your grace that they are gone befoze, confidering our whole
Life, the righ' way to death, lyfe is nothing els but the righte waye to death. Shoulde
it trouble any one & his fiend is come to his iourneies end?

But

Our life is nothyng els, but a continuall trauaill,& death   Death purcha=
obtaineth rest after all our laboure. Emong men that tra=   seth rest.
uaill by the high waie, he is best at ease(in my mynde)that
sonest cometh to his iourneis ende.Therfore, if your grace
loued your children (as I am wel assured you did)you must
reiopce in their rest,and geue God hartie thankes,that thei
are come so sone to their iourneis ende.Marie,if it were so
that man might escape the daunger of death, and liue euer,
it were another matter:but because we must all dye,either
first or last,and of nothyng so sure in this life, as we are all
sure to dye at length,and nothyng more vncertain vnto mã
then the certain tyme of euery mannes latter tyme : what
forceth when wee dye,either this daie,or to morowe,either
this yere,or the next,sauyng that I thinke them moste hap=   Death more
pie that die sonest, and death frendely to none so muche, as   frendly, the so
to theim whom she taketh sonest.At the tyme of an execuciõ   ner it cometh.
doen for greuous offences, what mattereth who dye firste,
when a dosen are condempned together,by a lawe, conside=
ryng thei muste all dye one and other.I saie still,happie are
thei,that are sonest ridde out of this worlde, and the soner
gone, the soner blessed . The Thracians lament greatly at   Thracians.
the birthe of their children, & reiopce muche at the burial of
their bodies,beyng well assured that this world is nothyng
els but miserie,& the worlde to come,iope for euer. Now a=   Children by
gain,the child newe borne,partly declareth the state of this   wepyng,de=
life,who beginneth his tyme with wailyng,& firste sheweth   clare our woo.
teares,before he can iudge the cause of his wo.If we beleue
the promisses of God,if we hope for the generall resurrecci=
on,and constantly affirme,that God is iust in all his woor=
kes:we cãnot but iopfully saie,with the iust man Job:The   Job.
lorde gaue them,the lorde hath taken them again,as it plea=
seth God,so maie it be,and blessed be the name of the lorde,
for now and euer.God dealeth wrongfully with no man,but
extendeth his mercie moste plentifully, ouer all mankynde.
God gaue you twoo children,as the like I haue not knowen
happie are you moste gracious ladie,that euer you bare thẽ.
God lent you them twoo for a tyme,and toke them twoo a=
gain at his tyme, you haue no wrong doen you, that he hath

The arte of Rhetorique.

Lent goodes, muste be restored at the awners will.

taken thē:but you haue receiued a wonderfull beneſite, that euer you had thē. He is very vniuſt that boroweth, and will not pay again, but at his pleaſure. He forgetteth muche his duetie, that boroweth a iewell of the kynges maieſtie, & will not reſtore it with good will, when it ſhall pleaſe his grace, to call for it. He is vnworthy hereafter to borowe, that will rather grudge, becauſe he hath it no longer, then ones geue thankes, bicauſe he hath had the vſe of it ſo long He is ouer courteous, that compteth not gainfull, the tyme of his borowyng: but iudgeth it his loſſe, to reſtore thynges again. He is vnthankfull, that thynkes he hath wrong doen, when his pleaſure is ſhortened, and takes the ende of his delite, to bee extreme euill. He loſeth the greateſt parte of his ioye in this worlde, that thynketh there is no pleaſure, but of thynges preſent: that cānot comfort hymſelf with pleaſure paſt, and iudge them to be moſte aſſured, conſideryng the memorie of them ones had, can neuer decape. His ioyes be ouer ſtraighte, that bee comprehended within the compaſſe of his ſighte, and thynketh no thyng comfortable, but that whiche is euer before his iyes. All pleaſure whiche man hath in this worlde, is very ſhorte, and ſone goeth it awaie, the remembraunce laſteth euer, and is muche more aſſured, then is the preſence or liuely ſight of any thyng. And thus your grace maie euer reioyce, that you had twoo ſuche, whiche liued ſo verteouſly, and died ſo Godly : and though their bodies bee abſent from your ſight, yet the remembraunce of their vertues, ſhall neuer decape from your mynde. God lendeth life to all, and lendeth at his pleaſure for a tyme. To this man he graunteth a long life, to this a ſhorte ſpace, to ſome one, a daie, to ſome a yere, to ſome a moneth. Now whē God taketh, what man ſhould be offended, conſideryng he that gaue frely, maie boldely take his awne when he will, and dooe no manne wrong. The Kynges Maieſtie geueth one.x.pounde another fourtie pounde, another thre ſkore pounde, ſhall he be greued, that receiued but tenne pound, and not rather geue thankes, that he receiued ſo muche? Is that man happier, that dieth in the latter ende of the monethe, then he is that died in the beginnyng of theſame Monethe? Doeth di

ſtaunce

ſtaunce of tyme, and long tariyng from God, make men more
happie, when thei come to God: By ſpace of paſſage we dif-
fer muche, and one liueth longer then another, but by death
at the laſt, we al are matched, and none the happier, that liueth the longer, but rather moſte happie is he, that died the
ſoneſt, & departed beſt in the faithe of Chriſt. Thinke therfore
your ſelf moſt happie, that you had two ſuche, and geue God
hartie thākes, that it pleaſed him ſo ſone, to take two ſuche.
Neceſſitie is lawles, and that whiche is by God appoyncted
no man can alter. Reioyce we, or wepe we, die we ſhall, how
ſone, no man can tell . Yea, we are all our life tyme warned
before, that death is at hande, and that when we go to bedde
we are not aſſured to riſe the nexte daie in the mornyng, no,
not to liue one houre lōger. And yet to ſe our foly, we would
aſſigne God his tyme, accordyng to our ſacietie, and not cō-
tent our ſelfes with his doynges, accordyng to his appoynct-
ment. And euer we ſaie, when any dye young, he might haue
liued longer, it was pitie he died ſo ſone. As though forſothe
he were not better with God, then he can bee with manne.
Therefore, whereas for a tyme your grace, muche bewailed
their lacke, not onely abſentyng your ſelf from all companie
but alſo refuſyng all kynde of comforte, almoſte dedde with
heauineſſe, your body beyng ſo worne with ſorowe, that the
long contānuance of the ſame , is muche like to ſhorten your
daies : I ſhall deſire your grace for Goddes loue, to referre
poure will to Goddes will , and whereas hetherto nature
hath taught you to wepe the lacke of your naturall childrē
lette reaſon teache you hereafter, to wipe awaie the teares,
and lette not phantaſie encreaſe that , whiche nature hath
commaunded moderately to vſe. To bee ſory for the lacke of
oure deareſt, wee are taughte by nature, to bee ouercome
with ſorowe , it commeth of oure awne fonde opinion, and
greate folie it is , with naturall ſorowe , to encreaſe all ſorowe , and with a litle ſickeneſſe, to purchaſe readie deathe.
The ſorowes of brute beaſtes are ſharpe , and yet thei are **The nature of**
but ſhorte. The Cowe lackyng her Caulfe , leaueth Lowe- **brute beaſtes.**
yng within three or foure daies at the fartheſt . Birdes of
the ayre perceiuyng their youngones taken from their neaſt,

l.ij.   chitter

The arte of Rhetorique.

chitter for a while in trees there aboute, and ſtreighte after thei flie abrode,and make no more a dooe. The Doo lackyng her faune,the Hynde her Caulfe, braie no long tyme after their loſſe,but ſeyng their lacke to be without remedy,thei ceaſſe their ſorowe within ſhort ſpace. Man onely emong al other,ceaſeth not to fauour his ſorowe, and lamenteth not onely ſo muche as nature willeth him,but alſo ſo muche as his awne affeccion moueth hym. And yet all folke do not ſo but ſuche as are ſubiect to paſſions,and furtheſt from forti: tude of mynde,as women commonly,rather then men, rude people,rather then godly folke:the vnlearned,ſoner then the learned:fooliſhe folke,ſoner then wiſe men:children,rather then yong men. Whereupon we maie well gather,that im:

Immoderate ſorowe , not naturall.

moderate ſorowe is not naturall, (for that whiche is natu: rall,is euer like in al)but through folie mainteined,encrea: ſed by weakeneſſe,and for lacke of reaſon, made altogether intollerable . Then I doubte not but pour grace, will ra: ther ende pour ſorowe, by reaſon: then that ſorowe ſhould ende you, through foly : And whereas by nature,you are a weake woman in body, you will ſhewe pour ſelf by reaſon, a ſtrong man in harte:rather endyng pour grief by godly ad: uertiſementes,and by the iuſt conſideracion of Gods won: derfull doynges: then that tyme and ſpace,ſhould weare a: waie pour ſorowes,whiche in deede ſuffer none continual: ly to abide in any one,but rather ridde the of life,or els eaſe

Tyme,a reme: die for fooles, to take awaie their ſorowe.

them of grief. The foole,the vngodly,the weake harted haue this remedy,pour medecine muſt be more heauenly,if you do (as you profeſſe)referre all to Goddes pleaſure,and ſaie in pour praier. Thy will bee doen in pearth,as it is in heauen. Thoſe whom God loueth,thoſe he chaſteneth,and happie is

Math.vi, Job.v.

that body,whom God ſcourgeth,for his amendement. The man that dieth in the faithe of Chriſt is bleſſed,and the cha: ſtened ſeruaunt,if he doo repent and amende his life,ſhalbe bleſſed. We knowe not what we dooe,when we bewaile the death of our deareſt,for in death is altogether all happines,

The great mi: ſerie of this worlde,makes wearines of life

and before deathe , not one is happie . The miſeries in this worlde declare, ſmall felicitee to be in theſame. Therefore, many men beyng ouerwhelmed with muche woe,and wret:

ched

ched wickednes:haue wished and praied to God,for an ende
of this life,and thought this worlde to be a let,to the heaue=
ly perfeccion,the whiche blisse all thei shall attain hereafter
that hope well here,and with a liuely faith declare their as=
suraunce.Your graces two sonnes,in their life wer so god=
ly,that their death was their aduauntage: for, by death thei
liued,because in life thei wer dedde. Thei died in faithe,not
wearie of this worlde,nor wishyng for death; as ouerloden
with synne : but paciently takyng the crosse,departed with
iope.At whose dipng, your grace maie learne an example of
pacience,and of thankes geuyng,that God of his goodnesse,
hath so graciously taken these pour two children, to his fa=
uourable mercy.God punisheth,partly to trie pour consta=
cie,wherein I wishe that pour grace,maie nowe bee as well
willyng to forsake theim,as euer you were willyng to haue
them.But suche is the infirmitie of our fleshe, that we hate
good comforte in wordes, when the cause of our comforte in
dede(as we take it)is gone.And me thinkes I heare pou cry

Impacience
without com=
forte.

notwithstandyng all my wordes,alacke my children are gone.
But what though thei are gone? God hath called, & nature
hath obeyed.Yea,pou crie still my children are dedde:Marie
therefore thei liued,and blessed is their ende,whose life was
so godly.No worthe,thei are dedde, thei are dedde.It is no
new thyng,thei are neither the first that died,nor pet the last
that shall die.Many went before,and all shall folowe after.
Thei liued together,thei loued together,and now thei made
their ende bothe together.Alas thei died,that wer the fruicte
of myne awne body,leauyng me comfortlesse, vnhappie wo=
man that I am.You do well,to cal the the fruict of pour bo=
dy,& pet pou nothyng the more vnhappie neither.For,is the
tree vnhappy,from whiche the appelles fall? Or is the pearth

Trees,not ac=
cursed,becaus
Apples fall
from theim.

accurssed,that bringeth furthe grene Grasse,whiche hereaf=
ter notwithstandyng doth wither.Death taketh no order of
peres,but when the tyme is appoynted,be it earely or late,
daie or nighte,awaie we muste.But I praie pou,what losse
hath pour grace? Thei died,that should haue died,pea, thei
died,that could liue no longer.But pou wished theim longer
life.Pea,but God made pou no suche promise,& mete it wer

L.iij.   not

not that he shuld be led by you, but you rather should be led
by him. Your children died, & that right godly, what would
you haue more? All good mothers desire, that their children
maie die Goddes seruauntes, the whiche youre grace hath
moste assuredly obteined. Now again mannes nature alte=
reth, and hardely tarieth vertue long in one place, without
muche circumspeccion, & youth maie sone be corrupted. But
you will saie. These were good and godly broughte vp, and
therefore moste like to proue godly hereafter, if thei had li=
ued still . Well, thoughe suche thynges perhappes had not
chaunced, yet suche thynges mighte haue chaunced, and al=
though thei happen not to al, yet do thei happe to many, and
though thei had not chaunced to your children, yet we knew
not that before, and more wisedome it had been, to feare the
worst with good aduisement, then euer to hope, and loke stil
for the best, without all mistrustyng. For, suche is the nature
of man, and his corrupt race, that euermore the one foloweth

Commodus

Nero.

soner, then thother. Commodus was a verteous childe, and
had good bryngyng vp, and yet he died a moste wicked man.
Nero wanted no good counsaill, and suche a master he had,
as neuer any had the better , and yet what one aliue , was
worse then he? But now death hath assured your grace, that
you maie warrant your self, of their godly ende, whereas if
God had spared them life, thynges might haue chaunced o=
therwise. In wishyng longer life, we wishe often tymes lon=
ger woe, longer trouble, longer toyl in this world, and wepe
all thynges well, you shall perceiue wee haue small ioye to
wishe longer life. This imaginacion of longer life, when the
life standeth not by nomber of yeres, but by the appoynted
will of God, maketh our foly so muche to appere, & our tea=
res so continually to fall fro our chekes. For if we thought
(as we should dooe in deede) that euery daie risyng, maie be
the ende of euery man liuyng, and that there is no difference
with God, betwixt one daie, and an hundreth yeres: we might
beare all sorowes, a greate deale the better. Therfore it wer
moste wisedome for vs all, and a greate poynct of perfeccion
to make euery daie an euen rekenyng of our life, and talke so
with God euery houre, that we maie bee of euen borde with
hym,

hym, through fulnes of faithe, and redy to go the next houre
folowyng, at his commaundemente, and to take alwaies his
sendyng in good part. The lorde is at hande. We knowe not
when he will come (at mid night, at cocke crowe, o2 at noone
daies) to take either vs, o2 any of ours. Therfo2e, the rather
that we maie be armed, let vs folowe the examples of other
godly men, and lay their doynges befo2e our iyes. And emõg
all other, I knowe none so mete fo2 your graces comfo2t, as
the wise and Godly behauiour of good Kyng Dauid, who Dauid.
when he was enfourmed, that his sonne was sicke, p2aied to ii.Regum.xii.
God hartly, fo2 his amendement, wept, fasted, & with muche
lamentacion, declared greate heauinesse. But when woo2de
came of his sonnes departure, he left his mournyng, he called fo2 water, and willed meate to be set befo2e hym, that he
might eate. Wherupõ, when his men marueiled why he did
so, considerying he toke it so greuously befo2e, when his child
was but sicke, and now beyng dedde, toke no thought at al,
he made this answere vnto theim: so long as my child liued,
I fasted, and watered my plantes fo2 my young hope, and I
saied to my self, who can tell, but that God perhappes will
geue me hym, and that my child shall liue, but now seyng he
is dedde, to what ende should I faste? Can I call hym again
any mo2e? Naye, I shall rather go vnto hym, he shall neuer
come againe vnto me. And with that Dauid comfo2ted his
wife Bethsabe, the whiche example, as I truste your grace
hath redde, fo2 your comfo2t, so I hope you will also folowe
it fo2 youre healthe, and bee as strong in pacience, as euer
Dauid was. The histo2ie it self shall muche delighte youre
grace, beeyng redde as it lieth in the Booke, better then my
bare touchyng of it can dooe, a greate deale. The whiche I
doubte not but your grace will often reade, and comfo2te o-
ther your self, as Dauid did his so2owfull wife. Job losyng Job.
his child2en, and all that he had, fo2gatte not to p2aise God
in his extreme pouertie. Tobias lackyng his iye sighte, in Tobias.
spirite p2aised GOD, and with open mouthe, confessed his
holy name to bee magnified th2oughout the whole yearthe.
Paule the Apostle of God, rep2oueth thë as wo2thy blame,
whiche mourne and lament, the losse of their dere. I would
not

i.Theſſa.iiii.

not brethren (ꝙ he)that you ſhould be ignorant,concernyng them whiche be fallen on ſlepe, that you ſorowe not as other doo,whiche haue no hope. If we beleue that Ieſus died,and roſe again,euen ſo thei alſo,whiche ſlepe by Ieſus,wil God bryng again with hym . Then your grace, either with lea= uyng ſorowe,muſt ſhewe your ſelf faithfull,or els with pel= dyng to your wo,declare your ſelf to be without hope. But I truſt your grace,beyng planted in Chriſt,will ſhew with ſufferaunce,the fruicte of your faithe,and comforte your ſelf

Ihon.xi.

with the wordes of Chriſt,I am the reſurreccion and the life he that beleueth on me,yea,though he wer dedde,yet ſhould he liue,and whoſoeuer liueth,and beleueth in me,ſhal neuer die.We read of thoſe that had no knowlege of God,and yet thei bare in good worth,the diſceaſe of their children.Anaxa=

Anaragoras.

goras hearyng tell,that his ſoune was dedde, no maruail ꝙ he,I knowe well I begot a mortall body.Pericles chief ru=

Pericles.

ler of Athens , hearyng tell that his twoo ſounes, beyng of wonderfull towardneſſe,within foure daies wer bothe ded, neuer greately chaunged countenaunce for the matter , that any one could perceiue,nor yet forbare to go abrode, but ac= cordyng to his wonted cuſtome, did his duetie in the counſail houſe,in debatyng matters of weighte,concernyng the ſtate of the common peoples weale . But becauſe your grace is a woman,I will ſhewe you an example of a noble woman , in

Cornelia.

whom appered wonderfull pacience. Cornelia,a worthy la= die in Rome, beyng comforted for the loſſe of her twoo chil= dren,Tiberius,and Caius Gracchus,bothe valiaunt ientle men,although bothe not the moſte honeſt menne,whiche died not in their beddes , but violently were ſlain in Ciuill bat= taill,their bodies lying naked and vnburied,when one emon= geſt other ſaied:Oh vnhappie woman,that euer thou ſhoul= deſt ſe this daie.Naie ꝙ ſhe,I wil neuer thinke my ſelf other wiſe,then moſte happy,that euer I brought furthe theſe two Gracchions.If this noble lady,could thinke her ſelf happie, beyng mother to theſe twoo valiaunt ientlemen, & yet both rebelles,and therefore iuſtly ſlain: Howe muche more maye youre grace, thynke youre ſelf moſte happie, that euer you broughte furthe twoo ſuche Brandons, not onely by natu= rall

The Arte of Rhetorique. Fol.45.

ral birth,but alſo by moſt godly education, in ſuch ſoꝛt that
the lyke. ij. haue not been foꝛ their towardnes vniuerſallie.
woꝛoſe deathe the general voice of all men declares howe
muche it was lamented. So that whereas you might euer
haue feared ſome daungerouſe ende, you are nowe aſſured
that they both made a moſt godly ende, the whiche thyng is
the ful perfection of a Chꝛiſtiã lyfe. I reade of one Bibulus **Bibulus.**
that hearyng of his two childꝛen to dye both in one daie,la=
mented the lacke of them bothe foꝛ that one daye,and mour=
ned no moꝛe. And what coulde a man doe leſſe than foꝛ two
childꝛen to lament but one daie: and yet in my mynde he la=
mented enough and euē ſo muche as was reaſon foꝛ hym to
do,whoſe doynges if all Chꝛiſtians woulde folowe, in my
iudgement they ſhoulde not onely fulfill natures rule, but
alſo pleaſe God highly. Poꝛatius Puluillus beeyng highe **Poꝛatius**
Puluillus.
Pꝛieſte at Rome when he was occupied about the dedica=
tyng of a Temple to their greate God Juppiter in the Ca=
pitoly,holdyng a poſt in his hande, and hard as he was vt=
teryng the ſolempne woꝛdes,that his ſonne was dead, euen
at theſame pꝛeſent:he did neither plucke his hande from the
poſt leſt he ſhoulde trouble ſuche a ſolempnitie, neither yet
turned his countenaunce from that publique religiõ to his
pꝛiuate ſoꝛowe,leaſt he ſhould ſeeme rather to doe the office
of a father,then the dutie of an highe miniſter. Paulus Æ= **Paulus Emi-**
milius after his moſte noble victoꝛie had of Kyng Perſe, **lius.**
deſired of God,that if after ſuche a triumphe there were a=
ny harme lyke to happen to the Romaines, the ſame might
fal vpon his owne houſe.Whereupon when God had taken
his two childꝛen from hym immediatly after, he thancked
God foꝛ graũtyng him his bound.foꝛ in ſo doyng he was a
meane that the people rather lamented Paulus Emilius
lacke,thẽ that Paulus oꝛ any bewailed any miſfoꝛtune that
the Romains had. Examples be innumerable of thoſe
whiche vſed lyke moderation in ſubduyng their affections, **Quintus Mar**
as Zenophon,Quintus Martius,Julius Ceſar,Tiberius **tius.**
Ceſar, Emperours bothe of Rome. But what ſeeke I foꝛ **Julius Ceſar.**
Tyberius Ce-
miſfoꝛtunate men,(if any ſuche be miſfoꝛtunate)ſeyng it is **ſar.**
an harder matter and a greater peece of woꝛke to finde out
m.i. happie

happie men, Let vs loke round about euen at home, and we
shal finde enowe subiect to this misfortune, for who liueth
that hath not lost? Therfore I woulde wishe your grace e=
uen nowe to come in againe with God, and although he be
angry, yet show you your self most obedient to his wil, cō=
sideryng he is Lorde ouer Kynges, Empereurs, and ouer
al that be bothe in heauen and in yearth, and spareth noone
whom he listeth to take, and no doubt he wil take all at the
last. His dart goeth daily, neither is any darte cast in vaine
whiche is sent amongest a whole armie standyng thicke to=
gether. Neither can you iustly lament that they lyued no
longer, for they lyued long enough, that haue liued well e=
nough. You muste measure your children by their vertues,
not by their yeres. For (as the wise man saith) a mans wise=
dom is the grey heeres, and an vndefiled life, is the old age.
Happie is that mother that hath had Godly children, and
not she that hath had long lyuyng children. For if felicitie
should stande by length of tyme, some tree were more happy
then is any man, for it liueth longer, and so likewyse brute
beastes, as the Stagge, who liueth (as Plinius dothe say)
two hundreth yeares, and more. If we woulde but consider
what man is, we shoulde haue small hope to lyue, and litle
cause to put any great assuraunce in this lyfe. Let vs se him
what he is: Is his body any thyng els but a lumpe of earth
made together in suche forme as we do see? A frail vessell, a
weake carion, subiect to miserie, cast doune with euery light
disease, a man to daie, to morowe none. A flower that this
daie is freshe, to morowe withereth. Good Lorde do we not
see that euen those thynges whiche nourishe vs, doe rotte &
dye, as herbes, birdes, beastes, water, and al other without
the whiche we cannot lyue. And how can we lyue euer, that
are susteined by dead thinges? Therfore when any one doth
dye, why do we not thynke, that this may chaunse to euery
one, whiche now hath chaunsed to any one. We be now as
those that stande in battail raie. Not one man is suer of him
selfe before an other, but al are in daunger in lyke maner to
death. That your children died before other that were of ri=
per yeares, we may iudge that their ripenes for vertue and

aj

all other giftes of nature were brought euen to perfection,
wherby death the soner approched, for nothyng long lasteth
that is sone excellent. God gaue pour grace two most excellent childrē, God neuer geueth for any long tyme those that
be right excellent. Their natures were heauenly, and therfore more meete for God then man. Among frute we se some
appels are sone ripe and fal from the tree in the middest of
summer: other be stil greene, & tary til winter, & hercupō are
cōmonly called wynter frute: Euen so it is with men, some
dye young, some dye old, & some die in their midle age. Your
sunnes wer euen.ii. suche alreadp, as some hereafter may be
with long cōtinuance of tyme. Thei had that in their youth
for the giftes of nature, whiche al men would require of thē
bothe scacelie in their age. Therfore beyng both now ripe,
they were now most ready for God. There was a childe in
Rome of a mans quātitie, for face, legges & o.her partes of
his body, wherupon wise men iudged he would not be long
liuyng. How could pour grace thynke, that when you sawe
auncient wisdō in the one, & most pregnant wit in the other
meruailouse sobriete in the elder, & most laudable gentlines
in the younger, them bothe most studious in learnyng, most
forward in al feates aswel of the body, as of the mind, beyng
two suche, & so excellent, that they were lyke long to continue with you? God neuer suffreth such excellēt & rare iew-
els long to enherite therth. Whatsoeuer is nie perfectiō the
same is most nigh falling. Uertue being ons absolute cānot
long be seen with these our fleshly ies, neither can that tary the latter end with other, that was ripe it self first of al &
before other. Fier goth out the soner, the clearer that it bur-
neth: & that light lasteth longest, that is made of most course
matter. In greene wood we may see that where as the fuel
is not most apt for burning, pet the fier lasteth lōger, than if
it were nourished with like quantitie of drie wood. Euē so
in the nature of man the mynde beeyng ripe, the body decai-
peth streight, and life goeth away beeyng ones brought to
perfection. Neither can there be any greater token of shorte
lyfe, than full ripenes of naturall witte: The whiche is to
the bodie, as the heate of the Sunne is to thynges yearthly.

Rype thynges last not long.

m.ii. Therfore

Therfore iudge right honourable ladie, that euen now they
both died, when they both wer most readie for God, neither
thinke that thei died ouer soone, becaufe thei liu:d no löger.
They died both Gods feruauntes,& therfore they died wel
and in good tyme. God hath fet their tyme, and taken them
at his tyme bleffed childzen as they be, to reigne with hym
in the kyngdom of his father przpared for them from the beginnyng. Unto whofe wil, J wifhe and J trufte your grace
doth wholy referre your wil, thankyng hym as hartely for
that he hath taken them, as you euer thanked hym, for that
he euer lent you them. J knowe the wicked wozdes of fome
vngodly folke haue muche difquieted your grace, notwithftandyng God beyng iudge of your naturall loue towardes
your childzen, and al your faithful frendes, and feruauntes
bearyng earneft witnes with your grace of the fame : there
vngodly talke the moze lightely is to bee eftemed, the moze
vngodly that it is. Nay your grace may reioyce rather, that
whereas you haue doen well, you heare euill, accozdyng to
Math.v. the wozdes of Chzifte: Bleffed are you, when men fpeake al
euil thynges againft you. And again confider GOD is not
ledde by the repozte of men to iudge his creatures, but perfwaded by þ true knowlege of euery mans confcience, to take
them foz his feruauntes, & furthermoze the harme is theirs
whiche fpeake fo lewdlie, and the bleffe theirs whiche beare
it fo paciëtly. For loke what meafure thei vfe to other, with
the fame they fhalbe meafured againe. And as thep iudge fo
fhal they be iudged. Be your grace therfoze ftrong in aduer-
fitie, and pray foz them that fpeake amiffe of you, rendzyng
Paciëce praife
worthie in ad-
uerfitie. Gode foz euil, and with charitable dealyng fhowe your felf
long fuffryng, fo fhal you heape cooles on their heades. The
boifteroufe Sea trieth the good mariner, and fharpe veratiö
declareth the true Chziftian. Where battaill hath not been
befoze, there neuer was any victozie obteined. Pow then beyng thus affailed, fhow your felf rather ftowte to withftäd,
than weake, to geue ouer: rather cleauyng to good, than yeldyng to euil. For: if God be with you, what fozceth who bee
againft you. For when al frendes faile, GOD neuer faileth
them that put their truft in him, and with an vnfained hart

cal.

cal to hym for grace.Thus doyng J aſſure your grace,God
wilbe pleaſed,and the Godly wil muche praiſe your wiſdō,
though the worlde ful wickedly ſaie their pleaſure . J praie
God your grace may pleaſe the Godlie,and with your ver-
tuouſe behauiour in this pour wydohode,winne there com-
mendation to the glory of God,the retoyſyng of your frendes,and the comforte of your ſoule.Amen.

    Thus , the rather to make preceptes plaine , J haue
added examples at large both for counſel geuyng,& for com-
fortyng.And moſt nedeful it were in ſuche kynd of Oraciōs
to be moſt occupied,conſidering the vſe hereof appereth full
ofte in al partes of our life,and confuſedly is vſed emong al
other matters.For in praiſyng a worthie man, we ſhal haue
iuſt cauſe to ſpeake of all his vertues, of thynges profitable
in this lyfe, and of pleaſures in generall. Lykewyſe in tra-
uerſyng a cauſe before a iudge, we cannot wante the aide of
perſuaſion,and good counſel,concernyng wealth,health,life
and eſtimacion, the helpe wherof is partely boꝛowed of this
place. But whereas J haue ſette forthe at large the places
of confirmacion concernyng counſel in diuerſe cauſes : it is
not thought that either they ſhould al be vſed in numbre as
they are,or in order as they ſtande:but that any one may vſe
theim and order theim as he ſhall thynke beſt, accordyng as
the tyme,place,and perſon,ſhal moſt of al require.

    ¶ Of an Oration iudicial.

The whole burdeine of weightie matters, and the
earneſt trial of al controuerſies,reſt onely vpon iud
gement.Therfore when matters concernyng lande,
gooddes, or life , or any ſuche thyng of lyke weight
are called in Queſtion, we muſt euer haue recourſe to this
kynde of Oration,and after iuſt examinyng of our cauſes ¡y
the places therof:loke for iudgement accordyng to the law.

    ¶ Oration Judicial what it is.

Oration Judiciall is, an earneſt debatyng in open
aſſemblie of ſome weightie matter before a iudge,
where the complainaunt commenſeth his action,&
the defendaunt thereupon aunſwereth at his peril
to al ſuche thynges as are laied to his charge.

             m.iij.   Of

The Arte of Rhetorique.

¶ Of the foundacion, or rather principall poincte in euery de∙
bated matter, called of the Rhetoricians the
State, or constitucion of the Cause.

NOt onely is it nedefull in causes of iudgement to
considre the scope whereunto wee must leauell our
reasons, & directe our inuencion: but also we ought
in euery cause to haue a respect vnto some one espe∙
cial poincte, and chief article: that the rather the whole drift
of our doynges may seeme to agree with our firste deuised
purpose. For, by this meanes our iudgement shalbe framed
to speake with discretion, and the ignoraunt shall learne to
perceiue with profite, whatsoeuer is said for his enstructiō.
But they that take vpon theim to talke in open audience, &
make not their accompte before, what thei wil speake after:
shal neither be well liked for their inuenciō, nor allowed for
their witte, nor estemed for their learnyng. For, what other
thyng do they, that boult out their wordes in suche sorte, &
without al aduisement vtter out matter: but showe them∙
selues to plaie as young boyes, or scarre crowes do, whiche
showte in the open and plaine feldes at all auentures hittie
missie. The learned therfore and suche as loue to becoump∙
ted Clerkes of vnderstandyng, and men of good circumspe∙
ction and iudgement: doe warely scanne what they chefely
mynd to speake, and by definition seke what that is where∙
unto they purpose to directe their whole doynges. For, by
suche aduised warenesse, and good iye castyng: they shall al∙
waies be able both to knowe what to say, & to speake what
they ought. As for example if I shal haue occasion to speake
in open audience of the obediēce due to our soueraigne kyng
I ought first to learne what is obedience, and after knowe∙
lege attained, to direct my reasons to the onely proue of this
purpose, and wholly to seke confirmacion of the same, & not
turne my tale to talke of Robbyn Hoode, & to showe what
a goodly archer was he, or to speake wounders of the man
in the Mone, suche as are most nedelesse & farthest from the
purpose. For then, the hearer lookyng to be taught his obe∙
dience, & hearing in the meane season mad tales of archerie,
and great meruailes of the man in the Mone: beyng half a∙
stonied

Definition of
a thyng must
first be knowe
ere we speake
our mynd at
large.

Rouyng with
our reason.

ftonied at his fo great ftraing wil perhappes fay to himfelf:
Now, whether the deuill wilt thou, come in man againe for
very fhame, & tel me no bytailes, fuche as are to no purpofe
but fhow me that whiche thou diddeft promife both to tea=
che & perfwade at thy firft entrie. Affuredly fuche fonde fe=
lowes there haue been, yea euē emong Preachers, that tal=
king of faith, thei haue fetcht their ful race from the .xij. fig=
nes in the Zodiake. An other talking of the general refurre=
ction hath made a large matter of our bleffed Lady, praifyng
her to be fo ientle, fo courtife, & fo kynd, that it were better
a thoufandfould to make fute to her alone thē to Chrift her
fonne. And what needed (I pray you) any fuche reherfal be=
yng both vngodly, & nothyng at al to the purpofe: for what
maketh the praife of our lady to the confirmaciō of the gene
ral dowme: Would not a man thinke him mad that hauyng
an earneft errand from London to Douer, would take it the
next way to ride firft into Northfolke, next into Effer, & laft
into Kent: And yet affuredly many an vnlearned & witte=
leffe mā hath ftraied in his talke much farther a great deale,
yea truely as farre, as hence to Rome gates. Therfore wife
are thei that folow Plinies aduife, who would that al men
both in writing & fpeakyng at large vpon any matter, fhould
euer haue an iye to the chief title & principal ground of their
whole entent, neuer fwaruing frō their purpofe, but rather
bringyng al thinges together to cōfirme their caufe fo much
as they can poffible. Pea, the wife & experte men wil afke of
thēfelfes, how hangeth this to the purpofe: to what end do
I fpeake it: what maketh this for cōfirmacion of my caufe:
& fo by oft queftionyng either chide their owne folie, if they
fpeake amiffe: or els be affured thei fpeake to good purpofe.

A State therfore generally is the chief grounde of a mat=
ter, and the prpncipal poincte whereunto both he that fpea=
keth fhoulde referre his whole wit, & thei that heare fhould
chefely marke. A Preacher taketh in hande to fhowe what
praier is, and how nedeful for man, to cal vpon God: Now,
he fhoulde euer remembre this his matter, applieng his rea=
fons wholy and fully to this end that the hearers may both
knowe the nature of praier, and the nedefulneffe of praier.

*Plinies coun=
fel for hande=
ling of caufes.*

*A State gene=
rally what it
is.*

The

The whiche when he hath doen,his promise is fulfilled,his time wel bestowed,and the hearers wel instructed.

¶ A State,oz constitution what it is in
matters of Judgement.

IN al other causes the state is gathered without contention,and seuerally handled vpon good aduisement as he shal thynke best that professeth to speake. But in matters criminall, where iudgement is required: there are two persons at the least,whiche must through contrarietie,stande and reste vpon some issue. As foz example: A seruyng man is apprehended by a lawyer foz felonie vpon suspicion.The lawier saith to the seruyng man: Thou hast done this robbery.Nay,(saith he)J haue not doen it. Vpon this conflicte ❧ matchyng together,ariseth this State,whether this seruing man hath done this robbery,oz no?Vpon whiche poincte the lawyer must stande, and seeke to proue it to the vttermost of his power.

A State therfoze in matters of iudgement is that thyng, whiche doeth arise vpon the first demaunde and denial made betwixt men,whereof the one part is the accuser,and the other part the person,oz persons accused.Jt is called a State because we doe stande and reste vpon some one poincte , the whiche must wholly and onely be proued of the one side,and denied of the other . J cannot better terme it in Englishe than by the name of an issue,the whiche not onely ariseth vpon muche debatyng and long trauerse vsed,whereupon all matters ar said to com to an issue:but also elswhere an issue is said to be then and so often as bothe parties stande vpon one poinct,the whiche doth aswel happen at the first begynnyng befoze any probacions are vsed,as it doth at the latter endyng after the matter hath at large been discussed.

¶ The diuision of States, oz issues.

NOw that we knowe what an Jssue is,it is nexte most nedeful to showe how many thei are in numbze.The wisest and best learned haue agreed vpon thze onely, and no lesse , the whiche are these folowyng.

The

The arte of Rhetorique. *Fol.*49.

The ſtate.
- i. Coniecturall.
- ij. Legall.
- iij Iuridiciall.

ANd for the more playne vnderſtandynge of theſe darcke wordes,theſe three queſtions folowinge,ex= pounde their meaninge altogether.

- i. Whether the thinge bee,or no.
- ij. What it is.
- iij. What maner of thinge it is.

IN the fyrſt we conſider vpon rehearſal of a matter whether anye ſuche thinge bee, or no. As if one ſhoulde be accuſed of Murther, good it were to knowe, whether anye murther were committed at all,or no, if it be not perfectlye knowne before:and after to go further,and examine whether ſuche a man that is accu= ſed,haue done the dede or no.

In the ſeconde place, we doubte not vpon the thinge done, but we ſtande in doubte what to call it. Sometimes a man is accuſed of felonye, and yet he proueth his offence to be but a treſpace, wherupon he eſcapeth the daunger of deathe.An other beynge accuſed for killynge a man,confeſ= ſeth his faulte to be manſlaughter, and denieth it vtterlye to be any murder, wherupō he maketh frendes to purchaſe his Pardon. Nowe the lawyers by their learninge muſte iudge the doubte of this debate, and tell what name he de= ſerueth to haue that hath thus offended.

In the thyrde place,not onely the dede is confeſſed,but the maner of doynge is defended. As if one were accuſed for killynge a man,to confeſſe the dede, and alſo to ſtande in it that he mypght iuſtely ſo do,becauſe he did it in his owne de= fence:wherupon ariſeth this Queſtion, whether his doing be rypght or wrong. And to make theſe matters more plaine, I will adde an example for euery ſtate,ſeuerally.

Of the ſtate Coniecturall.

N.i.   The

The arte of Rhetorique.

The Assertion.

Thou hast killed this manne.

The Aunswere.

I haue not killed him.

The State or Issue.

Whether he hath killed this man or no. Thus we see vpon the auouchinge and deniall, the matter standeth vpon an issue.

Of the state Legall.

Assertion.

Thou hast committed treason in this facte.

Aunswere.

I denye it to be treason.

State or issue.

Whether his offence done maye be called treason or no. Here is denied that any suche thinge is in the dede done, as is by word reported, and saide to bee.

Of the state Iuridiciall.

Assertion.

Thou hast kylled this manne.

Aunswere.

I graunte it, but I haue doone it lawfullye, because I killed him in mine owne defence.

State or issue.

Whether a man may kill one in his owne defence, or no, and whether this man did so, or no.

The Oration coniectural, what it is.

The Oration coniectural is, when matters be examined and tryed out by suspicions gathered, and some likelihode of thinge appearinge. A Souldiour is accused for killinge a Farmar. The Souldioure denieth it vtterly, & sayth he did not kyll him. Herevpon riseth the question, whether the Souldioure killed the Farmar or no, who is well knowen to be slayne. Nowe to proue this question, we muste haue suche places of confirmation, as hereafter do folowe.

☞ Places of confirmation, to proue thinges by coniecture.

Will

The arte of Rhetorique.   Fol.50.

{ i. Will, to do euill.
{ ij. Power, to do euil.

IN the will muste be considered the qualitye of the i.
man, whether he were like to do suche a dede oz no,
and what shoulde moue him to attempte suche an
enterpzyse, whether he did the murther vpon anye
displeasure befoze conceyued, oz of a sodayne anger, oz els
foz that he loked by his death to receyue some commoditie,
either lande, oz office, money, oz money woz th, oz anye other
gaineful thinge.

Some are knowen to want no will to kill a manne, be- ij.
cause they haue bene flesht heretofoze, passing as little vpō
the deathe of a man, as a Botcher dothe passe foz killinge of
an Oxe, beynge heretofoze either accused befoze a Iudge of
manslaughter, oz els quitte by some general pardon. Now,
when the names of such menne are knowen, they make wise
men euer after to haue them in suspection.

The countrey where the man was bozne declares some- iij.
time his natural inclination, as if he wer bozne oz bzought
vp emong the Tindale, and Riddesdale menne, he may the
soner be suspected.

Of what trade he is, by what occupation he liueth. iiij.

Whether he be a gamester, an alehouse haunter, oz a pa- v.
nion emong Ruffians.

Of what wealthe he is, and how he came by that whiche vi.
he hath, if he haue anye.

What apparell he weareth, and whether he loueth to go vij.
gaye, oz no.

Of what nature he is, whether he be hastye, headye, oz viij.
readye to pike quarels.

What shiftes he hath made from time to tyme. ix.

What moued him to do suche an haynous dede. x.

Places of Confirmation to proue whether he had
power to do suche a dede, oz no.

N.ij.   The

The arte of Rhetorique.

i. The grounde where the man was slaine, whether it was in the hygh wape, in a woode, or betwixt two hylles, or els where, nyghe to an hedge or secrete place.

ij. The tyme, whether it was earlye in the mornynge, or late at nyght.

iij. Whether he was there about that time or no.

iiij. Whether he ranne awaye after the deede done, or had a: nye bloude aboute him, or trembled, or stakerde, or was contrarie in tellyng of his tale, and how he kept his counte: naunce.

v. Hope to kepe his dede secrete, bi reason of the place, tyme, and secrete maner of dopynge.

vi. Witnesses examined of his bepnge, either in this or that place.

vij. By comparinge of the strengthe of the murtherer wyth the other mans weakenes, armoure with nakednes, & stout: nes with simplicitie.

viij. His Confession.

An example of an Oration Judiciall, to proue by Con: iectures the knowledge of a notable and mooste hay: nous offence, committed by a Souldiour

S Nature hath euer abhorred murder, and God in all ages most terriblye hath plagued bloudsheading: so I truste your wisedomes (mooste worthye Jud: ges) will spedelye seke the execution of this mooste hatefull synne. And where as God reuealeth to the syght of menne the knowledge of such offences by diuers likelihodes, and probable coniectures: I doubte not but you beyng cal: led of God to heare suche causes, wyll doe herein as rea: son shall require, and as this detestable offence shall moue you vpon rehearsall of the matter. The Manne that is well knowen to be slayne, was a worthye farmar, a good house keper, a welthye husbandemanne, one that traueyled muche in this worlde, meanynge vprightlye in all hys do: inges, and therfore beloued emonge all men, and lamented of manye when his deathe was knowen. This Souldi:
                                                                              our

oure beynge desperate in his doynges, and liuyng by spoyle
all his lyfe tyme, came newlie from the warres, whose han=
des hath bene latelye bathed in bloude, and nowe he kepeth
this countrey(where this farmar was slaine) and hath ben
here for the space of one whole moneth together, and by all
likelihodes he hath slaine this honest farmer. For, such men=
slesht vilaynes, make small accompte for kyllinge anye one,
and do it they will withoute anye mercye, when they maye
see their time. Yea, this wretch is bruted for his beastly de=
meanoure, and knowen of longe time to be a stronge thiefe.
Nether had he escaped the daunger of the law, if the kinges
free pardon had not preuented the execution. His name de=
clares his noughtye nature, and his wycked liuynge hathe
made him famous. For, who is he that hearynge of N. (the
notable offenders name myght here be rehearsed) doth not
thynke by and by, that he were lyke to do suche a dede? Nei=
ther is he onelye knowen vniuersallye to be nought, but his
soyle also (where he was borne) geueth him to be an euill
man: consideringe he was bredde and brought vp emong a
denne of theues, emonge the men of Tindale and Rydders=
dale, where pillage is good purchase, and murderynge is
counted manhode. Occupation hath he none, nor yet any o=
ther honeste meanes, whereby to maintayne him selfe: & yet
he liueth mooste sumptuouslye. No greater gamester in a
whole countrey, no such riotour, a notable whoremonger,
a lewde roister emong Ruffiãs, an vnreasonable waister, to
day ful of money, win a seuenight after not worth a grote.
There is no man that seethe him, but will take him for his
apparell to be a gentilman. He hath his chaunge of suies,
yea, he spareth not to go in his silkes and veluet. A greate
quareller, and frate maker, glad when he may be at defiaũce
with one or other, he hath made such shyftes for money ere
now, that I maruaile how he hath liued till this daye. And
now beyng at a low ebbe, & lothe to seme base in his estate,
thought to aduenture vpon this farmar, and either to win=
ne the saddle, or els to lose the horse. And thus beynge so
farre forwarde, wantinge no will to attempte this wicked
dede, he sought by all meanes possible, conuenient oportu=

nitye to compaſſe his deſire. And waytinge vnder a woode ſioe, nighe vnto the hyghe waye, aboute ſire of the clocke at night, he ſette vpon this farmer, at what time he was com= ming homewarde. ffo?, it appeareth not onelye by his owne confeſſion, that he was there aboute the ſelfe ſame time, where this man was ſlayne: but alſo there be men that ſaw him ride in greate haſte aboute the ſelfe ſame time. And be= cauſe GOD would haue thys murder to be knowen, looke J p?aye you what bloude he carieth aboute hym, to beare witneſſe agaynſte hym of hys mooſt wicked deede. Againe, hys owne confeſſion dothe playnelye goe againſte hym, fo? he is in ſo manye tales, that he can not tell what to ſaye. And often his coloure chaungeth, his bodye ſhaketh, and hys tongue foultereth wythin hys mouthe. And ſuche men as he b?yngeth in to beare witneſſe wyth hym, that he was at ſuche a place at the ſelfe ſame houre, when the ffarmar was ſlayne: they wyll not be ſwo?ne fo? the verye houre, but they ſaye, he was at ſuche a place, wythin two houres after. Now Lo?d, dothe not this matter ſeeme mooſt playne vnto al mē, eſpeciallye ſeing this deede was done ſuch a time, and in ſuche a place, that if the deuyl had not bene his good Lo?de, thys matter hadde neuer come to lyghte. And who wyll not ſaye that this Captife hadde little cauſe to feare, but rather power inoughe to doe his wycked feacte, ſeynge he is ſo ſturdye and ſo ſtronge, and the other ſo weake and vnweldy: yea, ſeyng this vilaine was armed, and the other man naked. Doubte you not (wo?thye Judges) ſeynge ſuch notes of his fo?mer lyfe to declare his inwarde nature, and perceiuing ſuche coniectures lawfully gathered vpon iuſte ſuſpicion: but that this w?etched Souldioure hath ſlayne thys wo?thye ffarmar. And therfo?e J appeale fo? iuſtice vnto your wiſdomes fo? the deathe of thys innocente man, whoſe bloude befo?e God aſketh iuſte auengement. J doubt not but you remember the wo?des of Salomon, who ſaith. Jt is as greate a ſynne to fo?geue the wicked, as it is euill to condempne the innocente: and as J call vnfaynedlye fo? ryghtfull Judgemente, ſo J hope aſſuredlye fo? iuſte exe= cution.

The

The arte of Rhetorique   *Fol.52.*

The Person accuſed beynge innocente of the cryme that is layed to his charge, may vſe the ſelfe ſame places for his owne defence, the whyche hys accuſer vſed to proue hym gyltye.

The interpretation of a lawe, otherwiſe called the State legall.

IN boultynge out the true meaninge of a lawe, we muſt vſe to ſearch out the nature of the ſame, by de fining ſome one worde, or comparing one law wyth an other, iudging vpon good triall, what is right, and what is wronge.

The partes.

i. Definition.
ii. Contrarye lawes.
iii. Lawes made, & thende of the law maker
iiii. Ambignitye, or doubtfulnes.
v. Probation by thinges like.
vi. Chalengynge or refuſinge.

Definition what it is.

WHen we vſe to define a matter, when wee can not agree vpon the nature of ſome word, the which we learne to know by aſkyng the queſtion what it is. As for example. Where one is apprehended for kil ling a man, we laye murder to his charge: wherupon the ac cuſed perſon when he graunteth the killing, and yet denieth it to be murder: we muſt ſtraight after haue recourſe to the definition, and aſke, what is murder, by defininge wherof, and comparing the nature of the word, with his dede done: we ſhall ſone know whether he committed murder or mans ſlaughter.

Contrarye lawes.

IT often happeneth that lawes ſeme to haue a cer taine repugnancie, wherof emõg many riſeth much cõtenciõ, wher as if both the lawes wer wel weied & cõſidered accordjng to their circũſtances, thei wold

N.iiii.   appeare

The arte of Rhetorique.

appeare nothing contrari in matter, though in wordes they seme to dissent. Christ geueth warning, & chargeth his disciples in the .x. of Math. that they preach not the glad tidinges of his comming into the world to the Gentils, but to the Iewes only, vnto whom he was sent by his father. And yet after his resurrection we do read in the last of Mat. that he commaunded his disciples to go into all the whole world, and preach the glad tidinges of his passion, & raunsome, paied for al creatures liuing. Now though these .ii. lawes seme contrary, yet it is nothing so. For if the Iewes would haue receiued Christ, & acknowleged him their sauioure, vndoutedly they had bene the onelye children of God, vnto whom the promise and couenaunt was made from the beginninge. But bicause they refused their Sauiour, and crucified the Lord of glory: Christ made the lawe generall, and called all men to life that woulde repent, promissinge saluation to all suche as beleued and were baptised. So that the particuler law, beyng nowe abrogated, muste neades geue place to the superioure.

Foure lessons to be obserued, where contrarye lawes are called in question.

{
i. The inferioure law must geue place to the superiour.
ii. The lawe generall muste yelde to the speciall.
}

{
iii. Mans lawe, to Gods lawe.
iiii. An olde lawe, to a newe lawe.
}

There be Lawes vtterde by Christes owne mouthe, the whiche if they be taken accordinge as they are spoken, seme to contepne great absurditie in them. And therfore the mind of the lawe maker muste rather be obserued, then the bare wordes taken onely, as they are spoken. Christ sayth in the v. of Mathew. If thy right eye be an offence vnto thee, plucke him out, and caste him awaye from thee. If one geue the a blowe of thy ryghte cheke, turne to him agayne thy lefte cheke

Mathe.v.

cheke. There be some Eunuches,that haue gelded theselfes Math.rix.
for the kyngdome of heauen.Go, and sell all that thou hast, Math.rvi.
and geue it to the poore.He that doeth not take vp his crosse
and folowe me,is not worthy of me.In all whiche sentences
there is no suche meanyng,as the bare wordes vttered seme
to yelde. Pluckyng out of the iye, declares an auoydyng of
all euill occasions : receiuyng a blowe vpon the lefte cheke,
comendes vnto vs,modestie and pacience in aduersitie.Gel=
dyng,signifieth a subduyng of affeccions,& tampyng the foule
luste of pleasure,vnto the will of reason.Go and sell all:de=
clares we should be liberal,and glad to part with our good=
des to the poore and neady.Bearyng the Crosse,betokeneth
sufferance of all sorowes,and miseries in this worlde.Now
to proue that the will of the lawe maker,is none other then
I haue saied : I maie vse the testimonies of other places in
the Scripture,and compare theim with these sentences,and
so,iudge by iuste examinacion,and diligent searche,the true
meanyng of the lawe maker.

¶Ambiguitee.

Smetymes a doubt is made,vpon some woorde or
sentece,when it signifieth diuerse thynges,or maie
diuersly be taken, wherupon ful oft ariseth muche
contencion.The lawyers lacke no cases,to fil this Lawyers.
parte full of examples.For, rather then faile,thei will make
doubtes ofte tymes,where no doubt should be at all.Is his
Lease long enough (q one): yea sir, it is very long , saied a
poore husbande man.Then(q he)let me alone with it,I wil
finde a hole in it,I warrant thee.In all this talke,I excepte
alwaies the good lawyers,and I maie well spare theim, for
thei are but a fewe.

¶Probacion by thynges like.

Hen there is no certain lawe by expresse wordes
vttered for some heinous offender,we maie iudge
the offence worthy deathe,by rehersall of some o=
ther Lawe , that soundeth muche that waie.As
thus.The ciuil lawe appoynteth ý he shalbe put in a sacke,
and cast in the Sea,that killeth his father:well, then he that
killeth his mother,should by all reason,in like sort be orde=
red

o.j.

red. It is lawfull to haue a Magiſtrate, therefore it is law: full to plead matters befoꝛe an officer. And thus, though the laſt cãnot be pꝛoued by expꝛeſſe woꝛdes, yet theſame is foũd lawfull, by rehearſall of the firſt.

¶ Chalengyng, oꝛ refuſyng.

We vſe this oꝛder, when wee remoue our ſewtes, from one Courte to another, as if a manne ſhould appele from the Comnon place, to the Chaunce: rie. Oꝛ if one ſhould bee called by a wꝛong name, not to anſwere vnto it. Oꝛ if one ſhould refuſe to anſwere in the ſpirituall court, and appele to the loꝛde Chauncelloꝛ.

¶ The Oꝛacion of right oꝛ wꝛong, called otherwiſe the ſtate Juridiciall.

After a deede is well knowen to be doen, by ſome one perſone, we go to the next, and ſearche whether it be right, oꝛ wꝛong. And that is, when the maner of do: yng is examined, and the matter tried thꝛough rea: ſonyng, and muche debatyng, whether it be wꝛongfully doen oꝛ otherwiſe.

¶ The diuiſion.

This ſtate of right oꝛ wꝛong, is twoo waies diuided, wherof the one is, when the matter by the awne na: ture, is defended to bee righte, without any further ſekyng, called of the Rhetoꝛiciãs, the ſtate abſolute. The other (vſyng litle foꝛce, oꝛ ſtrengthe to maintein the matter) is, when outward help is ſought, and bywaies vſed to purchaſe fauour, called otherwiſe the ſtate aſſumptiue.

¶ Places of confirmacion foꝛ the firſt kynd, are ſeuen.

j. Nature it ſelf.
ij. Goddes lawe, and mannes lawe.
iij. Cuſtome.
iiij. Aequitie.
v. True dealyng.
vj. Auncient examples.
vij. Couenauntes and deedes autentique.
Tullie

Tullie in his moste worthy Oracion, made in behalfe of Milo, declareth that Milo slewe Clodius moste lawfully, whom Clodius sought to haue slain moste wickedly. For:(ꝙ Tullie)if nature haue graffed this in man, if lawe haue confirmed it, if necessitie haue taught it, if custome haue kept it, if aequitie haue mainteined it, if true dealyng hath allowed it, if all common weales haue vsed it, if deedes auncient haue sealed this vp, that euery creature liuyng should sense it self, againſt outward violence: no mā can thinke that Milo hath dooen wrong, in killyng of Clodius, except you thinke, that when menne mete with theues, either thei muſt be slain of theim, or els condempned of you.

Places of confirmacion for the
seconde kynde, are foure.

{ Grauntyng of the faulte committed.
{ Blamyng euill companie for it.
{ Comparyng the fault, and declaryng that either
{ thei muſt haue doen that, or els haue doen worſe
{ Shiftyng it from vs, and shewyng that wee did
{ it vpon commaundement.

Onfeſſyng of the faulte, is when the accuſed perſon   Confeſſyng, graunteth his crime, and craueth pardon thereupon,   what it is. leauyng to aſke iuſtice, ⁊ leanyng wholy vnto mercie

Confeſſion of the faulte, vſed twoo maner of waies.

The firſt is, when one excuſeth hymſelf, that he did it not   The diuiſion. willyngly, but vnwares, and by chaunce.

The second is, when he aſketh pardone, for the fault doen conſideryng his seruice to the common weale, and his worthy deedes heretofore dooen, promiſyng amendement of his former euill deede: the whiche wordes, would not be vsed before a Iudge, but before a kyng, or generall of an armie. For the Iudges muſte geue sentence, accordyng to the Lawe: the Kyng maie forgeue, as beyng aucthour of the lawe, and hauyng power in his hande, maie do as he shall thinke beſt.

Blamyng other for the faulte doen, is when wee saie that   Blamyng o-
the accuſed perſone, would neuer haue doen suche a deede, if   ther, how it
other againſt whō alſo, this accuſacion is intended, had not   is ſaied.
o.ij.   been

been euill men, and geuen iuſt cauſe, of ſu he a wicked dede.

Comparyng the faulte.

Comparyng the faulte is when we ſaie, that by ſlayng an euill man, we haue doen a good dede, cuttyng awaie the corrupte and rotten member, for preſeruacion of the whole body. Or thus: ſome ſette a whole toune on fire, becauſe their

Saguntines.

enemies ſhould haue none aduautage by it. The Saguntynes beeyng tributarie to the Romaines, ſlewe their awne children, burnte their goodes, and fired their bodies, becauſe thei would not be ſubiecte to that cruell Haniball, and loſe their allegiaunce, due to the Romaines.

Shiftyng the fault from vs

Shiftyng it frō vs, is when we ſaie, that if other had not ſet vs on, wee would neuer haue attempted ſuche an enterpriſe. As often tymes the ſouldiour ſaieth, his Capitaines biddyng, was his enforcement : the ſeruaunt thynketh his Maiſters commaundemente, to bee a ſuffi- cient de- fence for his diſ- charge.

The

The seconde Booke.

Ow that J haue hetherto set furthe what Rhetorique is, whereunto euery Oꝛatoꝛ is moſte bounde, what the cauſes bee, bothe in their nature, and alſo by nomber, that comꝛ pꝛehende euery matter, & what places ſerue to confirme euery cauſe: J thinke it is moſte mete after the knowlege of all theſe, to frame an Oꝛaciō acꝛ coꝛdingly, & to ſhewe at large, the partes of euery Oꝛacion, (but ſpecially ſuche as are vſed in iudgement) that vnto eꝛ uery cauſe, apte partes maie euermoꝛe bee added. Foꝛ euery matter hath a diuerſe beginnyng, neither al cōtrouerſies, oꝛ matters of weight ſhould alwaies after one ſoꝛt be reherſed noꝛ like reaſons vſed, noꝛ one kynd of mouyng affecciōs, oꝛꝛ cupied before all men, & in euery matter. And therfoꝛe, wherꝛ as J haue bꝛiefly ſpoken of thē befoꝛe, J wil now largely de clare them, and ſhewe the vſe of theim in euery matter, that cometh in debate, & is nedeful, thꝛough reaſon to be diſcuſſed

C_An enteraunce, two waies diuided.

He firſt is called a plain beginnyng, when the heaꝛ [margin: A beginnyng, what it is.] rer is made apte, to geue good eare out of hande, to that whiche ſhall folowe.

The ſecond is a pꝛiuey twinyng, oꝛ cloſe creeping [margin: Inſinuacion.] in, to win fauoꝛ with muche circūſtaunce, called inſinuacion

Foꝛ in all matters that man taketh in hande, this conſideꝛ racion ought firſt to be had, that we firſt diligētly expend the cauſe, before wee go thꝛough with it, that wee maye bee be aſſured, whether it be lawfull, oꝛ otherwiſe. And not oneꝛ ly this, but alſo we muſt aduiſedly marke the menne, before whom wee ſpeake, the men againſt whom we ſpeake, and all the circumſtaunces, whiche belong vnto the matter. Jf the matter bee honeſt, godly, and ſuche as of righte ought to bee well liked, we maie vſe an open beginnyng, and will the heaꝛ rers to reioyce, & ſo go thꝛough with our parte. Jf the cauſe be lothſome, oꝛ ſuche as will not be well boꝛne withall, but nedeth muche helpe, and fauour of the hearers: it ſhalbe the ſpeakers parte, pꝛiuely to get fauour, and by humble talke, to wynne their good willes. Firſte, rꝛquiryng theim to geue

o.iij.   hym

him the hearing,and next,not ſtreightly to geue iudgement, but with mercie to mitigate,all rigoꝛ of the Lawe.Oꝛ in a cõplaint made,whiche the counſail ſhall greuouſly ſtomack, to exaggerate it ẏ moꝛe,if we ſe iuſt cauſe to ſet it foꝛward. And whereas many often tymes,are ſuſpect to ſpeake thyn: ges of malice,oꝛ foꝛ hope of gain , oꝛ els foꝛ a ſet purpoſe,as who ſhould ſaie,this I can do:the wiſeſt will euermoꝛe clere themſelfes,from all ſuche offences, and neuer geue any tokẽ ſo muche as in them lieth,of any light ſuſpicion.

In accuſyng any perſone,it is beſt to heape all his faultes together,and whereas any thyng ſemeth to make foꝛ hym,to extenuate theſame to the outermoſte. In defendyng any per: ſone, it is wiſedome to reherſe all his vertues firſt and foꝛe: meſt,and with aſmuche arte as maie be,to wipe awaie ſuche faultes,as were laied to his charge. And befoꝛe all thynges, this would be wel marked,that, whenſoeuer we ſhal large: ly talke of any matter,wee alwaies ſo inuent, and finde out our firſt enteraunce in the cauſe,that theſame be foꝛ euer ta: ken,euen from the nature and bowelles therof,that al thyn: ges,whiche ſhall firſt be ſpoken,maie ſeme to agree with the matter,and not made as a Shippe mannes hoſe,to ſerue foꝛ euery legge.Now whereas any long talke is vſed,the begin: nyng thereof is either taken of the matter ſelf , oꝛ els of the perſones,that are there pꝛeſent,oꝛ els of theim,againſt whõ the accion is entended. And becauſe the winnyng of victoꝛie,

Thꝛe thynges moſte mete foꝛ euery Oꝛatoꝛ. reſteth in thꝛee poynctes:Firſte,in apt teachyng the hearers, what the matter is,next in gettyng them to geue good eare, and thirdly in winnyng their fauour:We ce ſhall make theim

To make the hearers to vnderſtande the matter. vnderſtande the matter eaſely, if firſte of all we begin to ex: pounde it plainly,and in bꝛief wooꝛdes,ſettyng out the mea: nyng,make them harken to our ſaiynges. And by no meanes better,ſhall the ſtanders by,knowe what we ſaie,and cary a: waie that,whiche thei heare,then if at the firſte,wee couche together the whole courſe of our tale, in as ſmale roume as we can, either by definyng the nature and ſubſtaunce of our matter,oꝛ els by diuidyng it in an apte oꝛder,ſo that neither the hearers bee troubled with confoundyng of matter , and heappyng one thyng in anothers necke, noꝛ yet their memoꝛie dulled

dulled with ouerthwarte rehersall , and disorderly tellyng
of our tale. Wee shall make the people attentiue, and glad to
heare vs, if wee will promise thē, to speake of weightie mat=
ters, of wholsome doctrine, suche as thei haue heretofore wā
ted: yea, if we promise to tell them thynges, cōcernyng either
their awne profite, or thaduauncement of their countrey, no
doubte wee shall haue theim diligent hearers. Or els if thei
like not to heare weightie affaires, wee maie promise theim
straunge newes, and perswade them, we wil make thē laugh
and thinke you not, that thei wil rather heare a foolishe tale
then a wise and wholesome counsail. Demosthenes therfore
seyng at a tyme, the fondnes of the people to be suche, that he
could not obtein of them, to heare hym speake his mynde, in
an earnest cause, concernyng the wealthe of his countrey: re=
quired them to tary, and he would tell them a tale of Robin
Hode. Whereat thei all staied, & longed to knowe what that
should be. He began streight to tel them, of one that had sold
his Asse to another man, whereupon thei bothe went furthe
to the next Market toune, hauyng with them the saied Asse.
And the wether beyng somewhat hotte, the first awner, whi=
che had now sold his Asse, went of that side the Asse, whiche
kept hym best from the heate. The other beyng now the aw=
ner, and in full possession, would not suffer that, but requi=
red hym to geue place, and suffer him to take the best commo=
ditie, of his awne Asse, that he could haue, wherat the other
answered and saied, naie by sainate Marie sir, you serue me
not so, I sold you the Asse, but I solde you not the shadowe
of the Asse, & therfore pike you hence. When the people hard
this, thei laughed apace, and likte it very well. Whereupon
Demosthenes hauyng wonne theim together, by this merie
tope , rebuked their folie, that were so slacke to heare good
thinges, and so redy to heare a tale of a Tubbe, and thus ha=
uyng them attentiue, perswaded with them to heare hym, in
matters of great importauce, the whiche otherwise he could
neuer haue doen, if he had not taken this waie with hym.

We shall get the good willes of our hearers, foure maner
of waies, either beginnyng to speake of our selfes, or els of
our aduersaries, or els of the people, and company present,

o? laſt of all,if we begin of the matter it ſelf, and ſo go tho?rowe with it. We ſhall get fauour fo? our awne ſakes,if we ſhall modeſtly ſet furthe our bounden dueties, and declare our ſeruice docu, without all ſuſpicion of vauntyng,either to the common weale,as in ſeruyng either in the warres a? b?ode,o? els in bearyng ſome office at home, concernyng the tranquilitie of our countrey:o? in helpyng our frendes,kynſ folkes,and poo?e neighbours, to declare our goodnes, doen heretofo?e towardes them:and laſtly,if wee ſhewe without all oſtentacion,aſwell our good willes towardes the iudges there,as alſo pleaſures docu fo? thcim in tymes paſte,to the outermoſte of our power. And if any thyng ſeme to lette our cauſe,by any miſrepo?t, o? euil behauio? of our partes here tofo?e:beſt it were in moſte humble wiſe to ſeke fauour,and ſleightly to aduoyde all ſuche offences,laied to our charge.

We ſhall get fauoure, by ſpeakyng of our aduerſaries,if we ſhall make ſuche repo?te of theim,that the hearers ſhall either hate to heare of them,o? outerly enuy them,o? els al? together deſpiſe thcim. We ſhall ſoue make our aduerſaries to be lothed,if we ſhewe and ſet furth, ſome naughtie deede of theirs,and declare how cruelly, how vilie, and how ma? liciouſly thei haue vſed other men heretofo?e.

We ſhall make theim to be enuied, if we repo?te vnto the Iudges,that thei beare theimſelfes haulte,and ſtoute vpon their wealthy frendes,and opp?eſſe poo?e men by might,not regardyng their honeſtie, but ſekyng alwaies by hooke and croke,to robbe poo?e men of their fermes, Leaſes,and mo? ney. And by the waie declare ſome one thyng, that thei haue doen,whiche honeſt eares would ſcant abide to heare.

We ſhall make theim to bee ſette naught by,if we declare what luſkes thei are,how vnth?iftiely thei liue,how thei do nothyng from daie to daie,but eate,d?inke, and ſlepe,rather ſekyng to liue like beaſtes, then mynoyng to liue like men, either in p?ofityng their countrey,o? in tenderyng their awne commoditie,as by right thei ought to do.

We ſhall gette good will,by ſpeakyng of the Iudges and hearers: if we ſhall commende their wo?thy doopnges, and p?aiſe their iuſt dealyng,and faithfull execucion of the law,

and

& tel them in what eſtimacion the whole countrp hat'p them
foꝛ their vpꝛight iudgpng and determinpng of matters, and
therfoꝛe in this cauſe needes muſt it be that thep muſt aunꝛ
ſwere their foꝛmer dopnges, and iudge ſo of this matter, as
all good men haue opinion thep wil do.

We ſhal finde fauoꝛ bp ſpeakpng of the matter, if in handꝛ
lpng our owne cauſe, we commende it accoꝛdpnglp, and diſꝛ
pꝛaiſe the attẽpt of our aduerſarie extenuatpng al his chief
purpoſes, ſo muche as ſhalbe neceſſarie.

Now reſteth foꝛ me to ſpeake of the other parte of Entꝛ
raunce into an Oꝛation, whiche is called a cloſe, oꝛ pꝛiuie
gettpng of fauouꝛ wꝛ)en the cauſe is daungerouſe, and canꝛ
not eaſelp be heard without diſpleaſure.
Inſinuacion

A pꝛiup begpnnpng, oꝛ creppng in, otherwpſe called Inꝛ
ſinuation muſt then, and not els be vſed, when the iudge is
greaued with vs, and our cauſe hated of the hearers.

The cauſe ſelfe oftentpmes is not lpked foꝛ thꝛe diuerſe
cauſes, if either the matter ſelfe be vnhoneſt, and not meete
to be vtterd befoꝛe an audience, oꝛ els if the iudge hpmſelfe
bp afoꝛmer tale be perſwaded to take part agaiſnſt vs, oꝛ laſt
if at that tpme we are foꝛced to ſpeake, when the iudge is
weried with hearpng of other. foꝛ the iudge hpmſelf bepng
weried bp hearpng, wil be muche moꝛe greeued if anp thpng
be ſpoken either ouermuche, oꝛ els againſt his likpng. Pea,
who ſeeth not that a weried man will ſoone miſlike a right
good matter? Pf the matter be ſo hainouſe that it cannot be
hearde without offence, (as if I ſhoulde take a mans parte,
who were generallp hated) wpſedome were to lette hpm go
and take ſome other whom al men liked: oꝛ if the cauſe were
thought not honeſt, to take ſome other in ſtede therof which
were better lpked, til thep were better pꝛepared to heare the
other : ſo that euermoꝛe nothpng ſhoulde bee ſpoken at the
firſte, but that whiche might pleaſe the iudge, and not to be
acknowen ones to thpnke of that, whiche pet we minde moſt
of al to perſwade. Therfoꝛe when the hearers are ſomwhat
calmed, we map entre bp litle and litle into the matter, and
ſaie that thoſe thpnges whiche our aduerſarie doth miſlpke
inthe perſon accuſed, we alſo do miſlpke the ſame.

The Arte of Rhetorique.

And when the hearers are thus wonne, we may faie, that all, whiche was faied, nothyng toucheth vs, and that wee mynde to fpeake nothyng at al againft our aduerfaries, neither this waie, no; that waie. Neither were it wyfedome openly to fpeake againft theim, whiche are generally well eftemed and taken fo; honeft menne. And yet it were not a; miffe fo; the furtheraunce of our owne caufes clofely to fpeake our fantafie, and fo, ftreighte to aulter their hartes. Yea ; to tel the iudges the like in a like matter, that fuche & fuche iudgement hath bene geuen: And therfo;e at this time confpderyng the fame cafe, and the fame neceffitie, lyke iud; gement is looked fo;. But if the aduerfarie haue fo tolde his tale that the iudge is wholy bent to geue fentence with hym, and that it is well knowne vnto what reafons the iudge moft leaned and was perfwaded: we may firft p;omife to weaken that, whiche the aduerfarie hath made mofte ftrong fo; hym felfe, and confute that parte whiche the hearers didde moft efteme, and beft of all lyke. O; elles we may take aduauntage of fome part of our aduerfaries tale, and talke of that firfte, whiche he fpake laft : o; elles be; gynne fo, as though wee doubted what were beft firfte to fpeake, o; to what parte it were mofte reafon firfte of all to aunfwere, wonderyng, and takyng GOD to witte; neffe at the ftraungeneffe of his repo;te, and confirmacion of his caufe. Fo; when the ftandersby perceiue that the aunfwerer (whome the aduerfaries thought in their mind was wholly abafhed) feareth fo litle the obiections of his aduerfarie, and is ready to aunfwere Ad omnia quare, with a bolde contenaunce: they wil thynke that they them; felues rather gaue rafhe credite, and were ouerlighte in beleuyng the firfte tale : than that he whiche nowe aunfwe; reth in his owne caufe, fpeaketh without grounde, o; p;e; fumeth vpon a ftomacke to fpeake fo; hym felfe without iuft confideracion.

But if the tyme bee fo fpente, and the tale fo long in tellyng, that al menne be almoft weried fo heare any mo;e : than we muft make p;omife at the firft to be very fho;te, and to lappe vp our matter in fewe wo;des.

And

And if tyme may so serue it were good when men bee weried to make them somewhat merie, and to beginne with some pleasaunt tale, or take an occasion to iest wittely vpon some thyng then presently doen. Myrth ma= kyng good at the begynning

Or if the tyme wil not serue for pleasaunt tales, it were good to tell some straunge thyng, some terrible won= der that they all may quake at the onely hearyng of the same. For lyke as when a mannes stomacke is full and can brooke no more meate, he may stirre his appetite either by some Tarte sawce, or elles quicken it somewhat by some sweate dishe: euen so when the audience is weried with weightie affaires, some straunge woonders maye call vp their spirites, or elles some merie tale may cheare their hea= uie lookes. Straung thin= ges some tyme nedeful to be tolde at the first.

And assuredly it is no small connyng to moue the har= tes of menne either to mirthe, or saddenesse: for he that hath suche skill, shal not lightely faile of his purpose what= soeuer matter he taketh in hande.

Thus haue I taught what an Enteraunce is, and howe it shoulde be vsed. Notwithstandyng I thynke it not amisse often to reherse this one poincte, that euermore the begynnug be not ouermuche laboured, nor curiously made, but rather apte to the purpose, seemyng vpon present occa= sion, euermore to take place, and so to be deuised, as though we speake all together without any great studie, framyng rather our tale to good reason, than our toungue to vaine paintyng of the matter. Enteraunces apt to the purpose.

In all whiche discourse, whereas I haue framed all the Lessons and euery Enteraunce properly to serue for pleadyng at the Barre: yet assuredly many of them maye well helpe those that preache Goddes truthe, and exhorte men in open assemblies to vpright dealyng.

And no doubte many of them haue muche neede to knowe this Arte, that the rather their tale maye hange toguether, where as oftentymes they begynne as muche from the matter, as it is betwixte Douer and Barwycke, whereat some take pitie, and many for werines can skante

Enteraunces
apt for Preachers.

abyde their begynnyng,it is so long oz they speake any thyng
to the purpose. Therefoze the learned Clerkes of this our
tyme, haue thought it good that al Pzeachers shoulde take
their begynnyng vpon the occasion of suche matter as is
there written,declaryng why and wherfoze and vpon what
consideracion suche wozdes were in those daies so spoken,
that the reason geuen of suche talke then vtterde, might
serue wel to begynne there Sermon.Oz els to gather some
seueral sentence at the firste, whiche bziefly compzehendeth
the whole matter folowyng, oz elles to begynne with some
apte similitude,example,oz wittie sayyng . Oz lastely to declare what wente befoze, and so to showe that whiche foloweth after . Yea sometimes to begynne lamentablie with
an vnfained bewailyng of sinne, and a terrible declaryng of
Goddes threates:Sometymes to take occasion of a matter
newly done,oz of the company there pzesent,so that alwaies
the begynnyng be aunswerable to the matter folowyng.

Of Narration.

Narration.
i. Bziefe.
ii. Plaine.
iii. Pzobable

Bzeuitie howe
it might be
vsed.

After the pzeface & firste Enteraunce,the matter must
bee opened, and euery thyng lyuely tolde , that the
hearers may fully perceaue what we go about now
in repoztyng an acte done , oz vtteryng the state of a
controuersie,we must vse these lessons,whereof the firste is
to be shozte,the next to be plaine,and the thirde is,to speake
likely,and with reason,that the hearers may remember,vn-
derstande ,& beleue the rather,suche thynges as shalbe said.

And first whereas we sholud be shozte in tellyng the matter as it lyeth, the best is to speake no moze than needes we
muste, not rauyng it from the botome, oz tellyng bytales
suche as rude people full ofte doe , noz yet touchyng euery
poinct,but tellyng the whole in a grosse summe.And where
as many matters shal neither harme vs,noz yet do vs good
beyng bzought in,and repozted by vs:it were well done not
to medle with them at al,noz yet twyse to tell one thyng,oz
repozte that,whiche is odiouse to be tolde againe.Notwith-
standyng this one thyng woulde bee wel considered that in
seekyng to be shozt,we be not obscure.And therfoze to make

our

matter plaine, that all may vnderſtande it, the beſte were
firſt and formeſt to tell euery thyng in order ſo muche as is
nedeful, obſeruyng bothe the tyme, the place, the maner of
doyng, and the circumſtaunces thereunto belongyng. Wher=
in good heede woulde bee had that nothyng bee doubtfullie
ſpoken, whiche maie haue a double meanyng, nor yet any
thyng vtterde that may make aſmuche againſt vs, as with
vs, but that al our woordes runne to confirme whollp our
matter. And ſuerly if the matter be not ſo plainelp told that
al may vnderſtande it, we ſhall doe litle good in the reſte of
our report. For in other partes of y̆ Oration if we be ſome=
what darke, it is the leſſe harme, we may bee more plaine in
an other place. But if the Narration, or ſubſtaunce of the
tale bee not well percepued, the whole Oration beſydes is
darckened altogether. For to what ende ſhould we go about
to proue that whiche the hearers know not what it is? Nei=
ther can we haue any libertie to tel our tale again, after we
haue ones tolde it, but muſt ſtreight go furthe and confirme
that whiche we haue ſaid howſoeuer it is. Therfore the re=
portyng of our tale may ſoone appere plaine, if we firſte er=
preſſe our mynde in plaine woordes, and not ſeeke theſe rope
rype termes, whiche betraie rather a foole, than commende
a wyſe man: & again if we orderly obſerue circumſtaunces,
& tell one thyng after another from tyme to tyme, not tum=
blyng one tale in an others necke tellyng halfe a tale, and ſo
leauyng it rawe, backyng & hemmyng as though our wittes
and our ſenſes were a wooll gatheryng. Neither ſhoulde we
ſuffer our tongue to runne before our witte, but with much
wareneſſe ſette forthe our matter, and ſpeake our mynde e=
uermore with iudgement.

   We ſhal make our ſaiynges appere lykely, and probable:
Yf we ſpeake directely as the cauſe requireth, if wee ſhowe Probalitie
how it might
be vſed.
the very purpoſe of al the deuiſe, & frame our inuencion ac=
cordyng as we ſhal thynke them moſt wyllyng to allowe it,
that haue the hearyng of it.

   The Narration reported in matters of iudgement ſhall Narration in
iudgement.
ſeeme to ſtande with reaſon, if wee make our talke to agree
with the place, tyme, thyng, and perſone, if we ſhall ſhowe
p.iij.   that

Plaineneſ
how it might
be vſed.

that whatsoeuer we say, the same by al likelyhodes is true, if our coniectures, tookens, reasons, & argumentes be suche that neither in them there appere any fabling, nor yet that any thyng was spoken whiche might of right otherwyse be taken, and that wee not onely speake this, but that diuers other of good creditie will stande with vs in defense of the same, all whiche reportyng may sone bee lyked, and the tale so tolde, may be thougt very reasonable. Yea, we shall make our doynges seme reasonable, if we frame our worke to natures wil, and seke none other meanes, but suche onely, as the honest and wyse haue euer vsed and allowed, bryngyng in, and blamyng the euil alwaies for suche faultes chiefely, wherunto thei most of al are like to be subiect. as to accuse a spend al, of thefte: a whoremunger, of adulterie: a rash quareller, of manslaughter: & so of other. Sometimes it is good and profitable to be merie and pleasaunt in reportyng a matter, against some maner of man and in some cause. For neither against all men that offend, nor yet against all matters shoulde the wittie alwaies vse iestyng. And nowe for those that shall tel their mynde in the other kyndes of Oratorie,

Narration in praisyng and counsel geuyng.

as in the kynde Demonstratiue, Deliberatiue, in exhortyng or perswadyng: the learned haue thought meete, that they must also cal the whole summe of their matter to one especial poincte, that the rather the hearers may better perceiue

Preachers what order they vse.

wherat they leauel al their reasons. As if a Clarke do take in hande to declare Goddes hest, he will after his Entraunce, tell what thyng is chiefely purposed in that place, and nexte after, showe other thynges annexed thereunto whereby not onely the hearers may gette great learnyng, and take muche profite of his doctrine, but he hym self may knowe the better what to say, what order to vse, and when to make an ende.

Some do vse after the literal sense to gather a misticall vnderstandyng, and to expounde the saipnges spiritually, makyng their Narration altogether of thynges heauenly. Some rehersing a texte particularly spoke, applie the same generally vnto all states, enlargyng the Narration moste Godly by comparyng wordes long agoe spoken, with thynges

ges

ges and matters that are presently done. Notwithstandyng
the aunckent fathers becaufe they did onely expounde the
Scriptures for the mofte parte, made no artificiall Narration: but vfed to folowe suche order as the plaine text gaue
theim. So that if euery fentence were plainely opened to
the hearers, they went not muche farther, sauyng that
when any worde gaue them occasion to speake of some vice,
they woulde largely faie their mynde in that behaulfe: As
Chrisoftome and Bafile haue done, with other.

The ware markyng and heedie obseruacion of tyme,
place, and person may teache al menne(that be not paft teachyng,) howe to frame their Narration in all Controuer-
fies that are called in Question, and therfore when presente occasion shall geue good instruction, what neede more
leffons? And especially seeyng nature teacheth what is comely, and what is not comely, for all tymes.

Yea what tell I nowe of suche leffons, seeyng G O D
hath raised suche worthe Preachers in this our tyme, that
their Godly, and learned doopnges, may be a mofte iufte
example for al other to folowe: afwell for their lyuyng, as
for their learnyng. I feare me the preceptes are more in nõber, than wil be wel kepte or folowed this yeare.

¶ Of Diuifion.

After our tale is tolo, and the hearers haue wel learned what wee meane, the nexte is to reporte wherein
the aduerfarie and wee, cannot agree, and what it is
wherin we do agree. And then to part out suche principall pointes whereof we purpose fully to debate, and laie
theim out to be knowen: that the hearers may plainely see,
what we wil say, and perceiue at a worde, the fubftaunce of
our meanyng. Now Tullie would not haue a deuifion to be
made, of, or aboue thre partes at the mofte, nor yet leffe than
thre neither, if nede fo require. for if we haue thre chief groũ-
des wherupon to reft, applying al our argumentes therũto
we shal bothe haue matter enough to speake of, the hearers
shal with eafe vnderftãd our meanyng, & the whole Oratiõ
shal fone be it at an end. Notwithftandyng this leffon muft
not fo curiouflie be kepte, as though it were fynne to make
the

Diuifion of
thre partes at
the moft.

The Arte of Rhetorique.

the diuision of fower, oz fyue partes, but it was spoken foz this ende that the diuision shoulde be made of as fewe as may be possible, that menne may the better carie it away and the repozter with moze ease maie remember what he hath to saie. Nowe in pzaisyng, oz dispzaisyng, in perswadyng, oz disswadyng, diuisions muste also be vsed. As if one woulde enueighe against those women that will not geue their owne chidzen sucke, he might vse this deuision. Where as women commonly put their childzen furthe to nursyng, I will first pzoue that it is bothe against the lawe of nature and also against Goddes holie wil: Againe I wil showe that it is harmefull bothe foz the childes bodie, and also foz his witte, lastly, I wil pzoue that the mother selfe falleth into muche sickenesse therebp.

(marginal note) Of women rebuked that nurse not their owne childzen.

First, nature geueth milke to the woman foz none other ende, but that she shoulde bestowe it vpon her childe. And we see beastes feede there youngones, and why shoulde not women? GOD also commaundeth all women to bzyng vp their childzen.

Againe, the childzens bodies shalbe so affected, as the milke is whiche they recepue. Nowe, if the Nurse be of an euil complexion, oz haue some hidde disease, the childe suckyng of her bzest muste needes take parte with her. And if that be true whiche the learned doe saie, that the temperature of the mynde folowes the constitucion of the bodie, needes must it be that if the Nurse be of a naughtie nature, the childe muste take thereafter. But be it, the Nurse be of a good complexion, of an honest behauiour (whereas contrary wyse Maydens that haue made a scape are commonly called to bee Nurses) yet can it not bee but that the mothers mylke shoulde be muche moze naturall foz the childe, than the mylke of a straunger.

As by experience, let a man be long vsed to one kynde of dzynke, if the same man chaunge his ayze, and his dzynke, he is lyke to mislyke it. Lastly foz the mothers, howe are they troubled with soze bzestes besydes other diseases that happen thzoughe plentie of mylke, the whiche Phisitians can tell, and women full ofte haue felte. Lykewyse in

speakyng

speakyng of fastyng, I might vse this diuision. Firste, it is
godly to fast, becaufe the fpirite is moze free and apter foz a
ny good wozke. Again it is wholefome, becaufe thereby euill
humours are waifted, and many difeafes either clerely put
awaie, oz muche abated of their tyrannie. Laftly it is pzofita=
ble, becaufe men fpende leffe money, the leffe bankequetyng
that thei vfe. Therfoze, if men loue either to be wife, godly,
healthfull, oz wealthy. let the vfe faftyng, & forbeare exceffe.

Now vpon a diuifion, there might alfo be made a fubdiui=
fion, as where I faie, it is godly to fast, I might diuide god=
lineffe, into the hearyng of Goddes wozde, into pzaiyng de=
uoutly, and charitable dealyng with all the wozlde.

Again, fpeakyng of healthe, I mighte faie that the whole
body, is not onely moze luftie with moderate faftyng, but al
fo moze apte foz al affaies. The learned man ftudieth better
when he fafteth, then when he is full. The counfailoz heareth
caufes with leffe pain beyng emptie, then he fhalbe able af=
ter a full gozge.

Again, whereas the fiue fenfes, bzyng vs to the knowlege
of many thynges: the moze apte that euery one is, the moze
pleafure thei bzyng euer with the. The iyes fe moze clerely,
the eares heare moze quickely, the togue rouleth moze roud=
ly, and tafteth thinges better, and the nofe fmelleth euill fa=
uours the foner.

Philofophie is diuided into the knowlege of thynges na=   Philofophie
turall, thynges morall, and into that arte, whiche by reafon   diuided.
findeth out the truthe, commonly called Logique. Nowe of
thefe thzee partes of Philofophie, I might make other thze
fubdiuifions, and largely fet them out. But thefe maie fuf=
fice foz this tyme.

¶ Of Propoficions.

Uintilian willeth, that ftreight and immediatly af
ter the Narracion, there fhould alfo be vfed fuche
fentences, as might bee full of pithe, and contein in
the the fubftance of muche matter, the rather that
the hearers maie be ftirred vpo the only repozt, of fome fen=
tencious faipng, oz weightie text in the law. As in fpeakyng
largely againft extozciõ, one might after his reafons applied

to the purpoſe, bꝛyng in a pithie and ſentencious pꝛopoſicion
as thus . Thoſe handes are euill that ſcratche out the eyes:
and what other dooe thei, that by foꝛce robbe their Chꝛiſtian
bꝛethꝛẽ? Wo be to that realme, where might outgoeth right
Oꝛ thus, whẽ rage doth rule, and reaſon doeth waite, what
good mã can hope to liue long in reſt. Alſo an act of a realme
maie wel ſerue to make a pꝛopoſicion. As thus. The lawe is
plain: that man ſhall dye as an offendour, whatſoeuer he bee
that bꝛeaketh vp another mannes houſe, and ſeketh by ſpoyle
to vndo his neighbour. Now here is no man that doubteth,
but that thou haſt doen this deede, therfoꝛe, what nedes any
moꝛe, but that thou muſte ſuffer, accoꝛdyng to the lawe? In
diuidyng a matter, pꝛopoſiciõs are vſed, and oꝛderly applied
foꝛ the better ſetting furth of the cauſe. As if J ſhould ſpeke
of thankfulneſſe, J might firſt ſhewe, what is thankfulneſſe,

Thankfulnes, next how nedefull it is, and laſt, how commendable and pꝛo-
what it is. ſitable it is vniuerſally? Thankfulneſſe is a kynde of remẽ-
bꝛyng good will ſhewed, and an earneſt deſire to requite the
ſame. Without thankfulneſſe, no man would do foꝛ another.
The bꝛute beaſtes haue theſe pꝛoperties, and therefoꝛe man
cannot want thẽ, without his greate rebuke. Some pꝛopoſicions are plain ſpoken, without any cauſe, oꝛ reaſon added
therunto. As thus. J haue charged this man with felony, as
you haue hard, but he denieth it: therfoꝛe iudge you it, J pꝛay

Diuiſion of you. Sometymes a cauſe is added, after the allegyng of a pꝛo
pꝛopoſicions. poſiciõ. As thus, J haue accuſed this man of felonie, becauſe
he tooke my purſſe by the high waie ſide, and therfoꝛe J call
foꝛ iuſtice. Thus pꝛopoſicions might bee gathered, nexte and
immediately after the reherſall of any cauſe, and beautifie
muche the matter, beyng either alleged with the cauſe annered, oꝛ els beyng plainly ſpoken, without geuyng any reaſon
to it at all.

¶Of confirmacion in matters of iudgement.

Hen we haue declared the chief poynctes, where-
vnto wee purpoſe to referre all our reaſons, wee
muſte heape matter and finde out argumentes, to
confirme theſame to the outermoſte of our power,
makyng firſte the ſtrongeſt reaſons that wee can, and nexte
after,

after,gatherpng all probable caules together,that beepng in
one heape,thei maie seme strong,and of greate weighte. And
whatsoeuer the aduersarie hath saied againk vs,to answere
thereunto, as tyme and place bēe maie serue . That if his
reasons be light, and moze good maie bee doen in confutpng
his,then in confirmpng our awne: it were bek of all to sette
vpon hpm,and putte awaie by arte, all that he hath fondelp
saied without witte.ffoz proppng the matter,and searchpng
out the substaunce, oz nature of the cause,the places of Lo: Caules of cō
gique muke helpe to sette it fozward.But when the persone   firmacion two
shalbe touched,and not the matter, we muk seke els where,   waies vsed,
and gather these places together.

{
  i. The name.
  ij. The maner of liupng.
  iij. Of what house he is,of what countre
      and of what peres.
  iiij. The wealthe of the man.
  v. His behauiour oz daily enurpng with
      thpnges.
  vi. What nature he hath.
  vij. Whereunto he is moste geuen.
  viij.What he purposeth frō tyme to tyme.
  ix, What he hath doen heretofoze.
  x. What hath befaulne vnto hpm here:
      tofoze.
  xi. What he hath confessed , oz what he
      hath to saie foz hpmself.
}

IN well examinpng of all these matters,muche maie
be said,& greate likelihodes maie be gathered,either
to oz fro,the whiche places I vsed heretofoze, when
Ispake of matters in iudgement,againk the accused
souldiour.Now in tripng the truth, by reasons gathered of
the matter:we muk firk marke what was doen at that time
by the suspected persone,when suche and suche offenses wer
committed.Pea,what he did,befoze this acte was dooen. A:
gain,the tyme muke bee marked,the place, the maner of do:
png,and what hart he bare hpm.As thopoztunitie of dopng

        q.ij.   and

and the power he had to do this deede. The whiche all sette together, shal either acquitte him, oz finde him giltee. These argumentes serue to confirme a matter in iudgement, foz any hainous offence. But in the other causes which are occupied, either in pzaisyng, oz dispzaisyng, in perswadyng, oz diswadyng, the places of confirmacion, be suche as are befoze rehersed, as when wee commende a thyng, to pzoue it thus,

$$\left.\begin{array}{l} \text{Honest} \\ \text{Profitable.} \\ \text{Easie.} \\ \text{Necessarie.} \end{array}\right\} \text{ to be doen.}$$

A nd so of other in like maner, oz els to vse in stede of these, the places of Logique. Therefoze, when we go aboute to confirme any cause, wee maie gather these groundes aboue rehersed, and euen as the case requireth, so frame our Reasones.

Confutacion. In confutyng of causes, the like maie be had, as we vsed to pzoue: if we take the contrarie of the same. Foz as thynges are alleged, so thei maie be wzested, and as houses are buylded, so thei maie bee ouerthzowen. What though many coniectures be gathered, & diuerse matters framed, to ouerthzowe the defendaunt : yet witte maie finde out bywaies to escape, and suche shiftes maie be made either in auoydyng the daunger, by plain denial, oz els by obiectcions, and reboundyng again of reasons made, that small harme shall turne to the accused persone, though the presumptions of his offence be greate, and he thought by good reason to be faultie. The places of Logique, as I saied, cannot be spared, foz the confirmacion of any cause. Foz, who is he, *Places of Logique moste nedefull,* that in confirmyng a matter, wil not know the nature of it, the cause of it, theffect of it, what is agreyng therunto, what likenesse there is betwixt that, and other thinges, what examples maie bee vsed, what is contrary, and what can be saied aginst it. Therefoze, I wishe that euery manne should desire and seke to haue his Logique perfect, befoze he looke to pzofite in Rhetorique, consideryng the grounde and confirmacion of causes, is foz the moste part gathered out of Logique.

Of

The arte of Rhetorique.

¶Of concluſion.

Concluſion is the handſome lappyng vp together, and bꝛief heappyng of all that, whiche was ſaied beꝛfoꝛe, ſtirryng the hearers by large vtteraunce, and plentifull gatherpng of good matter, either the one waie, oꝛ the other.

There are twoo partes of a concluſion, the one reſteth in gatherpng together bꝛieflp, all ſuche argumentes as wer beꝛfoꝛe reherſed, repoꝛtpng the ſome of them, in as fewe woꝛdes as can be, and yet after ſuche a ſoꝛte, that muche varietie be vſed, bothe when the reherſall is made, as alſo after the matꝛter is fullp repoꝛted. ffoꝛ, if the repeticion ſhould bee naked, and onelp ſet furthe in plain wooꝛdes, without anp chaunge of ſpeache, oꝛ ſhift of Rhetoꝛique: neither ſhould the hearers take pleaſure, noꝛ yet the matter take effect. Therfoꝛe, when the Oꝛatour ſhall touche anp place, whiche maie geue iuſte cauſe to make an exclamacion, & ſtirre the hearers to be ſoꝛp to bee glad, oꝛ to be offended: it is neceſſarp to vſe arte to the outermoſte. Oꝛ when he ſhall come to the repeatpng of an heinous acte, and the maner thereof: he maie ſet the Judges on fire, and heate them earneſtlp againſt the wicked offendoꝛ. Thus in repeatpng, arte maie bee vſed, and nexte with the onelp reherſall, matters maie bee handeſomelp gathered vp together.

The other part of a concluſion reſteth, either in augmenꝛtpng and vehementlp enlargpng that, whiche befoꝛe was in fewe woꝛdes ſpoken, to ſet the Judge oꝛ hearers in a heate: oꝛ els to mitigate and aſſwage diſpleaſure conceiued, with muche lamentpng of the matter, and moupng theim therebp the rather to ſhewe mercie. Amplificacion is of twoo ſoꝛtes, whereof I wſll ſpeake moꝛe at large, in the nexte Chapiter. The one reſteth in woꝛdes, the other in matter. Suche woꝛꝛdes muſte bee vſed, as be of greate weight, wherein either is ſome Metaphoꝛe, oꝛ els ſome large vnderſtandpng is conteiꝛned. Yea, woꝛdes that fill the mouthe, and haue a ſound with them, ſet furthe a matter verp well. And ſometpmes woꝛdes twiſe ſpoken, make the matter appere greater.

Again, when we firſte ſpeake our mynde in lowe woꝛdes, and

The arte of Rhetorique.

& after vſe weightier,the fault likewiſe ſemeth to be greater As whē one had killed a ientleman, thus might another am= plifie his mynd. ffor one ſlaue to ſtrike another,wer worthy of puniſhement, but what deſerueth that wretche, whiche not onely ſtriketh a manne, but ſtriketh a ientlemanne, and not onely ſtriketh a ientleman,bnt cowardly killeth a ientle manne,not geuyng hym one wounde,but geuyng hym twen= tie. To kill any manne in ſuche ſorte,deſerueth deathe, but what ſaie you to him,that not onely killeth hym ſo,but alſo hangeth hym moſte ſpitefully vpon a tree .And yet not con= tent with that,but ſcourgeth hym,and mangeleth hym whē he is dedde,and laſt of all, maketh a ieſt of his moſte naugh= tie deede,leauyng a writyng there,aboute the dedde mannes necke.Now then ſeyng his crueltee is ſuche,that thomp kil= lyng,cannot content his deuiliſhe deede,and moſte dedly ma= lice:J aſke it for Gods loue,and in the waie of Juſtice,that this wicked Deuill,maie ſuffer worthy death,and bee puni= ſhed to the example of all other . Amplifiyng of the matter, conſiſteth in heappyng,and enlargyng of thoſe places,whiche ſerue for confirmacion of a matter . As the definicion, the cauſe,the conſequent, the contrary, the example,and ſuche other.

Again,amplificaciõ maie be vſed, whē we make the law to ſpeake,the dedde perſone to make his complaint, the coũ= trey to crie out of ſuche a deede . As if ſome worthy manne wer caſt awaie,to make the countrey ſaie thus:Jf England could ſpeake,would ſhe not make ſuche, & ſuche cõplaints? if the walles of ſuche a citee or toune, had a tongue, would thei not talke thus and thus ? And to bee ſhorte, all ſuche thynges ſhould be vſed,to make the cauſe ſeme greate,whi= che concerne God,the commõ weale,or the lawe of nature. ffor if any of theſe three bee hindered, we haue a large fielde to walke in.Jn praiſyng,or diſpraiſyng, wee muſte exagge= rate thoſe places towardes the ende , whiche make menne wonder at the ſtraungeneſſe of any thyng. Jn perſwadyng, or diſſwadyng, the reherſall of commoditees , and heappyng of examples together, encreaſe muche the matter . Jt were a greate labour to tell all the commoditees,and all the pro=

perteeſ

perties, whiche belong vnto the conclufion. ffo² fuche arte maie bee vfed in this behalfe, that though the caufe bee very euill, yet a wittie manne maie gette the ouerhande, if he bee cunnyng in his facultee.

The Athenians therfo²e did ftreightly fo²bid by a lawe, to vfe any conclufion of the caufe, o² any enterance of the matter to wynne fauour. Cicero did herein fo excell, that lightly he gotte the victo²ie in all matters, that euer he tooke in hande. Therefo²e as iufte p²aife arifeth by this parte, fo I doubte not, but the wittieft will take mofte paines in this behalf, and the honeft, fo² euer will vfe the defence of mofte honeft matters. Weapons maie bee abufed fo² murder, and yet weapons are onely o²deined fo² faufgard.

Of the figure amplificacion.

Mong all the figures of Rhetorique, there is no one that fo muche helpeth fo²warde an O²acion, and beautifieth thefame with fuche delitefull o²namentes, as dooeth amplificacion. ffo² if either wee purpofe to make our tale appere vehemente, to feme pleafaunt, o² to be well fto²ed with muche copie: nedes muft it be that here we feke helpe, where helpe chiefly is to be had, and not els where. And nowe becaufe none fhall better bee able, to amplifie any matter then thofe, whiche befte can p²aife, o² mofte difp²aife any thyng here vpon yearth, I thinke it nedefull, firfte of all to gather fuche thynges together, whiche helpe beft this waie. Therefo²e in p²aifyng, o² difp²aifyng, we mufte bee well fto²ed euer with fuche good fentences, as are oft² vfed in this our life, the whiche through arte beyng encreafed, helpe muche to perfwafion. As fo² example, where it is faied (ientle behauioure wynneth good will, and clerely quencheth hatred) I mighte in commendyng a noble ientlemanne fo² his lowlineffe, declare at large howe commendable, and howe p²ofitable a thyng, ientle behauioure is, and of the other fide, how hatefull and howe harmefull, a p²oude difdainfull manne is, and howe beaftly a nature he hath, that beeyng but a manne, thinketh hymfelf better then any other manne is, and alfo ouer good to haue a matche

X

Lowlinesse. oz felowe in this life. As thus, if lowelinesse and Charitie maintayne life, what a beaste is he, that throughe hatered will purchace deathe? If God warneth vs to loue one ano: ther, and learne of him to be ientle, becaufe he was tetle and humble in harte: howe cruell are thei, that dare withstande his commaundement? If the subiect rebell against his kyng, we crie with one voyce, hang hym, hang hym, and shall wee not thynke hym worthy the vileft death of all, that beeyng a creature, contempneth his creatour, beyng a mortall manne neglecteth his heauenly maker, beyng a vile moulde of claie, setteth lighte by fo mightie a God, and euer liuyng Kyng? Beaftes and birdes without reason, loue one another, thei shroude, and thei flocke together, and shall men endued with suche giftes, hate his euen christian, and eschewe companie? When Shepe dooe straie, oz cattell doo striue one against a: nother, there are Dogges ready to call them in, yea, thei wil bite them (as it hath been full often seen) if twoo fight toge: ther: and shall man wante reason, to barke against his lewde affeccions, oz at the least shal he haue none to checke hym for his faultes, and force him to forgeue? Likewise if you would

Backbityng. rebuke one that geueth eare to backbiters and slaunderers, ye mufte declare what a greate mischief an euill tongue is, what a poyfone it is, yea, what a murder, to take a mannes good name from hym. We compte hym worthy death, that poyfoneth a mannes body, and shal not he suffer the like pain that poyfoneth a mannes honeftie, and feketh to obscure and darken his eftimacion? Menne bee well accepted emong the wife, not for their bodies, but for their vertues. Now take a waie the thyng, whereby menne are commended: and what are menne, other then brute beaftes? For beaftes do nothyng against nature, but he that goeth against honeftie, thefame manne fighteth against nature, whiche would that all menne should liue well. When a manne is killed fecretly, wee aske Iudgement for the offendour, and shall thei escape without Iudgement, that couertly murder a mannes foule? That feparate hym from GOD, that Iudge hym to helle, whose life hath euer been mofte heauenly? When oure purffe is piked, we make strieght fearche for it agayne, and empzifone

the

the offendoure, and ſhall we not ſeke recouerye of our good name, when euyll tongues haue ſlayned it? If our fame be of more price, then is either golde or groſſes, what meane we to be ſo careleſſe in keppyng the one, and ſo carefull in keppyng the other? Fonde is his purpoſe that beinge in the rayne, caſteth his garmente in a Buſhe, and ſtandeth naked him ſelfe, for ſauynge the gloſſe of his gaye coate. And yet what other thing do they that eſteme the loſſe of money, for greate lacke: and counte not the loſſe of their honeſtie for anye wante at all? Thus we ſee, that from vertues and vyces, ſuche amplifications maye be made, and no doubt he that can prayſe or diſpraiſe anye thinge plentifullye, is able moſte copiouſlye to exaggerate anye matter.

Agayne, ſentences gathered and heaped together commende muche the matter. As if one ſhoulde ſaye: Reuengemente belongeth to God alone, and therby exhorte manne to pacience: He myghte brynge in theſe ſentences with him, and geue greate cauſe of muche matter. No man is hurte but of him ſelfe, that is to ſaye: aduerſitie or wronge ſuffe= ringe is no harme to him that hathe a conſtaunt harte, and liues vpright in all his doynges.

He is more harmed that dothe wronge, then he that hath ſuffereth wronge.

He is the ſtowter that contemneth, then he is that committeth wronge.

Yea, he gayneth not a little, that had rather ſuffer much loſſe, then trye his ryght by contention.

Gaine gotte by fraude, is harme and no gaine.

There is no greater victorye, then for manne to rule hys affections.

It is a greater matter to ouercome anger, then to winne a fortreſſe or a tower.

There is no greater token of a noble harte, then to contemne wronge.

He that requitteth euill for euill: throughe hatred of an euil mayne, is made euyll him ſelfe, and therfore worthy to be hated.

He that contemneth his enemye in battayle, is counted

Sentences ga=
thered to help
Amplificaon.

Reuengemente
forbidden.

a goodman of warre, and a wise.

He that requiteth good for euill, is an aungell of God.

He that mindeth reuengemente, is at the next doore to manslaughter.

God is moued wyth nothynge soner to forgeue vs oure offences, then if we for his sake forgeue one another.

The requitinge of iniuries hath no ende.

Strife is best ended throughe Pacience

Anger is a madnesse, differing from it in this point only, that anger is shorte, and tarieth not longe, madnesse abideth still.

It is folye to suffer the fome of a horse, or the striking of his fote, and not abyde anye thynge that a foole dothe, or a noughtye disposed felowe speaketh.

No man trusteth a dronkard: And yet seyng the dronkenes of rage, and madnesse of anger, are much more daungerous then surfetinge with wyne: he dothe folyshely that trusteth his owne wytte anye thynge, when he is in a rage. Good dedes shoulde all waies be remembred, wronge doing shoulde sone be forgeuen, and sone be forgotten.

Againe for liberalitye, these sentences might serue. It is the propertie of a God to helpe man. He hathe receyued a good turne by geuynge, that hath bestowed his liberalitye vpon a worthye man.

He geueth twise, that geueth sone and chearefully.

God loueth the gladde geuer.

It is a poynte of liberalitie, sometymes to lose a good turne.

He that geueth to hym that wyll euyll vse it, geueth no good thing, but an euil thing.

Nothyng is more safelye layed vp, then is that whiche is bestowed vpon good folke.

Be not afrayed to sowe good fruite.

Nothinge is better geuen to Christe, then is that whiche is geuen to the pore.

No one man is borne for him selfe.

He is vnworthye to haue, that hath onelye for him selfe.

The

The arte of Rhetorique. **Fol.66.**

The thirde kinde of Amplifiynge is when wee gather suche sentences as are communelye spoken, oʒ elles vse to speake of suche thynges as are notable in thys lyfe. Of the first these maye be examples. In lamenting the miserye of wardeshyppes, I might saie it is not foʒ noughte so com= munelye said: I wil handle you like a warde. She is a steppe mother to me: that is to saye, she is not a naturall mother: who is woʒsse shodde then the shomakers wife? that is to saye: gentilmens childʒen full ofte are kepte but meanelye. Trotte sire, and trotte damme, how should the fole amble, that is, when bothe father and mother were noughte, it is not like that the childe wil proue good, without an especiall grace of God.

Likeryshe of tongue, lighte of taile: that is, he oʒ she that will fare daintelye, will ofte liue full wantonlye. Sone rype, sone rotten. Honoure chaungeth maners. Enoughe is as good as a feaste. It is an euill coke that can not licke his owne fingers. I will soner truste mine eye, then myne eare. But what nede I heape all these together, seynge Heywoʒ= des Prouerbes are in prynte, where plentye are to be had= de: whose paynes in that behalfe, are woʒthye immoʒtall prayse.

Thinges notable in this life are those, the which chaunce to fewe. As this: To see a man of an hundʒed yeres of age. A yonge chylde as sober as a man of fiftye yeres. A woman that hath hadde, xxiiij. chyldʒen. A man once woʒthe thʒee oʒ foure thousande pownde, now not woʒthe a grote. A yong man sayʒer then anye woman. A woman that hath had seué oʒ eyght husbandes. A man able to dʒaw a parde in his bow besides the feathers. A man merye nowe, and deade wythin halfe an houre after. There is none of all these, but serue muche to make oure talke appeare vehemente, and encrease the weight of communication. As foʒ example, If one wou= lde perswade an olde man to contemne the vanities of thys woʒlde, he might vse the examples of sodayne death, & shew that childʒé haue dyed in their mothers lappe, some in their cradell, some strypplinges, some elder, & that not one emonge a thousande commeth to thʒe score yeres.

R.ij.   Dʒ

Prouerbes al leged, helpe Amplificatió.

Thynges no= table oʒ stra= unge, helpe - foʒward Am= plification.

The arte of Rhetorique.

Oz be it that some lyue an hundzed yeares, beyonde the whiche not one in this last age passeth, what is there in this lyfe, foz the whiche anye manne shoulde desire to liue longe, seynge that olde age bzingeth this onelye commoditye wyth it, that by longe liuinge, we see many thinges, that we woulde not see, and that manye a manne hath shoztened his life, foz wearines of this wzetched woZlde. Oz what thoughe some pleasures are to be hadde in this life, what are they al to the pleasures of the lyfe to come? Lykewise in speakinge of euill happe, I myght bzynge him in that was once woz: the thzee thousande pounde, and is not nowe woZthe thzee grotes, and perswade menne either to set lyghte by riches, oz elles to comfoZte theim, and perswade theim not to take thought, seyng great harmes haue happened to other here: tofoze, and time maye come when God will sende better. These sentences aboue rehearsed, being largely amplified, encrease much any suche kinde of matter.

what is amplification.

Amplification is a figure in Rhetozique, which con: sisteth mooste in Augmentynge and diminishynge of anye matter, and that diuers wayes.

The deuision of Amplification.

AL Amplification and diminishynge eyther is taken oute of the substaunce in thinges, oz els of woZdes. Oute of the substaunce and matter, affections are deriued: oute of woZdes, suche kindes of amplifica: tion, as I wyl nowe shewe, and partly haue shewed befoZe, when I spake of the Conclusion, oz lappynge vp of anye matter.

The firste kinde of Amplification is, when by chaunging a wooZde, in augmentynge we vse a greater, but in dimini: shynge, we vse a lesse. Of the firste, this may be an exam: ple. when I see one soze beaten, to saye he is slayne: to call a naughtye felowe, thiefe, oz hangemanne, when he is not
knowen

knowen to be anye suche. To call a womanne that hathe made a scape, a commune harlot: to call an Alehouse haun-ter, a dronkarde: to call one that is troubl_d with choler, and often angrye, a madde manne: to call a pleasaunte gen-tilman, a rayipnge iester: to call a couetous man, a deuill.

Of the latter, these examples shalbe: when one hath sore **Diminution** beaten his felowe, for the same manne to saye that he hathe scant touched him: when one hath sore wounded another, to saye that he hurt him but a little: when one is sore sicke, to be saide he is a little crased. In lyke maner also, when we geue vices, the names of vertue, as when I cal him that is a cruell or mercilesse man, somewhat soore in iudgement. when I call a naturall foole, a playne symple man: when I call a notable flatterer, a fayre spoken man: a glutton, a good felowe at hys table: a spende all, a liberall gentilman: a snudge, or pynche penye, a good husbande, a thriftye man.

Nowe in all these kindes, where woordes are amplified, **Correction** they seme muche greater, if by corretion the sentence be vt-terde, and greater wordes compared with them, for whome they are vtterde. In the whiche kynde of speache, we shal seme as thoughe we wente vp by stayres, not onelye to the toppe of a thinge, but also aboue the toppe. There is an ex-ample hereof in the seueth action that Tullie made againse Uerres. It is an offence to bynde a Citezen of Rome with chaynes, it is an haynous deede to whyppe him: it is worse then manslaughter to kyll him: what shall I call it to hang hym vp vpon a gibet? If one woulde commende the auctho-ritye whiche he alledgeth, he myght saye thus. These wor-des are no fables vtterde emonge men, but an assured truth lefte vnto vs by wryptynge, and yet not by anye commune writynge, but by suche as all the worlde hathe confirmed and agreed vpon, that it is autentique, and canonicall: ney-ther are they the wordes of one, that is of the commen sort, but they are the wordes of a doctour in the church of God, and yet not the woordes of a deuine, or doctoure of the com-mune sorte, but of an Apostle: and yet not of one that is the worste, but of Paule, that is the best of al other: and yet not Paules, but rather the wordes of the holye ghost, speakyng by the mouthe of Paule. He that loueth to enlarge by this kinde, must marcke well the circumstaunces of thinges, and heappnge them altogether, he shall with ease espye how one thinge riseth aboue an other. And because the vse hercof extendeth largelye, I wil largelye vse examples . As thus. If a gentleman and officer of the kinges, beynge ouerchar= ged at Supper with ouermuche drynke, and surfetyng with gorge vpon gorge, should vomite the next daye in the Par= liamente house: I myght enueyghe thus: O shameful dede, not onelye in sighte to be lothed, but also odious of all men to be hearde. If thou haddest done this dede at thyne owne house beynge at Supper wyth thy wyfe and children , who would not haue thought it a filthy dede: but now for the to do it in the Parliamente house, emong so manye gentilmē, & such, pea, the best in al England: beyng bothe an officer of the kynges, and a man of muche aucthoritye , and there to caste oute gobbets (where belchinge were thoughte greate shame) pea , and suche gobbets as none coulde abyde the smell, and to fyll the whole house wyth euill sauoure, and thy whole bosome with muche filthines , what an abhomi= nable shame is it aboue all other: It had bene a fowle dede of it selfe to vomite where no suche gentilmen were : pea, where no gentilmen were: pea, wher no Englysh men were: pea, wher no men were : pea, wher no cōpany were at al: or it had ben euil, if he had borne no maner of office, or had ben no publique officer, or had not bene the kinges officer : but being not onely an officer, but a publike officer, and that the kynges officer: pea, & suche a kinges, & doyng such a dede: I cā not tel in ỹ worold what to say to him. Diuers examples maye be inuented like vnto this. As thus, against an heade officer in a noble mans house, I myght enueigh thus. Now Lorde, what a man is he, he was not ashamed beyng a gen= tilman, pea, a man of good peres, and much aucthoritie, and the heade Officer in a Dukes house , to playe at dyce in an alehouse wyth boyes, bawdes, and verlets. It had bene a a greate faulte to playe at so vile a game, emonge suche vile persons, beynge no gentilman, beynge no officer, beyng not of suche peres: But beynge bothe a man of fayre landes, of

an auncient houſe, of great aucthoꝛitie, an officer to a Duke,
yea,and to ſuche a Duke, and a man of ſuch peres,that his
white heeres ſhoulde warne him to auoyde all ſuche folye,
to play at ſuche a game,with ſuche royſters, and ſuch ver=
lets,yea,and that in ſuch a houſe as none come thither but
theues,bawdes,and Ruffians:nowe befoꝛe God I can not
ſpeake ſhame enoughe of him. There is an other kynde of
Amplification when vnto the hygheſt, there is added ſome
thinge higher then it is. As thus. There is not a better
pꝛeacher emonge them all, excepte Hughe Latimer,the fa=
ther of all pꝛeachers. There is no better Latine man with=
in England,excepte Gualter Haddon the lawer.

Againe, we amplifye a matter not aſcendyng by degrees,
but ſpeakinge that thinge onely, than the whiche no greater
thinge can be ſpoken. As thus. Thou haſte killed thyne
owne mother,what ſhall I ſaye moꝛe,thou haſt kylled thine
owne mother. Thou haſt deceaued thy ſoueraine Loꝛd and
kinge, what ſhall I ſaye moꝛe, thou haſt deceiued thy ſoue=
raine Loꝛde and kinge.

Sometymes wee amplifie by comparynge, and take oure
grounde vpon the weakeſt and leaſt,the whiche if they ſeme
greate, then muſte that neades appeare greate, whyche wee
woulde amplifie and encreaſe.As Tullie againſte Catiline.
My ſeruauntes in good ſouth,if they feared me in ſuch ſoꝛt,
as all the Citezens do feare thee: I would thinke it beſt foꝛ
me to foꝛſake my houſe.Thus by vſing the leſſe firſt,this ſē=
tence is encreaſed,fewe ſeruauntes are cōpared with all the
citezens,bondmen are compared with free men : Tullie the
maſter,is compared with Catiline the traytour,which was
neither loꝛd noꝛ ruler ouer the Citezens: and Tullies hou=
ſe is compared with the Citye.

By comparing of examples,we vſe alſo to encreaſe oure
matter. As thus.Did the Maioꝛ of London thꝛuſt thꝛou=
ghe Iacke Straw beinge but a verlet rebell, and onely diſ=
quietinge the Citye: and ſhall the kynge ſuffer Capitayne
Kete to liue in Englandes grounde,and enioye the fruites
of his realme, beinge a moſt tyrannous traytoure,and ſuch
a rebell as ſought to ouerthꝛow the whole Realme?

R.iiij. Here

The arte of Rhetorique.

Here is Jacke Strawe compared with Capitaine Kett, the Citye of London, with the whole Realme, the Maior with the kinge. So that if he which is a priuate perfon, and hathe no power of deathe, mpghte punpshe wpth deathe the disquietpnge of a Citye: the kpnge him selfe haupnge all power in his hande, mape iustelpe punishe hpm that seketh to ouerthrowe his whole realme.

The places of Logique helpe ofte for Amplification. As, where men haue a wronge opinion, and thpnke theft a greater faulte then slaunder, one mpght proue the contrarpe as well bp circumstaunces, as bp argumentes. And first he might shewe that slaunder is thefte, and that euerpe slaunderer is a thiefe. For as well the slaunderer as the thiefe, doe take awap an other mannes possession againste the owners will. After that he might shewe that a slaunderer is worse then anpe thiefe, becaufe a good name is better then all the goodes in the worlde: and that the losse of monep mape be recouered, but the losse of a mannes good name, can not be called backe againe, and a thefe mape restore that agapne whiche he hath taken awape, but a slaunderer can not geue a man his good name againe, whiche he hath taken fro him. Agapne, he that stealeth goodes or cattell, robbes onelp but one man, but an euill tongued man infecteth all their mindes: vnto whofe eares this reporte shall come. Besides this, there are lawes & remedies to subdue theues: but there is no lawe agapnste an eupll tongue. Agapne, all suche hapnous Offences are euer the more greuouslpe punished, the more clossie, and more craftelpe thep are committed. As it is thought a greater faulte to kpll one with popfon, then to kpll him with the swerde, and a more haphous offence to commit murder, then to commit manslaughter: we mape gather an argument alfo from the instrumente or maner of dopng. As a thefe hath done this offence wpth hps hande, a slaunderer hath done it with his tongue. Agapne, bp the iudgement of al menne, enchauncement is a notable euill: But thep that infecte a prpnce or a kinge wpth wpcked counsaple, are not thep more wpcked enchaunters, considerpnge thep doe as muche as if one shoulde Popfon a

Conduite

Slaunder, a greater offèce then thefte

conduite head,o2 a Riuer from whence al men featche their water. And yet they do mo2e,fo2 it is a greater fault to poi= son the mynde,than the bodie. Thus by the places and cir= cumstaunces,great matter might be made.

By contrraries set together,thynges oftentymes ap= pere greater. As if one shoulde set Lukes Ueluet against Geane veluet,the Lukes wil appere better, and the Geane wil seeme wo2ser. O2 sette a faire woman against a foule, and she shal seeme muche the fairer,and the other muche the fouler. Acco2dyng whereunto there is a saiyng in Logique: Contraria inter se opposita magis elucescunt.That is to say, Contraries beyng set,the one against the other, appere mo2e euident. Therefo2e if any one be disposed to set furthe chastitie,he may b2yng in,of the contrarie parte,who2dome, and show what a fouly offence it is to liue so vnclenly, and then the defo2mitie of who2edome shall muche sette fo2the chastitie:o2 if one be disposed to perswade his felow to lear= nyng and knowlege, he may showe of the contrarie what a naked w2etche,man is,yea how muche a man is no man,and the life no lyfe,when learnyng ones wanteth.The lyke helpe we may haue by comparyng lyke examples together either of creatures liuyng, o2 of thynges not liuyng : As in spea= kyng of constauncie, to showe the Sonne who euer kepeth one course:in speakyng of inconstaunce to showe the Moone whiche keepeth no certaine course . Againe, in pounge Sto2kes wee may take an example of loue towardes their *Sto2kes.* damme, fo2 when she is olde, and not able fo2 her crooked bil to picke meat,the poungones fede her. In poungUipers *Uipers,* there is a contrary example (fo2 as Plinie saieth) they eate out their dammes wombe, and so come fo2the. In Hennes there is a care to b2yng vp their chickens,in Egles the con= trarie,whiche caste out their egges if thei haue any mo then th2e:and al because they woulde not be troubled with b2yn= gyng vp of many.

There is also a notable kynde of amplification when we woulde extenuate and make lesse,great faultes,which befo2e we did largely encrease: to thende that other faultes might seeme the greatest aboue all other. As if one had robbed his
s.i.   maister,

maifter,thzuft his felow thzough the arme,accõpaned with harlottes, kepte the tauerne till he had been as dzonke as a ratte:to fay after a large inuectiue againft al thefe offences. Pou haue heard a whole court roule of ribauldzie and pet al thefe are but fle bitynges in refpect and comparifon of that which I fhal now fhow pou. who doth not loke foz a marueiloufe great matter & a moft hainoufe offence,when thofe faultes that are thought mofte greuoufe are counted but fle bitynges in refpect and comparifon of that whiche he mynzdeth to reherfe? In like maner,one might exhozt ý people to godlineffe , and whereas he hath fet fozthe al the commodities that folowe the fame,as in fhowyng a quiet confcience not gilty of any great faulte,the libertie of fpirite,the peace whiche we haue with GOD, the felowfhip with al the electe,foz the feruant of Sathan,to be the fonne of GOD the comfozte of the foule, the greateneffe wherof no man is able to conceiue:to fay at lengthe,and what can be greater, what can be moze excellent,oz moze bleffeful? & pet al thefe are fmal matters if thei be cõpared with the bleffed enheritaunce of the euerliuingGod pzepared foz al thofe that liue Godlie here vpon earthe,faftenyng there whole truft vpon Chzifte aboue,whiche bothe is able,and will faue all thofe that cal vnto him with faith. We do encreafe our caufe by reafonyng the matter and cafting our accompt,when either by thynges that folow,oz by thynges that go befoze,oz elles by fuche thynges as are annered with the matter, wee geue fentence how great the thyng is.By thynges goyng befoze I iudge when I fee an enuioufe,oz hafty man fight wich an other as haftie , that there is lyke to be bloudfhed . As who fhould faie,can enuioufe,oz haftie men matche together,but that they muft needes trie the matter with bloudfhedyng? Affuredly it can not be otherwyfe but that bloude muft appeafe their rage. Likewyfe feeyng two wyfe men earneftly talkyng together, I cannot otherwyfe iudge but that their talke muft nedes be wittie,and concerne fome weightie matter.foz to what ende fhoulde wyfe men iopne,oz wherefoze fhoulde they laie their heades together , if it were not foz fome earneft caufe? Wh it a fhame is it foz a ftrong man, of

muche

muche health & great manhode, to be ouercome with a cuppe
of dzynke. Frō thynges iopned with the caufe, thus. A wo:
man hauyng her houfbande empzifoned, and in daunger of
death, foubdenly fteppe befoze the Kyng and craued his par:
don. Bold was that womā whiche durft aduenture to knele
befoze a Kyng, whofe houfband had fo greuoufly offended.
Though wo.nen by nature are fearful, pet in her appered a
manly ftomake, and a good bolde harte, pea euen in greateft
daunger. By thynges that folowe, thus, al England lament
the death of Duke Henrie and Duke Charles twoo noble
bzethzen of the houfe of Suffolke. Then may we wel iudge
that thefe two ientlemen were wonderfully beloued, when
they both were fo lamented.

There is a kynde of Amplifyng, when in fpeakyng of.ij.
that fought together, wee pzaife hym muche that had the
wozfe, becaufe we would the other to haue mozepzaife. Cō:
fiderpng foz a man to beate a bope, it were no pzaife, but foz
a talle man to matche with an other, that were as talle as
hym felfe: that were fomwhat wozthe. Therfoze J would
haue the Scottes wel pzaifed, whome the Englifhmen haue
fo often banquifhed. He that pzaifeth muche the ftronghold
of Boleine, muft nedes thereby pzaife kyng Henry the.viij.
of England, who by martial power, wonne it, and kepte it
al his lyfe tyme. Oz thus. Suche a one kepes a marueiloufe
good houfe, foz the wozft bote in his houfe dzynkes one and
thefame dzynke with his mafter, and al one bzead, pea euery
one hath his meate in filuer, chamber veffels, and all are of
filuer. We iudge by apparel, by armour, oz by harneffe what
a man is of ftature, oz biggenes. We iudge by occafion, the
goodnes of men, as when they might haue doen harme, thei
would not, when they might haue flaine, thei fought rather
to faue. Frō the place where one is, encreafe may be gatherd
As thus. Beyng euen in the Court, he was neuer moued to
gāmyng, beyng at Rome, he hated harlottes, where there is
by repozt fo great plentie as there are ftarres in the elemēt.

From the tyme thus, he muft nedes be well learned in
the lawes of our Realme that hath been a ftudent this thir:
tie wynter.

The Arte of Rhetorique.

From the age:affuredly,he is lyke to be good,for beepng but a childe he was euer moft godlie.

From the ftate of lyfe:no doubt but he is honeft, for beepng but a feruaunt he lyued fo vpzightely ,as none coulde iuftly blame his lyfe.

From the hardeneffe of a thyng. That whiche is almoft onely pzoper to Aungels muft nedes be harde for man:there foze chaftitie is a rare gifte,and harde foz man to kepe.

From the ftraungeneffe of a thyng.Eloquēce muft nedes bee a wonderful thyng,when fo fewe haue attained it.

Lykewyfe notable aduentures doen by a fewe, are moze pzaife wozthy than fuche as haue been done by a great nom; be.Therfoze the battail of Mufkelbozow againft the Scot; tes where fo fewe Englifhmen were flaine, and fo many Scottes difpatched:muft nedes be moze pzaife wozthie,than if the nomber of Englifhmen had been greater.

Uehemencie of woozdes full often helpe the matter foz; warde, when moze is gatherde by cogitacion, than if the thyng had been fpoken in plaine woozdes. When wee heare one fay fuche a mā fwelled feyng a thyng againft his mynd. we gather that he was then,moze than half angrie.Againe, when wee heare one faie,fuche a woman fpittes fier,we ga; ther ftreight that fhe is a Deuill.The Pzeacher thunderde in the Pulpite,belyke then he was metely hoote. But con; cernyng all fuche fpeaches , the knowlege of a Metaphoze, fhall bzyng men to muche knowlege,(whereof J wil fpeake herzafter emong the figures) and therefoze J furceafe to fpeake of it in this place.

We encreafe our caufe by heappyng of woozdes & fenten; ces together,couchyng many reafons into one cozner which befoze were fcaterde abzode,to thentent that our talke might appere moze vehement . As when by many coniectures and great pzefumptions we gather that one is an offendoz, hea; **Amplification by coniectures** ppng them al into one plumpe,whiche befoze were fparpled abzode,and therefoze did but litle good. As thus:To pzoue by cōiectures a murder committed,J might thus fay againft a fufpected perfon.My Lozdes do not weye my woozdes and fentences feuerally , but confider them all altogether . If

the

the accuſed perſone here ſhall receiue profite by this other
mans deathe, if his lyfe heretofore hath euer been euill,his
nature couetouſe, his wealthe moſt ſlendre, and that this
dead mans gooddes could turne to no mans auaile ſo muche
as vnto this accuſed perſon,and that no man could ſo eaſely
diſpatche him,and that this man could by no better meanes
compaſſe his deſier, and that nothyng hath been vnattemp=
ted whiche might further his naughtie purpoſe, & nothyng
doen that was thought needeleſſe, and ſeeyng a meete place
was chefely ſought for,and occaſion ſerued very wel, & the
tyme was moſt apt for ſuche an attempte and many meanes
heretofore deuiſed to compaſſe this offence, and greate hope
bothe to kepe it cloſe, and alſo to diſpatche it, and beſydes
that, ſeeyng this man was ſeen alone a litle before in the
ſame place, where this other man was ſlaine, and that this
mans voice whiche did ſlaye hym was hard a litle before in
the ſame place where this other man was ſlaine, and ſeyng
it is well knowne that this man came home late the ſame
night, and the nexte daie after beyng examined, did anſwere
confuſedlie, fearefullie,and as though he were amaſed, and
ſeeyng al theſe thynges are partely ſhowed by witteneſſes,
partely by good reaſon,partely by his owne confeſſion,and
partely by the reporte that comonly goeth of hym, whiche
by lyke is not ſpoken without ſome ground:It ſhalbe your
partes wozthie iudges wayng al theſe thynges together to
geue certaine iudgement of hym for this offence, and not to
thynke it a matter of ſuſpicion.For it might haue been that
thre of foure of theſe coniectures beyng proued, might geue
but onely a cauſe of ſuſpicion, but whereas all theſe toge=
ther are plainely proued by hym,it can not be otherwiſe but
that he hath offended.

It is an excellent kynd of Amplifiyng when thynges en=
creaſed, and thynges diminiſhed are both ſet together, that
the one may the rather beautifie the other. As if, when
Gods goodneſſe towardes vs wer largely amplified,we did
ſtreight extenuate our vnthankfulneſſe towardes him again.
As thus: Seeyng God hath made man a creature vnto his
owne likeneſſe, ſeeyng he hath geuen hym lyfe, and the ſpi=

rite of vnderstandyng, endewyng hym with h s manifolde graces, and redemyng hym not with vile money, but with his owne precioule bodie, sufferyng deathe, and bloodshed; dyng vpon the Crosse, the rather that man might lyue for euer: what an vnthankefull parte is it, yea what an hai; noule thyng is it for man so ofte to offende, so ofte to wal; lowe in suche his wickednesse, and euermore for Goddes louyng kyndnesse, to showe hym selfe of all other creatures most vnkynde.

Lykewyle contraries beyng rehersed and the euill imme; diatly vtterde after the good, make muche for encrease. As many men now a daies for sob;ietie, folowe gluttonie, for chastitie, take leacherp, for truthe, lyke falsehode, for gentle; nesse, seeke crueltie, for iustice, vse wrong dealyng, for hea; uen, hell, for God, the Deuill:to whome they will without peraduenture, if Goddes grace be not greater.

¶ Of mouyng affections.

affections
mouyng.

Becaule the beautie of Amplifiyng, standeth apte mouyng of affections: It is needefull to speake somewhat in this behaulfe, that the better it may be knowne what they are, and howe they maie bee vsed. Affections therefore (called Pallions) are none other thyng, but a stirryng, or foreyng of the mynde, either to de; sier, or elles to detest, and lothe any thyng, more vehemently then by nature we are commonly wonte to doe. We desier those thynges, we loue them, and lyke them earnestly, that appere in our iudgement to be goodlie, we hate and abhorre those thynges, that seeme naughte, vngodlie, or harmefull vnto vs. Neither onely are wee moued with those thynges which we thinke either hurtful, or profitable for our selues, but also we reiopce, we sorie, or we pitie an other mannes happe.

And euermore there are twoo thynges whiche moue vs, either this waie, or that waie. The matter selfe whiche doth happen, or is lyke to happen: and the person also whome the matter dothe concerne. As for example: If a wicked wretche haue his desertes, we are al glad to heare it, but if an inno; cent

cent shoulde be cast away, we thynke muche of it, and in slo=
make repine against wrong iudgement. If an euil man finde
muche fauour, we enuie his good happe, yea it greeueth vs,
that any suche shoulde haue suche fauour showed: And not
onely doe we hate the euil, that are come to any wealth, but
also we enuie commonly all suche as come to any preferre=
ment, especially if either they haue been as poore men as
we are, or elles came of a meaner house than we haue done.
No one man woulde haue any to be better than hym selfe,
and euery one enhableth his owne goodnes to deserue lyke
dignitie with the best. And whereas some haue gotte before,
startyng soubdeinly from an inche to an elle, we spare not
to saie that flattery made theim speede, and though they
haue muche gooddes, yet are they cleare voide of all good=
nes, and therefore muche good may it do theim, we woulde
not come by gooddes in suche sorte to wynne al the worlde.
for the Deuill and they (saie wee) shall parte stakes with
theim one daie. And thus wee can neuer bee content to geue
our neighbour a good woorde. Yea though they haue ser=
ued right well, and deserued a greate rewarde, wee muste
needes finde some faulte with theim to lessen their praises,
and saye that though their desertes bee great, yet their na=
tures are nought: none so proude, though fewe bee so har=
dy: none so enuiouse, though fewe so faithfull: none so co=
uetouse, though fewe so liberall: none so gluttonouse,
though fewe kepe suche an house. And thus, thoughe wee
graunt them one thyng, yet we will take another thyng as
fast againe from them.

Suche a man is an excellent felowe (saieth one) he can
speake the tongues wel, he plaies of instrumentes fewe men
better, he seyneth to the Lute maruilouse swetely, he en=
dites excellently: but for all this (the more is the pitie) he
hath his faultes, he will bee dronke ones a daie, he loues
women well, he will spende Goddes coope if he had it, he
will not tarye longe in one place, and he is somewhat
large of his tongue. That if these faultes were not,
surely he were an excellent fellowe. Euen as one shoulde
saie: If it were not for lyeng and stealyng, there were not

Which prai=
syng:disprai=
syng vsed.

aιι

an honeſter man than ſuche a one is that perchaunce hath
ſome one good qualitie to ſet hym forwarde. Theſe buttes
bee to brode, and theſe barres be ouer bigge, for looke what
is geuen to one by commendyng, the ſame is ſtreight taken
away by buttyng. Therfore ſuche are not to be lyked that
geue a man a ſhoulder of mutton, and breake his heade with
the ſpitte when thei haue doen. And yet this is manya más
nature, eſpecially where enuie hath any grounded dwellyng
place, whoſe propertie is alwaies to ſpeake nothyng of o-
ther without reproche and ſlaunder.

In mouyng affections, and ſtirryng the iudges to be greued, the weight of the matter muſt be ſo ſet forth, as though
they ſaw it plaine before their eyes, the report muſt be ſuche
and the offence made ſo hainouſe, that the like hath not been
ſeene heretofore, and al the circuſtaunces muſt thus be heaped together: The naughtines of his nature that did the
dead, the cruel orderyng, the wicked dealyng and malicious
handelyng, the tyme, the place, the maner of his doyng, and
the wickedneſſe of his wil to haue doen more. The man that
ſuffeined the wrong, how litle he deſerued, how wel he was
eſtemed emong his neighbours, howe ſmall cauſe he gaue
hym, how great lacke men haue of hym. Now, if this be not
refourned, no good man ſhal lyue ſauſe, the wicked wil ouer-
flowe al the world, & beſt it were for ſauegard to be noughte
alſo, and to take parte with them, for no good man ſhal goe
quiet for them, if there be not ſpedie redreſſe found, and this
faulte puniſhed to therample of al other.

Quintiliane coucheth together in theſe few wordes the
ful heape of ſuche an heauouſe matter, by gatheryng it vp
after this ſorte.

i.	what is doen.
ij.	By whome.
iij.	Againſt whome.
iiij.	Upon what mynde.
v.	At what tyme.
vi.	In what place.
vij.	After what ſorte.
viij.	How muche he would haue doen.

It

Deſcription of an euil & wic-ke offence doen.

The arte of Rhetorique.

If one bee beaten blacke and blewe, wee take it gre: uouslp: but if one be slain. we are muche more treu: bled. Again, if a slaue or ruffine shall do suche a dede we are displeased, but if an officer, a preacher, or an hed ientleman, should vse any slaucrie, wee are muche more agreued. Pea, or if a very notable euill man, commit suche an horrible offence, we thynke hym worthy to haue the lesse fauor. If a sturdy felowe be stroken, we are not so muche di: squieted, as if a child, a woman, an aged man, a good man, or a chief officer, should be euil vsed. If the offence be commit: ted vpon a prepensed mynde, and wilfully, wee make muche more a do, then if it were doen by chaunce medly. If it be doen vpon an holy daie, or els vpon the daie of Assise, or vpon the daie of a kynges coronacion, or about suche a solempne tyme or if it bee dooen in the nighte, rather then at Noone daies, we make the matter greater, then if it had been dooen at a: nother tyme. In the courte if one strike a man, it is thought greater, then if he should strike hym in the open streate. The maner of doopng also, doeth muche moue the pacience of men as if one should cowardly kill one, and strike hym sodainly. he were worthy greater blame, then if he should manfully set vpon hym: or if one kill his felowe secretly with a gunne, he wer worthy more hatred, then if he killed hym with a sword or if he wounded hym sore, or cruelly mangeled hym, we crie out muche more, then if he had barely killed hym. And last of al, if his will had been to haue doen muche more then he did: we encrease our anger againg his rage muche more, then e: uer we would els haue doen.

what is doen.
By whom,
Against whom
Vpon what mynde.
At what time.
In what place
After what sorte.
How muche he would.

Of mouyng pitee.

Nowe in mouyng pitie, and stirryng menne to mercie, the wrong doen must first be plainly told: or if the Judges haue susteined the like extremitee, the best wer to will them to re: membre their awne state, how thei haue been abused in like ma: ner, what wronges thei haue suffered by wicked doers: that by hearyng their awne, thei maie the better hearken to others.

Again, whereas all other miseries, that befall vnto man, are greuous to the care, there is nothing more heinous, then to heare that the most honest men, are sonest ouerthrowen by

t.i. the

thē that are moſte wicked,and vertue put to flight, through the onely might of vice. That if the like hath not happened, vnto the hearers of this cauſe, yet it wer mete to ſhewe thē that the like maie happē,and ſo require them to geue iudgemēt in this cauſe,as thei would doo in their awne, and remēber that harme may chaunce to euery one,that perhappes chaunceth to any one. And no doubt euery man remēbring hymſelf,and his awne caſe,will loke well about hym, and geue iudgement,accordyng to right.

Neither can any good be doen at all, when we haue ſaied all that euer we can, excepte we bryng theſame affeccions in our awne harte, the whiche wee would the Iudges ſhould

He that will ſtirre affecciōs to other,muſte firſt be moued hymſelf.

beare towardes our awne matter.For how can he be greued, with the report of any heinous acte,either in ſtomackyng the naughtineſſe of the deede,or in bewailyng the miſerable miſfortune of the thyng,or in fearyng muche,the like euill hereafter:excepte the Oratour hymſelf vtter ſuche paſſions outwardly,and from his harte fetche his complaintes,in ſuche ſort,that the matter maie appere,bothe more greuous to the eare,& therwith ſo heinous,that it requires earneſtly ſpedy reformacion:There is no ſubſtaunce of it ſelf, that wil take fire, excepte ye put fire to it. Likewiſe no mannes nature is

Heate,cauſeth heate.

ſo apt,ſtreight to be heated,except the Orator himſelf,be on fire,and bryng his heate with hym.It is a common ſaiyng, nothyng kyndeleth ſoner then fire.And therefore a fierie ſtomack,cauſeth euermore a fierie tongue.And he that is heated with zeale and godlineſſe,ſhall ſet other on fire with like affeccion.No one man can better enuiegh againſt vice,then he can do,whiche hateth vice with al his harte.Again,nothyng

A wepyng iye prouoketh moyſture.

moyſteth ſoner then water.Therefore a wepyng iye cauſeth muche moyſture , and prouoketh teares . Neither is it any meruaile:for ſuche men bothe in their countenaūce, tongue, iyes,geſture,and in all their body els, declare an outwarde grief,and with wordes ſo vehemently and vnfeinedly,ſettes it forward, that thei will force a man to be ſory with them, and take part with their teares, euen againſt his will. Notwithſtandyng,when ſuche affecciōs are moued, it wer good not to ſtande long in thē. For though a vehement talke maie

moue

moue teares,yet no arte can long holo theim.ffoz as Cicero
doth faie,nothyng dzieth foner,then teares,efpecially when
we lament another mans caufe,& be fozy w him foz his fake
But now that I haue taught men to be fozy,I wil attēpt
again to make them merp, and fhewe what learned men faie
concernyng laughter,in delityng the hearers whē tyme and
place fhall beft require.

¶Of delityng the hearers,and ftirryng them to laughter.

Onfiderpng the Dulneffe of mannes nature,that nei= Laughter
ther it can be attentiue to heare,noz yet ftirred to like moupng.
oz allowe,any tale long tolde,except it be refrefhed,oz
finde fome fwete delite:the learned haue by witte and
laboz deuifed muche varietee.Therefoze fometymes in tel=
lyng a weightie matter,thei bzyng in fome heup tale,& moue
thē to be right fozy,wherby the hearers are moze attentiue.
But after when thei are weried, either with tedioufneffe of
the matter,oz heuines of the repozt:fome pleafant matter is
inuēted both to quicken them again,& alfo to kepe theim frō
facietie.But furely fewe there be, that haue this gift in due
tyme to chere men.Neither can any do it,whom nature h th
not framed,& geuen an aptnes therunto.Some mannes coū=
tenaūce will make paftyme,though he fpeake neuer a wozde
Pea,a foolifhe wozde,vttered by an apte mannc,oz a gefture
ftraungely vfed by fome pleafant body,fettes men ful oft v=
pon a laughter. And whereas fome thinke it a trifle, to haue
this gift,& fo eafy,that euerp varlet oz common iefture is a=
ble to matche with the beft:yet it appereth that thei,whiche
wittely can be pleafant,& when time ferueth,can geue a me=
ry anfwere,oz vfe a nippyng taunte,fhalbee able to abafhe a
righte wozthy man,& make hym at his wittes ende, thzough
the fodein quip & vnloked frūpe geuen.I haue knowen fome
fo hit of the thūbes,that thei could not tell in ẙ wozld whe=
ther it were beffe to fighte,chide,oz to go their waie.And no
meruaile:foz wher ẙ ieft is aptly applied, the hearers laugh
immediatlp,& who would gladly be laughed to fcorne?fome
can pzetely by a wozd fpoken, take occafiō to be right merp.
Other can ieft at large,& tel a round tale pleafantly,though
thei haue none occafion at that tyme geuen . But affuredly

t.ij. that

that mirth is moze wozth,whiche is moued by a wozd new=
ly fpoken,then if a long tale fhould pleafauntly be told.ffoz
afmuche as bothe it cometh vnlooked foz,and alfo declares a
quickeneffe of witte,wozthy commendacion. There are fiue
thynges,whiche Tullie noteth,concernyng pleafaunt talke.

⎧ i. What it is to delite the hearers.
⎪ ij. Whereof it cometh.
⎨ iij. Whether an ozatoz may moue laughter
⎪ iiij.How largely he maie go,and what mea
⎪   fure he muft vfe.
⎩ v. What are the kyndes of fpoztyng , oz
       mouyng to laughter.

Now to tell you in plain woozdes,what laughter is,how
it ftirreth and occupieth the whole body,how it altereth the
countenance,and fodainly bzafteth out,that we cannot kepe
it in: Let fome mery man on Goddes name,take this matter
in hande.ffoz it paffeth my cunnyng,and I thynke euen thei
that can beft moue laughter,would rather laugh merily whē
fuche a queftion is put furthe, then geue anfwere earneftly,
what,and how laughter is in deede.

The occafion of laughter , and the meane that maketh vs
merie(whiche is the fecond obferuacion) is the fondnes,the
filthines,the defoznitee, and all fuche euill behauioz, as we
fe to bee in other . ffoz wee laugh alwaies at thofe thynges,
whiche either onely oz chiefly touche handfomely, and wit=
tely fome efpeciall fault,oz fonde behauioz in fome one body,
oz fome one thing.Sometymes we ieft at a mānes body that
is not well pzopozcioned , and laugh at his countenaunce,if
either it be not comely by nature.oz els he thzough foly,can=
not wel fet it.ffoz if his talke be fond,a mery man can want
no matter to hit hym home,ye maie be affured. Some ieft is
made,when it toucheth no man at al,neither the demaunder
neither the ftāders by,noz yet any other,and yet deliteth as
muche the hearers,as any the other can do. Now when wee
would abafhe a man,foz fome woozdes that he hath fpoken,
and can take none aduauntage of his perfone, oz makyng of
his body, wee either doulte hym at the firfte,and make hym
beleue,that he is no wifer then a Goofe : oz els wee confute
                                                    wholy

wholy his saipnges, with some pleasaunt iest, oꝛ els we exte=
nuate and diminishe his doynges, by some pretie meanes, oꝛ
els we cast the like in his dishe, and with some other deuise,
dashe hym out of countenance: oꝛ last of all, we laugh him to
skoꝛne out right, and sometymes speake almost neuer a woꝛd
but onely in countenaunce shewe our selfes pleasaunt. But
how soeuer we make spoꝛt, either the delite is vttered by cou̅=
tenaunce, oꝛ by poyntyng to some thyng, oꝛ els shewed at
large by some tale, oꝛ els occasio̅ taken by some woꝛd spoken

Mirthe howe many waies it is moued.

The .iij. question is, whether it standeth with an Oꝛatoꝛs
pꝛofessio̅, to delite the hearers with pleasaunt repoꝛtes, and
wittie saipnges, oꝛ no. Assuredly it behoueth a ma̅, that must
talke muche, euermoꝛe to haue regard to his audience, & not
onely to speake so muche as is nedefull, but also to speake no
longer then thei be willyng to heare. Euen in this our tyme,
some offende muche in tedyousnesse, whose parte it were to
co̅foꝛt all men with cherefulnes. Yea, the pꝛeachers of God,

Pꝛeachers.

mynd so muche edefiyng of soules, that thei often toꝛget, we
haue any bodies. And therefoꝛe, some doo not so muche good
with tellyng the truthe, as thei doe harme with dullyng the
hearers, beyng so farre gone in their matters, that oftenty=
mes thei cannot tell when to make an ende. Plato therefoꝛe,

Platoes sai= yng to Anti= sthenes.

the father of learnyng, and the well of all wisedome, when
he hard Antisthenes make suche a long oꝛacio̅, that he starke
weried all his hearers, phy foꝛ shame man (ꝙ he) doest thou
not knowe, that the measuryng of an oꝛacion, standeth not in
the speaker, but in the hearers. But some perhapps wil saie
vnto me pascite quantum in uobis est, to whom J answere,

i. Peter. v.

estote prudentes. And now bicause our senses be suche, that

Math.x.

in hearyng a right wholsome matter, wee either fall a slepe,
whe̅ we should moste harken, oꝛ els are weried with stil hea=
ryng one thyng, without any change, and thinke that the best
part of his tale, resteth in makyng an ende: the wittie & lear=
ned haue vsed delitefull saipnges, and quicke sentences euer
emong their weightie causes, co̅sideryng that not onely good
wil is got therby (foꝛ what is he that loueth not mirth?) but
also men woounder at suche a head, as hath mennes hartes at
his commaundement, beyng able to make theim merie when

t.iij. he

he liſt, and that by one woꝛde ſpeakyng, either in aunſweryng ſome thyng ſpoken befoꝛe, oꝛ els oftentymes, in geuyng the onſet, beyng not pꝛouoꝛed thereunto. Again, we ſe that men are full oft abaſhed, and putte out of countenaunce, by ſuche tauntyng meanes, and thoſe that haue ſo dooen, are compted to be fine men, and pleaſaunt felowes, ſuche, as fewe dare ſet foote with them.

Thus knowyng, that to moue ſpoꝛte, is lawfull foꝛ an oꝛato:, oꝛ any one that ſhall talke, in any open aſſembly: good it were to knowe, what compaſſe he ſhould kepe, that ſhould thus be merie. Foꝛ feare he take to muche ground, and go be-

Jeſtyng when it ſhould bee ſpared. yonde his boundes. Therfoꝛe, no ſuche ſhould be taunted, oꝛ ieſted with all, that either are notable euill liuers, and heynous offendours: oꝛ els are pitifull caitifes, & wꝛetched beggers. Foꝛ euery one thinketh it a better and a meter deede, to puniſhe naughtie packes, then to ſkoffe at their euill demeanoure: and as foꝛ wꝛetched ſoules, oꝛ pooꝛe bodies, none can beare to haue thē mocked, but thinke rather, that thei ſhould be pitied, except thei fooliſhely vaunt thēſelfes. Again, none ſuche ſhould be made any laughyng ſtockes, ẏ either are honeſt of behauiour, oꝛ els are generally welbeloued. As foꝛ oꝛ-ther, we maie be bold to talke with them, & make ſuche game and paſtime, as their good wittes ſhal geue good cauſe. But yet this one thyng, we had nede euer to take with vs, that in all our ieſtyng we kepe ameane, wherin not onely it is mete to auoyde al groſſe bourdyng, and alehouſe ieſtyng, but alſo to eſchue al foliſhe talke, & ruffin maners, ſuch as no honeſt eares can ones abide, noꝛ yet any wittie man can like well, oꝛ allowe.   ¶ The diuiſion of pleaſaunt beꜣauiour.

Mirthe ma-kyng, twoo waies vſed. Pleaſauntneſſe, either appereth in tellyng a rounde tale, oꝛ els in takyng occaſiō of ſome one woꝛde. The matter is told pleaſauntly, when ſome mannes nature (whereof the tale is tolde,) is ſo ſet furthe, his countenaunce ſo counterfeited, and all his ieſture ſo reſembled, that the hearers might iudge the thing, to be then liuelly dooen, euen as though he were there, whereof the tale was told. Some can ſo liuely ſet furthe another mannes nature, and with ſuche grace repoꝛte a tale; that fewe ſhalbe able to

foꝛbeare

forbeare laughter,whiche knowe bothe parties, though thei
would the cōtrarp neuer fo fain, Row in counterfeitpng af:
ter this fort,if fuche moderacion be not vfed,that the hearer
maie iudge moze by hymſelf,then the pleaſant diſpoſed man
is willpng fully to fet furth:it will not be well liked,for he
that exceveth and telleth all:pea,moze then is nevefull,with:
out al repect,oz conſiveracion had:theſame ſhalbe taken for a
common ieſture, ſuche as knowe not howe to make an ende,
when thei once biginne, bepng better acquaiuted with bible
bable,then knowpng the frute of wiſedomes loze,

Pleaſantneſſe in a faipng,is ſtirred by the quicke alterpng　**Pleaſauntnes**
of ſome one woze,oz of ſome one ſentēce,But euen as in re:　**in a faipng.**
poztpng a tale,oz counterfeitpng a manne, to muche is euer
naught:ſo ſcurrilitie oz(to ſpeake in old plain engliſh)kna:
uerp in ieſtpng would not be vſed,where honeſtie is eſtemed
Therfoze though there be ſome wit, in a pzetie deuiſed ieſte:
pet we ought to take hede,that we touche not thoſe,whō we
would be moſte loth to offend,And pet ſome had as Leue loſe
their life,as not beſtowe their conceiued ieſt,and oftentimes
thei haue,as thei deſire,But ſhall J ſap of ſuche wilful men,
as a Spaniard ſpake of an earneſt Goſpeller, that foz woozde
des ſpoken againſt an Eccleſiaſticall lawe,ſuffered death in
Smithe fielde? Ah miſer,non potuit tacere & uiuere.? Ah
wzetche that he was,could he not liue,and hold his peace?

Again,to ieſt when occaſiō is geuen,oz when the ieſt maie
touch al mē:it is thought to be againſt al good maner,Ther　**Difference be.**
foze the conſideracion of time,& moderacion of paſtpme,& ſel:　**twirte a com-**
dome vſpng of drie mockes,euen when nede moſte requireth,　**mon ieſter and**
make a difference,and ſhewe a ſeuerall vnderſtandpng , be:　**a pleaſaunt**
twirte a common ieſter,and a pleaſaunt wiſe man,　**wiſe manne.**

Now the time requireth,to ſhew what kindes there are of
moupng laughter,& makpng the hearer to be merp:notwith:
ſtāding this would firſt be learned,that out of diuerſe plea:
ſant ſpeches,aūcient ſaipnges alſo maie be gathzed,As foz e:
rāple we maie by one woze,bothe pzaiſe a faithfull ſeruaūt
and if he be naught,we maie alſo ieſt of him,& diſpzaiſe him,
Accozding to that merp faipng of Nero,vpō his man $ was
light fingered, J haue one at home ($ he)emōg all other,to
　　　　　　　　　　　　　　　　　　　　whom

whom there is no cofer lockt, no? do?e fhut in all mp houfe,
meanyng that he was a picklocke, and a falfe verl:t, and pet
thefe wo?des might haue been fpoken of a faithfull feruaunt.

Pleafaunt an-
fweres made,
cotrary to our
lokyng, delite
vs muche.

We fhall delite the hearers, when thei looke fo? one anfwere, and we make theim a cleane contrarp, as though wee
would not feme to vnderftande, what thei would haue. As
when one commyng fro a faire, and beyng afked in good fad-
neffe of another, howe ho?fes went there. Marie q̃ he, fome
trotte, and fome amble. And thus beyng deceiued of our lookyng (fo? who would haue lookte fo? fuche an anfwere?) we
are oft delited with our awne errour. Again, one Pontidius
beyng fo?e greued, that another ma had comitted aduoutrie
came to a frend of his, and faied fadlp: Ah lo?de, what thinke
pou fir of hym, that was taken in bedde of late. with another
mannes wife? Marie q̃ the other, J thynke him to be a verp
fluggard. Pontidius hearyng him faie fo, was abafhed at the
ftraungeneffe of his anfwere, and lokyng fo? no fuche thyng
was d?iuen to laugh at his awne errour, although befo?e, he
was muche greued with thaduouterers mofte wicked deede.

One beyng fo?e greued with the euill behauiour of a certain ientlema, fpake his pleafure largelp againft hym, wher-
vpon another merie man, diffeblyng to take his part, faid he
was an honefter ma then fo. Pea (q̃ thother) what one thing
hath he, wherbp to p?oue himfelf honeft at al? Marie (q̃ the
man) he hath the kynges pardon, q̃ what faie pou to that?

Diogenes.

Whe is it beft to dine (q̃ one) to Diogenes? Marp (q̃ he)
fo? a riche man, when he lift: fo? a poo?e man when he canne.

A noble man that whilome kept a chapell, beyng difpofed
to ferue God, went to his clofette deuoutelp, and made hym
felf redp to p?aie, wherupon one came doune in haft, and faid
to the Chaunter, pou mufte begin fir. The Chaunter beyng
a merie man, anfwered thus, as though he were angrp. Begin q̃ he? J will begin with none, except thei begin with me
And fo made the whole Quier, that then was redp fo? fpn-
gyng, to fall ftreight a laughyng. The whiche is all one, fo?,
fyng we, o? laugh we, what maketh matter, fo we be merie?

wo?des doubt
fully fpoken.

Wo?des doubtfullp fpoke, geue ofte iuft occafio of muche
laughter. Ah (q̃ a certain man) do pou fe ponder felowe, q̃ do

pou

The arte of Rhetorique. Fol.77.

you knowe him? Yea,(quod the other)I knowe him verye
well. I shall tell you sir (saide the gentilman)there is not
a manne of greater vnderstandinge within this Citye then
he is. Tushe it is not so (quod he.) No, (saide the other)
marcke well the bought of his legge, and you shall see hys
vnderstandinge worthye to be compared with the beste, and
greatest of them all.

Sometimes it is well liked, whan by the chaungynge or
a letter,or taking: awaye some parte of a worde,or addinge
sometimes a sillable, we make an other meaninge. As one
saide that meante full vnhappelye, enueighynge againste
those that helde of Christes spirituall beynge in the Sa=
crameñt:some(quod he)wil haue a Trop: to be in these wor=
des: This is my bodye: But surely I would wishe the T,
were taken awaye, and they had that for their labour, whi=
che is lefte behinde.

Chaungyng
of a letter, or
altering parte
of a word, or
adding a silla=
ble.

What carpe you master Person (quod a gentilman)to a
Prieste that hadde his woman on horsebacke behynde him,
haue you gotte your male behinde you ? No syr (quod the
Prieste)it is my female.

The interpretation of a worde doth oft declare a witte.
As when one hath done a robbery,some wil saye,it is pitie,
he was a handsome man,to ŷ which another made answere
you saye truthe syr, for he hathe made these shyftes by hys
handes,and gotte his liuyng wyth lyght fingeringe,& ther=
fore beinge handsome as you saye he is, I woulde God he
were handsomelye hanged.

Interpretati=
on of a word.

Sometimes it is delightfull when a mannes word is ta=
ken,and not his meaninge. As when one hadde sayde to an
other(whose helpe he must nedes haue) I am sory sir to put
you to paynes: The other aunswered,I will ease you syr of
that sorowe,for I will take no paynes for you at all.

Wordes takẽ
and not the
meanyng.

The turning of a word,& denyinge that wherwith we are
charged,& aunswering a much worsse, doth often moue the
hearer.There was one Ballus (as Quintiliin dothe tell)
whiche seinge a Ladye called Domitia to be very nighe her
selfe,spake his pleasure of her. Wherupon she being greued
charged hym wyth these woordes, that he shoulde saye she

An aunswere
from euyll to
worsse.

v.l.   was

The arte of Rhetorique.

Snudgynge wittely rebuked.

wis suche a pynche penye, as woulde sell her olde shone for money, whereupon he aunswered, No forsothe mad ame(quod he)I saide not so, but these were my wordes, I saide you bought olde shone, suche as you coulde get best cheape for money.

The Hollanders woordes ars worthye rehearsall, who beynge a pore man(as Erasmus telleth the tale)had a cow or two goyng in the communes, wherupon it happened that an Oxe of a riche mans, who then was Maior of the towne hadde gored the pore mannes cowe, and almoste kylled her.

A wittie deuised tale to get right iudgmẽt

The pore man beingin this case halfe vndone, thought notwithstanding by a wittye deuise to get right iudgement of maister Maior for the losse of his cowe, if he gotte nothynge elles, and therfore thus he framed his tale. Sir so it is that my cowe hath gored and almoste kylled your Oxe. what hath she(quod he)by sainte Marye thou shalte pay for him then. Naye (quod the poore man) I crye you mercye, youre Oxe hathe gored my cowe. Ah(quod the Maior)that is an other matter, we wyl talke of that hereafter at more leasure

These wordes were spoken of purpose, but now you shal heare what an olde woman spake of simplicitie. In the dotynge worlde, when stockes were saintes, and dumme walkes spake, this olde grandamme was deuoutelye kneling vpon her knees before the ymage of our Ladye. Wherupon a merye felowe asked her what she meante to crouche & knele there. Marie (quod the olde mother) I praye to our Ladye, that she maye praye to her Sonne for me: with that he

A beldames blynd answere

laughed at her ignoraunce. Wherupon she thinkinge that her wordes were spoken amisse, corrected her owne sayinge in this wise. Naye(quod she)I praye to Christe in heauen, that he will praye for me to this good Ladye here.

Wordes ouerthwartly aunswered.

Wordes rehearsed contrarie to that which was spoken, & (as a man would say)ouerthwartly answered, do much abash the opponent,& delite the hearers. As when Sergius Galba being sicke,& therfore keping his house, had appointed certaine of his fredes to hear a matter of one Libo Scri bonius, Tribune of the people, a man muche noted for hys noughtye and vncleane life: this Libo saide to him in this wise.

167

The arte of Rhetorique. Fol.78.

wiſe. Good Loꝛde, whẽ ſhall wee ſee you Sir abꝛoade,
out of youre Parloure. Marye (quod he) when thou ke=
peſte thy ſelfe oute of an other mannes chambꝛe, meanynge
that he was ouer familiar with an other mans wife. Thus
we ſe howe and in what maner pleaſaunt ſawes are gathe=
red and vſed, vpon the occaſion of diuers woꝛdes ſpoken.

⸿ Pleaſaunte ſpoꝛte made by rehearſynge of a whole matter

The nature & whole courſe of a matter being large=
lye ſet oute with a comelye behauoure doth much
delite the hearers, and geu:th good cauſe of greate
paſtime. And this difference is betwene a ieſte in a
woꝛd, and a ieſt vtterde in a longe tale. That whiche is ſtill
deliteful, with what woꝛdes ſoeuer you tell it, is conteined
in the ſubſtaunce oꝛ nature of a lõge tale: that which loſeth
his grace by alteration of a woꝛde, is conteyned in the na=
ture of a wooꝛde. They that can liuely tell pleaſaunt tales
and merye dedes done, and ſet theim oute as well with ge=
ſture as with voyce, leauynge nothynge behynde, that maye
ſerue foꝛ beautifiynge of their matter: are mooſte mete foꝛ
thys purpoſe, wherof aſſuredlye there are but fewe. And
whatſoeuer he is that canne aptelye tell his tale, and wyth
countenaunce, voyce, and geſture, ſo temper his repoꝛte,
that the hearers maye ſtyll take delyte: him counte I a man
woꝛthye to be hyghlye eſtemed. Foꝛ vndoubtedlye no man
can dooe anye ſuche thinge, excepte they haue a greate mo=
ther wytte, and by experience confirmed ſuche their comeli=
nes, wherunto by nature they were moſt apte. Many a mã
readeth hiſtoꝛies, heareth fables, ſeeth woꝛthye actes done
euen in this our age, but few can ſet them out accoꝛdingly,
and tel them liuely, as the matter ſelfe requireth to be told
The kindes of delitinge in this ſoꝛte are diuers: wherof I
will ſet foꝛth many, as hereafter they ſhall folowe.

Difference be-
twixt a ieſt in
a woꝛd, and a
ieſt in a longe
tale.

Spoꝛte moued by tellinge olde tales.

If there be any olde tale oꝛ ſtraunge hiſtoꝛy wel & wit=
tely applied to ſome mã liuing, al mẽ loue to hear it of
life. As if one wer called Arthur, ſome good felow that

The arte of Rhetorique.

were well acquainted wyth kynge Arthures boke, and the knightes of his rounde table, woulde waunte no matter to make good fporte, and for a nede woulde dubbe him knyght of the rounde table, or els proue him to be one of his kynne, or els (whiche were muche) proue him to be Arthure hym felfe. And fo likewife of other names, mery panions woulo make madde pattime.

Deformitie of bodye moueth myrthe. Oftentimes the deformitie of a mans bodye geueth mat= ter enoughe to be ryght merye, or els a picture in fhape lyke an other man, will make fome to laughe right hartely. One being greued with an other man, faide in his anger, I will fet the oute in thy coloures, I will fhewe what thou arte. The other beinge therwith muche chafed, fhewe (quod he) what thou canfte: with that he fhewed him, (pointinge with his finger) a man with a bottell nofe, blobbe cheaked, and as redde as a Bouchers bowle, euen as like the other manne, as anie one in all the worlde coulde be. I neede not to fape that he was angrye. An other good felowe beinge merelye difpofed, called his acquaintaunce vnto him & faid: Come hither I faie, and I wil fhewe thee as verye a lowte as euer thou faweft in all thy lyfe before, with that he offe= red him at his commynge a ftele glaffe to loke in. But fure= lye I thynke he loked awrye, for if I hadde bene in hys cafe, I woulde haue tolde him that I efpied a muche greater lo= wte, before I fawe the glaffe.

Augmentyng or diminif= hynge In augmentynge or diminifhinge without all reafon, we geue good caufe of muche paftyme. As Diogenes feynge a pirtye towne, hauinge a greate payre of Gates at the com= minge in: Take hede quod he, you menne of this towne, left pour towne runne out of pour gates. That was a maruey= lous bygge Gate I trow, or els a wonderfull little towne, where fuche paffage fhoulde be made.

A Frier difpofed to tell mifteries, opened to the People that the foule of man was fo little, that a leuen thoufande might daunce vpon the naple of his thumbe. One maruey= linge much at that, I prape you mafter Frier quod he, wher fhall the piper ftande then, when fuche a number fhall kepe fo fmall a roume.

Mirth

Mirthe is moued when vpon a trifle or a worde spoken, an vnknowen matter and weightye affayre is opened. As if one shoulde finde fault with some mannes sumptuous buildinge, or other suche thinge: whiche hadde founde muche fauoure at the same mans hande: an other myght saye, well sir, he that builded this house, saued your worship from hanginge when the time was. A nececessarie note for him thankefullye to remembre the builder of that house, & not slaunderouslye to speake euil of him.

It is a pleasaunt dissembling, when we speake one thing merelye, and thyncke an other earnestlye, or elles when we prayse that which otherwise deserueth disprayse, to the shaming of those that are taken not to be most honest.

As in speakinge of one that is well knowen to be nought, to saye emong all men that are sene to, there is one that lacketh his rewarde. He is the diligentiest felowe in hys callinge of all other, he hath trauepled in behalfe of his countrey, he hath watched daye and night to further his comune weale, and to aduaunce the dignitye therof, and shall he go emptye home? Who stode by it at suche a felde, who played the man and cryed, stoppe the thiefe, when suche a man was robbed? Who seeth good rule kept in suche a place? can as nye here charge him with bawdrye? Whiche of you all dare saye or can say that euer you sawe him dronke, if then these be true, ought not suche to be sene to: and rewarded accordingelye? For praysinge the vnworthye, I remember once that our worthy Latimer did set out the deuyll for his diligence wonderfullie, and preferred him for that purpose before all the Bishoppes in England. And no doubte, the wicked be more busye and stirryinge, then the children of light be in their generation.

What talke you of suche a man (saythe an other) there is an honest man ye maye be assured. For if a man had neade of one, he is ready at a pynche, his body sweates for honestye, if you come to him in a hotte sommers day, you shal se his honestye in such sort to reeke, that it woulde pitye any christian soule liuinge. He hath more honestye with him then he neades, and therfore bothe is able and will lende, where it

v.iij.   pleaseth

Openynge a weyghtye or vnknowen thynge

Dissemblynge

170

The arte of Rhetorique.

pleaseth him best. Beware of him aboue all menne that e
uer you knewe. He hathe no felowe, there is none suche, I
thinke he wil not liue longe, he is so honest a man, the more
pitye that suche good felowes shoulde knowe what deathe
meaneth. But it maketh no matter, when he is gone, all
the worlde will speake of him, hys name shall neuer dye, he
is so well knowen vniuersallye.

Thus we maye mockingelye speake well of him, when
there is not a noughtyer felowe wythin all Englande a;
gayne, and euen as well sette out his noughtines this way,
as thoughe we hadde in verye dede vttered all his noughty
conditions plainelye, and without iestinge. Amonge al that
euer were pleasaunte in this kinde of delite, Socrates bea;
reth the name, and maye worthelye chalenge prayse. Sir
Thomas More with vs here in England, had an excellent
gifte not onely in this kinde, but also in all other pleasaunt
delites, whose witte euē at this houre is a wonder to al the
worlde, & shalbe vndoubtedly, euen vnto the worldes ende.
Unto this kinde of dissembling, is nexte adioyninge a ma;
ner of speache, when wee geue an honeste name to an euyll
dede. As when I woulde call one accordingly that is of a
noughtye behauoure, to saye: Ah sirrha, you are a marchant
in dede: wher as I thinke a marchauntes name is honest.
Some olde felowes whē they thinke one to be an herittique
they will saye, he is a gospeller. Some newe felowes when
they thinke one a Papist, they wil call him straight a catho;
lique, & be euen with him at the landes ende. Contrariwise
some will geue an euil name to a good thinge: As a father
louynge his Sonne tenderlye, and hauynge no cause to be
greued with him, will sometimes saye to him: Come hither
sir knaue, and the mother merelye beynge disposed, wyll
saye to her swete Sonne: Ah you little horeson, wyll you
serue me so. where as I thyncke some womenne that ofte
so saye, wil sweare vpon a booke they are none suche, and
almoste I hadde sayde, I dare sweare for some of theim
my selfe, if God hadde not forbidden me to sweare at all.

This Kynde also is prettye. when we gather an other
                                                        thinge

thinge by a mannes tale, then he woulde gladly we (houlde
gather. When Liuius Salinato2 a Romayne capitaine
hadde kepte the Caſtell of Tarentum loſinge the towne to
Annibal his enemye, and that Maximus therupō had layed
ſiege to the ſame towne, and gotte it againe by the ſwerde:
then Salinato2 whyche thus kepte the Caſtell, deſiered
him to remember, that th2oughe his meanes he gotte the
towne, Why houlde I not (quod he) thyncke ſo? fo2 if you
had neuer loſt it, I had neuer gotte it.

Q. Fabius Maximus.

To diſſemble ſometymes as thoughe wee vnderſtode
not what one meant, declareth an apte witte, and much deliteth ſuch as heare it. Diogenes was aſked on a time what
wyne he loued beſte to d2incke. Marye (quod he) an other
mannes wyne, meanynge that he loued that d2yncke beſte,
that coſte him leaſte. The ſame Diogenes likewyſe was
aſked what one houlde geue hym to lette him haue a blowe
at his heade. Marye a Helmet quod he.

Diogenes.

One Octauius a Libian bo2ne (as witneſſeth Macro-
bius) ſayde vnto Tullie when he ſpake hys mynde vpon a
matter. Sir I heare you not, I p2aye you ſpeake lowder.
No (quod Tullie)? that is maruaile to me, fo2 as I do remember, you2 eares are well bo2ed tho2owe, meanynge that
he was nayled vpon a Pillarie, o2 elles hadde holes made
in his eares, whyche myght well ſerue (as Tullie teſted) to
receiue open ay2e.

Whē Mettellus toke muſter & required Ceſar to be there,
not abiding ÿ he ſhould be abſent, thoughe his eyes greued
him, and ſaid: What man do you ſe nothing at all? Yes marye quod Ceſar, as euil as I ſe, I can ſe a lo2dſhip of yours
the which was iiij. o2 v. miles from Rome) declaringe that
(his building was ouer ſumptuous, and ſo howge withall,
(muche aboue his degree) that a blind man myght almoſt ſe
it. Nowe in thoſe dayes ouercoſtlye building was generally hated, becauſe men ſought by ſuche meanes to get fame &
beare rule in the commune weale.

The like alſo is of one Naſica who when he came to the
Poet Ennius, and aſkinge at the gates if Ennius were at
home

home, the maide of the house, beinge so commaunded by her mister, made aunswere that he was not within. And when he perceyued that she so saide by her maisters commaunde= mente, he wente straight his waye, and saide no more.

Nowe shortelye after when Ennius came to Nasica and called for him at the dore, Nasica cried out alowde & sayde, *Ennius plea= saunt answer to Nasica* Sirha, I am not at home? what manne (quod Ennius) I heare the speake. Do not I knowe thy voyce? Then (quod Nasica) Ah shamelesse man that thou arte, when I sought thee at thy home, I did beleue thy maide when she said thou wast not at home, and wilte not thou beleue me when I tel thee myne owne selfe that I am not at home?

It is a pleasaunte hearynge, when one is mocked with *A man mocked with the same he bryngeth.* the same that he bryngeth. As when one .M. Opinius ha= uinge an euill name for hys light behauoure had saide to a pleasaunte man Egilius that semed to be wanton of liuing, and yet was not so: Ah my swete darling Egilia, when wilt thou come to my house swete wenche, with thy rocke & thy spindle? I dare not in good faith (quod he,) mi mother hath forbidde me to come to anye suspected house where euil rule is kepte.

Those iestes are bitter whiche haue a hid vnderstanding in them, wherof also a man maye gather muche more then is spoken. A homelye felowe made his woful lamentation to Diogenes in most pitiful sorte, because his wife had hanged her selfe vpon a figge tree, hopinge to finde some comforte *Diogenes bob gyth aunswer in despyte of women.* at his hande. But Diogenes hearinge this straunge deede, for the loue of God (quod he) geue me some slippes of that tree, that I might set them in some orcharde. The frute li= ked hun well, and belyke he thought that such slippes wou= lde haue bene as good to dispatche noughtye womenne, as lime twigges are thought mete to catch wild birdes withal.

An Archideacon, beyng nothinge so wise as he was wel= thy, nor yet so learned, as he was worshipfull, asked a yonge man once, whether he hadde a good witte, or no. Yes mary sir (quod he) your wytte is good inoughe if you kepe it still, and vse it not, for euerye thinge as you knowe is the worsse for the wearinge. Thou sayest euen truth (quod he) for that

is

is the matter that I neuer vsed preachyng, for it is nothyng
but a waistyng of witte, and a spendyng of wynde. And yet
if I woulde preache, I thynke I could do as wel as the best
of them. Yea sir (q̃ he) but yet I would ye should not proue
it for feare of straynyng your selfe to muche : why? Doest
thou feare that (q̃ he?) nay thou maist be assured, I wil ne=
uer preache so long as I lyue, God beeyng my good Lorde.
There are ouer many Heretiques, for good meanyng men
to speake any thyng now a daies. You saie euen truth (q̃ the
young man) and so went forthe, but to tel al, I had neede to
haue tyme of an other worlde, or at the left to haue breathe
of an other bodie.

An vnlearned Oratour made an Oratiõ on a tyme, thyn
kyng that he had with his wel doyng delited muche al men,
& moued them to mercie & pitie, & therfore sittyng doune, he
asked one Catulus if he had not moued the hearers to mer=
cie. Yes marie (q̃ he) & that to great mercie & pitie bothe, for
I thynk there is none here so hard harted, but thought your
oratiõ very miserable, & therfore nedeful to be greatly pitied.

Churlishe aunsweres, lyke the hearers some tymes ve=
ry wel. When the father was cast in iudgement, the sonne
seyng hym wepe : why wepe you father? (q̃ he) To whome
his father aunswered : what? Shall I syng I praie the,
seeyng by a lawe I am condempned to dye. Socrates ly=
kewyse beeyng moned of his wyfe because he shoulde dy= an
innocent and gilteleße in the lawe : why for shame woman
(q̃ he) wilt thou haue me to dye giltie & deseruyng. When
one had falne into a ditche, an other pitiyng his fall, asked
hym, and said : Alas how got you into that pit? why, Gods
mother (q̃ the other) doest thou aske me how I gotte in, nay
tel me rather in the mischief how I shal gette out .

There is an other contrarie vnto this kynd, when a man
suffereth wrong, & geueth no sharpe answere at al. As when
Cato was stroken of one that caried a chest (some saie a lõg
powle) when the other said, after he had hit hym : Take hede
sir I pray you : why (q̃ Cato) doest thou cary any thyng els.

Folie and lacke of naturall wit, or els wante of honestie
geue good matter of myrthe often tymes. When Scipio be=

yng Pretor had appoincted vnto a certaine Sicilian, one
to be his lawyer that was of a good house, and had an euill
witte, litle better than half a foole : I praie you(ꝗ the Si=
cilian to Scipio) appoint this lawier for myne aduersarie,
and let me haue none at al hardely.

Wishyng. In speakyng againſt an euill man, & wiſhyng ſomewhat
thereupon, a ieſt may ſeeme delitefull. When an euill man
had accuſed many perſons, and none toke any harme by hym
but rather were acquited from tyme to tyme, and taken the
ſooner for honeſt men: Now would to Chriſtes paſſion(ꝗ a
naughtie fellow)that he were myne accuſer, for then ſhould
I bee taken for an honeſt man alſo, through his accuſacion.
Demonides hauyng crooked feete, loſt on a tyme bothe his
ſhoone, wherupō he made his praier to God that his ſhoone
might ſerue his feete that had ſtolne them away. A ſhrewde
wiſhe for hym that had the ſhoone, and better neuer weare
ſhoone, than ſteale them ſo dearely.

Coniectures. Thynges gathered by côiecture to ſeeme otherwiſe than
they are, delite muche the eares being wel applied together.
One was charged for robbyng a Churche, and almoſt eui=
dently proued to be an offendour in that behaulfe. the ſaied
man to ſaue hymſelf harmeleſſe, reaſoned thus: Why(ꝗ he)
how ſhould this be, I neuer robbed houſe, nor yet was euer
faultie in any offence beſides, how then ſhoulde I preſume
to robbe a Churche? I haue loued the Churche more than
any other, & wil louers of the Churche robbe the Churche?
I haue geuen to the Churche, howe happeneth that I am
charged to take frō the Churche hauyng euer ſo good mind
to church dignitie? aſſure your ſelues thei paſſed litle of the
Churche, that would auenture to robbe the Churche. Thei
are no Churche men, they are maſterleſſe men, or rather S.
Niclas Clarkes, that lacke liuyng, and goyng in proceſſion
takes the Churche to be an Hoſpitall for waie fairers, or a
praie for poore and nedie beggers: but I am not ſuche man.

**Thynges
wantyng.** Thynges wantyng, make good paſtyme beyng aptely v=
ſed. Alacke, alacke, if ſuche a one had ſomewhat to take to, &
were not paſt grace: he would doe well enough without all
doubt. I warrant hym, he wantes nothyng ſaieth an other
of a

of a couetouſe man but one thyng,he hath neuer enough.

Suche a man hath no fault, but one,and if that were a=
mended,all were well : what is that ꝗ an other ? In good
(faith) he is nought.

To geue a familiar aduiſe in the waie of paſtyme, deli= *Familiare ad-*
teth muche the hearers. Whē an vnlerned lawyer had been *uiſe geuyng.*
hourele and almoſt loſt his voice with ouerlong ſpeakyng,
one Granius gaue him counſel to drynke ſweete wine could,
ſo ſone as he came home. Why(ꝗ he)I ſhall loſe my voice,
if I do ſo. Marie(ꝗ he)and better do ſo,then vndo thy cliēt
and loſe his matter altogether.

But emong all other kyndes of delite there is none that
ſo muche comforteth and gladdeth the hearer, as a thyng *Thynges ſpo-*
ſpoken contrarie to therpectation of other. Auguſtus Empe= *ken contrario*
rour of Rome ſeeyng a handſome poung man there, whiche *to expection.*
was muche like vnto hymſelfe in contenaunce, aſked hym if
euer his mother was in Rome , as thoughe he had been his
baſtard. No forſouth(ꝗ he)but my father hath been here ve=
ry ofte: with that themperour was abaſſhed,as though the
emperours own mother had been an euil womā of her body

When an vnlearned Phiſicion(as England lacketh none
ſuche) had come to Pauſanias a noble Ientleman, and aſ=
ked him if he were not troubled muche with ſicknes. No ſir
(ꝗ he) I am not troubled at al, I thancke God, becauſe I
vſe not thy counſaill. Why doe pe accuſe me (ꝗ the Philiſ=
cion) that neuer tryed me? Mary (ꝓ Pauſanias) if I had
ones tryed the , I ſhoulde neuer haue accuſed the. for then
I had been deade, and in my graue many daies agone.

An Engliſh Phiſiciō ridyng by the way, & ſeyng a great
cōpany of men gatherd together, ſent his mā to know what
the matter was, whereupō his man vnderſtandyng that one
there was appointed to ſuffer for killyng a mā: came ridyng
backe in al poſt haſte, and cried to his maſter, long before he
came at him: Get you hence ſir, get you here for Gods loue.
What meanes thou(ꝗ his maſter). Mary(ꝗ the ſeruaunt)
ponder man ſhal dye for killyng of one man, and you I dare
ſaye, haue kilde a hundreth menne in your daies: Gette you
hence thereore for Gods loue, if you loue your ſelfe.

The Arte of Rhetorique.

Examples bee innumerable that ſerue foz this purpoſe.

A man map bp hearpng a loude lpe, pzetelp mocke the lpe bp repoztpng a greater lpe. When one bepng of a lowe degre and his father of meane welthe, had vaunted muche of the good houſe that his father kepte, of two Beeſes ſpent we: kelie, and halfe a ſcoze Tunne of wpne dzonke in a peare, an other good fellowe hearpng hpm lpe ſo ſhamefullp: J deede (p he) Beeſe is ſo plētiful at mp maſter pour fathers houſe that an Oxe in one daie is nothpng, and as foz wpne, Beg: gers that come to the dooze are ſerued bp whole gallondes. And as J remēber pour father hath a ſpzpng of wpne in the middeſt of his Court, God continue his good houſe keppng.

Oftentpmes we map graunt to an other, the ſame that they wil not graunt to vs. When a baſe bozn felowe whoſe parentes were not honeſt, had charged Lelius that he did not liue accozdpng to his aunceſters: pea, but thou doeſt liue (p Lelius) accozdpng to thp elders.

One beepng a ientlemen in bpzthe, and an vnthziſte in condicions, called an other man in repzoche begger & ſlaue. Jn dede Sir (p the pooze man) pou are no begger bozne, but J feare me pe wil dpe one.

An other lpkewpſe called Diogenes varlet and caitif, to whome Diogenes aunſwered in this wpſe. Jn dede ſuche a one haue J been as thou now art, but ſuche a one as J now am, ſhalt thou neuer be.

Saluſt beepng a ientleman bozne, and a man of muche welth, and pet rather bp birthe, noble: than bp true dealpng honeſt: enuied muche the eſtimacion whiche Tullie had e: mong al men, and ſaid to hpm befoze his face: Thou art no ientleman bozne, and therefoze not meete to beare Office in this commune weale: Jn dede (p Tullie) mp nobilitie be: gpnnes in me, and thpne dothe ende in the. Meanpng there: bp that though Saluſt were bozne noble, pet he were lpke to dpe wzetched, whereas Tullie beepng bozne both pooze, and baſe, was lpke to dpe with honour, becauſe of his ver: tue, wherein cheeflp conſiſteth nobilitie.

There is a pleaſaunt kpnde of diſſemblpng when twoo meetes together, and the one cannot well abpde the other: and

and yet they both outwardely ſtriue to vſe pleaſaunt beha=
uiour, and to ſhow muche courteſie: yea to cõtende on both
partes, whiche ſhould paſſe other in vſyng of faire wordes,
and makyng liuely countenaunces: ſekyng by diſſemblyng,
the one to deceiue the other.

When we ſee a notable lye vtterde, we checke the offen=
dour openly with a pleaſaunt mocke. As when one Ulibius
Curius did ſpeake muche of his yeares and made hym ſelfe
to be much yonger then he was: (ꝙ Tullie) why than maſter
Ulibius as farre as I can gather by my reckenyng, when
you and I declaimed together laſt, you were not then borne
by al likelyhoode, if that be true whiche you ſaie.

When Fabia Dolobella ſaid to theſame Tullie that ſhe
was but thirtie yeres of age (as women by their good wil=
les would neuer be olde) I thynke ſo (ꝙ Tullie) for I haue
heard you ſaie no leſſe, xx.yeres ago.

A Souldiour that though his eſtimacion ſtoude moſte
in the vertue of his hande gunne, made a marueilouſe brag=
gue of it, and ſaid he was able to ſhowte leauel a great deale
farther than any one there would beleue hym to ſaye truth:
wherpõ he called for his man to beare witneſſe of the ſame,
and aſked hym whether it were ſo, or no. In deede (ꝙ his
man) you ſay truth, but then you muſte remember Sir, you
had the wynde with you when you ſhotte ſo farre. Welpke
he thought, there woulde neuer come ſuche a wynde again.

Checkyng a
lyar with an
open mocke.

Of diſpoſicion and apte orde ryng of thynges.

I Haue trauailed hetherto in teachyng the right way
to fynde meete matter for euery cauſe, vſyng ſuche
Arte as my ſlender witte coulde beſte yelde. And
now, nexte and immediatly after inuention, I thinke
meete to ſpeake of framyng and placyng an Oration in or=
der, that the matter beeyng aptely ſattelde, and couched to=
gether: might better pleaſe the hearers, and with more eaſe
be learned of all men. And the rather I am earneſt in this
behaulfe, becauſe I knowe that al thynges ſtande by order,

and

and without ozder nothyng can be. Foz by an ozder wee are
bozne, by an ozder wee lyue, and by an ozder wee make our
end. By an ozder one ruleth as head, and other obey as mē=
bers. By an ozder Realmes ſtande, and lawes take fozce,
yea by an ozder the whole wozke of nature and the perfite
ſtate of al the elementes haue their appointed courſe. By an
ozder we deuiſe, we learne, and frame our doopnges to good
purpoſe. By an ozder the Carpenter hath his Squyze, his
Rule, and hiſ Plummet. The Tailour his mette Parde, ⁊
his meaſure: The Maſon his Fozmer, and his Plaine, and
euerȳ one accozdyng to his callyng frameth thynges there=
after. Foz though matter be had, and that in greate plentie:
yet al is to no purpoſe, if an ozder be not vſed. As foz exam=
ple : what auaileth Stoone, if Maſons doe not wozke it?
what good dothe clothe, if Tailours take no meaſure, oz
do not cutte it out? Though Tymber be had foz makyng a
Shippe, and al other thynges neceſſarie, yet the ſhippe ſhal
neuer be perfite, till wozke men begynne to ſet to their han=
des, and ioyne it together. In what a comenly ozder hath
God made man, whoſe ſhape is not thought perfite, if any
parte be altered? yea al folke would take hym foz a monſter,
whoſe feete ſhould occupie the place of his handes. An armȳ
neuer getteth victozie, that is not in araie, and ſette in good
ozder of battail. So an Ozation hath litle fozce with it, and
dothe ſmally pzofite, whiche is vtterde without all ozder.
And needes muſt he wander, that knowes not howe to goe,
neither can he otherwyſe chouſe, but ſtumble: that groppng
in the darke, can not tel where he is: yea he muſt nedes both
leaue muche vnſpoken, repeate often, thynges ſpokē befoze,
not knowing what, noz wher to ſpeake beſt: that geues hȳ
ſelfe rather to take the chaunce of foztune, than to folowe
the right way of aduiſed counſell. what ſhoulde a man do
with a weapon that knoweth not howe to vſe it? what
though one haue mountaines of golde, what auaileth hym
to haue ſuche heapes, if he cannot tel how to beſtow them?
It is not enough to haue learnyng, but it is al to vſe lear=
nyng. Therefoze becauſe this parte of beſtowyng matter,
and placyng it in good ozder, is ſo neceſſarie ; I will ſhowe
what

The Arte of Rhetorique. *Fol.* 84.

what the learned haue saied in this behaulfe so muche as I shall thynke nedeful.

Disposicion what it is.

Isposicion (as Tullie doth define it) is a certaine bestowyng of thynges, and an apte declaryng, what is meete for euery parte, as tyme and place do beste require.

Diuidyng of Disposicion.

There are two kyndes of disposyng, and placyng of matter. The one is when we folowe the appointed rule of Rethorique, the whiche nature doth almost teache vs: The other is wholy faschioned by the discretion of hym that makes the Oration.

Rethorique doeth teache vs, and nature also leadeth vs thereunto, first to speake somwhat before we open our matter, after that to tell the cause of our entent, settyng forthe the matter plainly that al may vnderstand it, then to proue our owne cause by good reason, and to confute all suche thinges as are contrarie to our purpose: last of al to gather the whole in a somme, concludyng the matter briefely, and so to make an ende. Nowe to place those reasons, whiche shoulde both serue to confirme and to confute, and to tel in what parte of the Oration it were best to vse this reason, and that reason, that the rather wee might proue, teache, and perswade: a right wyse man had nede to take this matter in hande. For euen as the tyme, the place, the iudge, and the matter it selfe shal geue cause: so must a wyse body take his aduantage. Sometymes it shalbe expedient to vse no preface at al, or els when the matter is wel knowne, it will be good to leaue the matter vntolde, and streight to seeke the confirmacion, vsyng some stronge reason for the same purpose. Yea sometymes it may do good to neglecte the naturall order, and begynne firste to proue the cause, and afterwarde to tell it better, than it was tolde before.

If the iudge, or the hearers shalbe weried with other reportes before, it is beste to goe to the matter, and proue it out

(margin note:) Rhetorique what it teacheth, for oredryng of thynges.

it out of hande with as briefe reafons, and as ſtrong as can be gatherde poſſible . And in prouyng of our matters , we had nede euermoze rather to waie our reafons, than to nõ= ber them,and thynke not that then we ſhall doe beſte,when haue the moſt, but then looke to doe beſt, when we haue the ſtrongeſt.And firſt of al the ſtrongeſt ſhould be vſed,and the other placed in the middeſt of the Oration, the whiche bee= yng heaped together wil make a good muſtar. And yet this

alſo would be learned, whereas we vſed the beſt reaſons at the firſt,we ſhoulde alſo reſerue ſome that were lyke good, foz the later end:that the hearers might haue them freſhe in their remembraunce, when they ſhoulde geue iudgement. The ſlender reaſons that can do leſſe good, and yet not all, (foz ſome may better be omitted) woulde bee placed in the middeſt (as I ſaied) that bothe they might bee leſſe mar= ked, oz beeyng heaped there together, they might doe moze good, eſpecially when bothe weightie reaſons went befoze, and weightie reaſons alſo,folowed after. Now a wyſe man that hath good experience in theſe affaires , and is able to make hym ſelfe a Rhetozique foz euery matter,will not bee bounde to any preciſe rules, noz kepe any one ozder, but ſuche onely as by reaſon he ſhall thynke beſt to vſe, beeyng maiſter ouer Arte,rather then Arte ſhoulde be maiſter ouer hym,rather makyng Art by witte,than confoundyng witte by Arte.And vndoubtedly euen in ſo doyng,he ſhal do right wel,and contente the hearers accozdyngly . Foz what mat= tereth whether we folowe our Booke,oz no, if wee folowe witte, and appoint our ſelfe an ozder, ſuche as may declare the truthe moze plainely ? Yea ſome that be vnlearned and yet haue right good wittes : will deuiſe with theim ſelues without any Booke learnyng,what they wil ſaie,and how muche they wil ſay, appointyng their ozder, and partyng it into thze, oz foure partes, oz moze,if neede be,ſuche as they ſhal thynke eſpecial pointes,and moſt meete to bee touched. Whoſe doynges as I can wel like,& muche commende them foz theſame:ſo I would thynke them muche moze able to do muche better:if thei either by learning folowed a Paterne, oz els knewe the preceptes , whiche leade vs to right ozder.

Rules

Rules wer therfore geuen, and by muche obseruacion gathe: red together, that thofe whiche could not fee Arte hid in another mannes doynges, fhould yet fe the rules open, all in an order fet together: & therby iudge the rather of their do: **Thuſe of arte.** ynges, and by earneſt imitacion, feke to refemble fuche their inuencion. I cannot deny but that a right wife man vnlear: ned, fhall doo more good by his naturall witte, then twentie of thefe common wittes, that want nature to help arte. And I know that rules wer made firſt by wife men, and not wife men made by rules. For thefe preceptes ferue onely to helpe our nede, fuche as by nature haue not fuche plentifull giftes And as for other, vnto whom nature is more fauorable, thei are rather put the foner in remembraunce, that fuche leſſons are, then fo taught as though thei neuer knewe theim, or els neuer would vfe them. And therfore a certain learned man, & of muche excellencie, beeyng aſked what was fuche a figure, and fuche a trope in Rhetorique: I cannot tell (q he) but I am affured, if you loke in the boke of myne oracions, you fhall not faile but finde theim. So that though he knewe not the name of fuche and fuche figures, yet the nature of the was fo familiar to his knowlege, that he had thufe of them, when foeuer he had nede. Nowe though this man could well thus doo, beyng of fuche notable vnderſtandyng, yet it were foly that all fhould folowe his waie, whiche want fo good a wit. And I thinke euen he himfelf, fhould not haue loſt by it nei: ther, if he had feen that in a glaſſe, whiche he often vfed to do without knowlege. Man is forgetfull, and there is none fo wife, but counfaill maie dooe hym good. Yea, he fhall dooe muche better, that knoweth what arte other men haue vfed, what inuencion thei haue folowed, what order thei haue kept, and how thei haue beſt doen in euery part. If he like not theirs, he maie vfe his owne, and yet none dooeth fo euill (I thynke) but fome good maie be got by hym. The wife therfore wil not refufe to heare: and the ignoraunt for want, had nede to feke a will.

¶The ende of the .ii. boke.

p.i.   The

The arte of Rhetorique.
¶ The third boke.

¶ Of apte chusyng and framyng of wordes and
sentences together, called Elocucion.

AND now we are come to that parte of
Rhetorique, the whiche aboue al other is moste
beautifull, wherby not onely wordes are aptly
vsed, but also sentences are in right order fra=
med. For whereas Inuencion, helpeth to finde
matter, and Disposicion serueth to place argumentes: Elo=
cucion getteth wordes to set furthe inuencion, & with suche
beautie commendeth the matter, that reason semeth to bee
clad in purple, walkyng afore, bothe bare and naked. Ther=
fore Tullie saieth well, to finde out reason,& aptly to frame
it, is the part of a wise man, but to commende it by wordes,
and with gorgious talke to tell our conceipte, that is onely
propre to an Orator. Many are wise, but fewe haue the gift
to set furthe their wisedome. Many can tell their mynde in
Englishe, but fewe can vse mete termes, and apt order: suche
as all men should haue, and wise men will vse: suche as ne=
des must be had, when matters should be vttered. Now then
what is he, at whom all men wonder, and stande in a mase, at
the viewe of his wit? Whose doynges are best estemed? whō
do we moste reuerence, and compt halfe a God emong men?
Euen suche a one assuredly, that can plainly, distinctly, plē=
tifully, and aptly vtter bothe wordes and matter, and in his
talke can vse suche conposicion, that he maie appere to kepe
an vniformitiee, and (as I might saie) a nomber in the vtte=
ring of his sentēce. Now an eloquēt man beyng smally lear=
ned, can do muche more good in perswadyng, by shift of wor=
des, and mete placyng of matter: then a greate learned clerke
shalbe able with great store of learnyng, wantyng wordes to
set furth his meanyng. Wherfore I muche maruaile that so
many seke the only knowlege of thynges, without any mynd
to commende or set furthe their entendement: seyng none cā
knowe either what thei are, or what thei haue, without the
gift of vtterance. Yea, bryng thē to speake their mynde, and
enter in talke with suche as are said to be learned, & you shal
finde in thē suche lacke of vtterance, that if you iudge theim

by

by their tongue,and expreſſyng of their mynde:you muſt neꝫ
des ſaie thei haue no learnyng. Wherin me thinkes thei do,
like ſome riche ſnudges, that hauyng great wealth,go with
their hoſe out at heeles,their ſhoes out at toes,and their coꝫ
tes out at bothe elbowes.ffoꝛ who çan tell, if ſuche men are
woꝛth a grote,when their apparel is ſo homely,and al their
behauioꝛ ſo baſe? I can call thẽ by none other name,but ſloꝫ **Barbarous**
uens,that maie haue good geare,and nether cã, noꝛ yet will **clerkes,no bet**
ones weare it clenly. What is a good thyng to a mainne,if he **ter then ſloues**
neither knowe thuſe of it,noꝛ yet (though he knowe it)is aꝫ
ble at all to vſe it? If we thinke it comelineſſe,and honeſtie
to ſet furthe the body with handſome apparell , and thynke
theim woꝛthie to haue money, that bothe can and will vſe it
accoꝛdyngly: I cannot otherwiſe ſe, but that this part deſerꝫ
ueth pꝛaiſe,whiche ſtandeth wholy in ſettyng furthe matter
by apte woꝛdes and ſentences together,& beautifieth the tonꝫ
gue with greate chaunge of colours,and varietie of figures.

C Foure partes belongyng to Elocucion.

     i.   Plainneſſe.
     ij.   Apteneſſe.
     iij.   Compoſicion.
     iiij.Exoꝛnacion.

Mong al other leſſons, this ſhould firſt be learned,ỹ **Plaines what**
E we neuer affect any ſtrãge ynkehoꝛne termes,but ſo **it is.**
ſpeake as is commonly recciued:neither ſekyng to be
ouer fine,noꝛ yet liuyng ouer careleſſe,vſyng our ſpeache as
moſt men do,& oꝛdꝛyng our wittes,as the feweſt haue doen.
Some ſeke ſo farre foꝛ outlãdiſhe Engliſhe,that thei foꝛget
altogether their mothers lãguage.And I dare ſwere this,if
ſome of their mothers were aliue,thei were not able to tell,
what thei ſay,& yet theſe fine Engliſhe clerkes,wil ſaie thei
ſpeake in their mother tongue,if a mã ſhould charge thẽ foꝛ
coũterfeityng the kynges Engliſh.Some farre ioꝛneid ien-
tlemẽ at their returne home,like as thei loue to go in foꝛrein
apparell, ſo thei wil pouder their talke wt ouerſea lãguage.
He that cometh lately out of ffrance,wil talke ffreche Engliſh,& neuer bluſhe at the matter.Another choppes in with
Angleſo Italiano:the lawyer wil ſtoꝛe his ſtomack with the

praiyng of Pedlers. The Auditour in makyng his accompt and rekenyng, cometh in with sise soulo, and cater denere, for vi.s iiij.d. The fine Courtier wil talke nothyng but Chauncer. The misticall wise menne, and Poeticall Clerkes, will speake nothyng but quaint prouerbes, and blynd allegories, delityng muche in their awne darkenesse, especiallp, when none can tell what thei dooe saie. The vnlearned or foolishe phantasticall, that smelles but of learnyng (suche felowes as haue seen learned men in their daies) will so Latine their tongues, that the simple cannot but wonder at their talke, and thynke surely thei speake by some Reuelacion. I knowe them that thynke Rhetorique, to stande wholy vpon darke woordes, and he that can catche an ynke horne terme by the taile, hym thei compt to bee a fine Englishe man, and a good Rhetotician And the rather to set out this folie, I will adde here suche a letter, as Willyam Sommer himself, could not make a better for that purpose. Some will thinke & swere it to, that there was neuer any suche thyng writté, well I wil not force any man to beleue it, but I will saie thus muche, and abide by it to, the like haue been made heretofore, and praised aboue the Moone.

An ynkehorne letter. Wonderyng, expedyng, and reuolutyng with my self your ingent affabilitee, and ingenious capacitee, for mundane affaires : I cannot but celebrate and extolle your magnificall dexteritee, aboue all other. For how could you haue adepted suche illustrate prerogatiue, and dominicall superioritee, if the fecunditee of your ingenie had not been so fertile, & wonderfull pregnaunt. Now therfore beeyng accersited, to suche splendent renoume, & dignitee splendidious: I doubt not but you will adiuuate suche poore adnichilate orphanes, as whilome ware condisciples with you, and of antique familiaritie in Lincolne shire . Emong whom I beeyng a Scholasticall panion, obtestate your sublimitee to extoll myne infirmitee. There is a sacerdotall dignitee in my natiue countrey, contiguate to me, where I now contemplate: whiche your worshipfull benignitee, could sone impetrate for me, if it would like you to extend your scedules, and collaude me in them to the right honorable lorde Chauncellor, or rather Archigrã-matian

macian of Englande. You knowe my literature,you knowe
the pastozall pzomocion, J obtestate your clemencie,to inui=
gilate thus muche foz me,accozdyng to my confidence,and as
you know my condigne merites,foz suche a compendious li=
uyng. But now J relinquishe to fatigate your intelligence
with any moze friuolous verbositie,and therfoze ke that ru=
les the climates be euermoze pour beautreur,pour foztresse,
and pour bulwarke.Amen.

What wise man readyng this letter,will not take him foz
a very Caulse,that made it in good earnest,& thought by his
ynkepot termes,to get a good personage. Doeth wit reste in
straunge wozdes,oz els standeth it in wholsome matter, and
apt declaryng of a mannes mynd? Do we not speake,because
we would haue other to vnderstande vs,oz is not the tongue
geue foz this ende, that one might know what another mea=
neth? And what vnlearned man can tell, what half this let=
ter signifieth? Therfoze,either we must make a difference of
Englishe,and saie some is learned Englishe,and other some
is rude Englishe,oz the one is courte talke,the other is coū=
trey speache,oz els we must of necessitee banishe al suche af=
fected Rhetozique,and vse altogether one maner of lāguage.

When J was in Cambzige,and student in the kynges Col=
lege,there came a man out of the toune,with a pinte of wine
in a pottle pot,to welcome the pzouost of that house, that la=
tely came from the courte.And because he would bestow his
pzesent like a clerke,dwellyng emong the schoolers: he made
humbly his thze curtesies,and said in this maner.Cha good
euen my good lozde,and well might pour lozdship vare:Un=
derstandyng that pour lozdeship was come,& knowyng that
pou are a wozshipfull Pilate,and kepes a bominable house:
J thought it my duetie to come incantiuantee , & bzyng pou
a pottell a wine,the whiche J beseche pour lozdeship take in
good wozthe.Here the simple man beyng desirous to amende
his mothers tongue , shewed hymself not to bee the wisest
manne,that euer spake with tongue.

Another good felowe in the contrey,beyng an officer,and
Maiour of a toune,and desirous to speake like a fine learned
man,hauyng iust occasion to rebuke a runnegate felow, said
                                        p.iij,   after

after this wise in a greate heate. Thou pngram and vacacis
on knaue, if J take thee any more within the circumcision of
my dampnacion : J will so corrupte thee, that all vacacion
knaues shall take ilsample by ther.

Another standyng in muche nede of money, and desirous to
haue some helpe at a ientlemanns hand, made his complaint
in this wise. J praie you sir be so good vnto me, as forbeare
this halfe yeres rent. for so helpe me God and halidome, we
are so taken on with contrary Bisshoppes, with reuiues, and
with subsides to the kyng, that al our money is cleane gone.
These wordes he spake for contribucion, relief, and subsidie.
And thus we see that poore simple men are muche troubled,
and talke oftentymes, thei knowe not what, for lacke of wit
and want of Latine & frenche, wherof many of our strauge
woordes full often are deriued. Those therefore that will
eschue this foly, and acquaint themselfes with the best kynd
of speache, muste seke from tyme to tyme, suche wordes as are
commonly receiued, and suche as properly maie expresse in
plain maner, the whole conceipte of their mynde. And looke
what woordes wee best vnderstande, and knowe what thei
meane: thesame should sonest be spoken, and firste applied to
the vtteraunce of our purpose.

Now whereas woordes be receiued, aswell Greke as Latine, to set furthe our meanyng in thenglishe tongue, either
for lacke of store, or els because wee would enriche the language: it is well doen to vse them, and no man therin can be
charged for any affectacion, when all other are agreed to fol-
lowe thesame waie. There is no man agreued, when he heareth (letters patentes) & yet patentes is latine, and signifieth
open to all men. The Communion is a felowship, or a commyng together, rather Latine then Englishe : the Kynges
prerogatiue, declareth his power royall aboue all other, and
yet J knowe no man greued for these termes, beeyng vsed in
their place, nor yet any one suspected for affectacion, when
suche generall woordes are spoken. The folie is espied, when
either we will vse suche woordes, as fewe men doo vse, or vse
theim out of place, when another might serue muche better.
Therfore to auoyde suche folie, we maie learne of that most
excellent

The arte of Rhetorique.　　　　　　　　*Fol.88.*

excellent Oratoꝛ Tullie, who in his thirde booke, where he
speaketh of a perfect Oratoure, declareth vnder the name of
Craſſus, that foꝛ the choyſe of woꝛdes, foure thinges ſhould
chiefly be obſerued. Firſt, that ſuche woꝛdes as we vſe, ſhuld
bee pꝛoper vnto the tongue, wherein wee ſpeake, again, that
thei be plain foꝛ all men to perceiue: thirdly, that thei be apt
and mete, moſte pꝛoperly to ſette out the matter. Fourthly,
that woꝛdes tranſlated from one ſignificacion to another,
(called of the Grecians, Tropes) bee vſed to beautifie the
ſentence, as pꝛecious ſtones are ſet in a ryng, to comnmende
the golde.

*Foure thinges
obſerued, foꝛ
choyſe of woꝛ
des.*

❧ Aptenſſe what it is.

Uche are thought apt woꝛdes, that pꝛoperly agre vnto that thyng, whiche thei ſignifie, and plainly expꝛeſſe
the nature of theſame. Therfoꝛe thei that haue regard
of their eſtimacion, do warely ſpeake, and with choyſe, vtter
woꝛdes moſte apte foꝛ their purpoſe. In weightie cauſes,
graue woꝛdes are thought moſte nedefull, that the greatneſſe
of the matter, maie the rather appere in the vehemencie of
their talke. So likewiſe of other, like oꝛder muſte be taken.
Albeit ſome, not onely do not obſerue this kynde of aptnes,
but alſo thei fall into muche fondneſſe, by vſyng woꝛdes out
of place, and applyng them to diuerſe matters without all
diſcrecion. As thus. An ignoꝛant felowe comyng to a ſentle-
mannes place, & ſeyng a greate flocke of ſhepe in his paſtour
ſaied to the owner of theim, now by my truthe ſir, here is as
goodly an audiēce of ſhepe, as euer I ſaw in al my life. who
will not take this felowe meter to talke with ſhepe, then to
ſpeake emong mennes. Another likewiſe ſeeyng a houſe faire
buylded, ſaied to his felowe thus: good loꝛde, what a handſome
phꝛaſe of buildyng is this? Thus are good woꝛdes euil
vſed, when thei are not well applied, and ſpoke to good purpoſe. Therfoꝛe I wiſhe that ſuche vntoward ſpeakyng, maie
geue vs a good leſſon, to vſe our tongue warely, that our
woꝛdes and matter maie ſtill agree together.

Aptnes.

*Unapte vſyng
of apt woꝛdes*

❧ Of Compoſicion.

When we haue learned vſuall and accuſtomable woꝛdes
to ſet furthe our meanyng, we ought to ioyne them together
in

The arte of Rhetorique.

in apt ozder, that the eare maie delite, in hearpng the harmo=
monie. J knowe some Englisl) men, that in this popnct haue
suche a gift in the Englishe, as fewe in Latine haue the like
and therfoze, delite the wise and lerned so muche, with their
pleasaunt composicion : that many reiopce, when thei maie
heare suche, and thpuke muche learnpng is gotte, when thei
maie talke with suche. Composicion therefoze , is an apte
iopnpng together of woznes in suche ozder, that neither the
eare shal espie anp ierre, noz pet anp man shalbe dulled with
ouerlong dzawing out of a sentence, noz pet muche consoun=
ded with mpngelpng of clauses, suche as are nedelesse, bepng
heaped together without reason, and vsed without nomber.
Foz, bp suche meanes the hearers will be foiced, to foigette
full oft, what was saied first, befoze the sentence be halfe en=
ded: oz els bee blpnded with confoundpng of many thpnges
together. Some again will bee so shozte, and in suche wise
curtall their Sentences , that thei had nede to make a com=
mentarie immediatly of their meanpng, oz els the moste that
heare them, shalbe foiced to kepe counsaill.

&ome will speake ozacles, that a man cannot tell, whiche
waie to take theim, some wll be so fine, z so Poeticall with
all, that to their sempng , there shall not stande one heire a=
misse, z pet euery bodp els shall thinke the meter foz a ladies
chamber, then foz an earnest matter, in anp open assemblie.

&ome wil roue so muche, and bable so farre without oz=
der , that a manne would thpnke, thei had a greate loue, to
heare themselues speake.

&ome repeate one woozde so often, that if suche wooides
could be eaten, and chopte in so ofte, as thei are vttered out,
thei would choke the widest thzofe in all England. As thus.
Jf a man knewe, what a mans life wer, no man foz anp ma=
nes sake, would kill anp man, but one ma would rather help
another man, considzpng man is boine foz man, to help ma, z
no to hate man. what man would not be choked, if he chopt
al these men at ones into his mouth, z neuer dzonke after it?
&ome vse ouermuche repeticio of some one letter, as pitiful
pouertie pzaieth foz a penp, but puffed pzesupcio, passeth not
a popnct, paperpng his panche, w pestilet pleasure, pzocuring

his

his paſſe poꝛte to poſte it to Hell pytte,there to be puniſhed
with paines perpetuall. Some will ſo ſette their woꝛdes
that they muſte be fayne to gape after euerye woꝛde ſpokē,
endinge one woꝛde with a vowell,and beginninge the next
wyth an other, whyche vndoubtedlye maketh the talke to
ſeme mooſte vnpleaſaunte. As thus Æquitie aſſuredlye eꝫ
uerye iniurye auoydeth. Some will ſet the carte befoꝛe the
hoꝛſe,as thus.My mother and my father are both at home,
euen as thoughe the good man of the houſe ware no bꝛeaꝫ
ches,oꝛ that the graye Mare were the better Hoꝛſe. And
what thoughe it often ſo happeneth (God wotte the moꝛe
pitye)yet in ſpeakinge at the leaſte,let vs kepe a natural oꝛꝫ
der,and ſet the man befoꝛe the woman foꝛ maners ſake.

An other cominge home in haſte after a long iourney,
ſayeth to hys manne : Come hither ſir knaue,helpe me of
with my bootes and my ſpurres. I pꝛaye you ſir geue him
leaue firſte to plucke of youre ſpurres, ere he meddle wyth
your bootes, oꝛ els your man is like to haue a madde plucꝫ
kinge. Who is ſo folyſhe as to ſaye the counſayle and the
kynge,but rather the Kinge and his counſayle, the father
and the ſonne,and not contrary.And ſo likewiſe in al other
as they are in degree firſte,euermoꝛe to ſet them foꝛmoſt.

The wiſe therfoꝛe talkinge of diuers woꝛthye menne toꝫ
gether,will firſte name the woꝛthieſt,and kepe a decent oꝛꝫ
der in repoꝛtynge of their tale. Some ende their ſentences
all alike,makyng their talke rather to appeare rimed meter
then to ſeme playne ſpeache, the whiche as it muche deliꝫ
teth beynge meaſurablye vſed, ſo it muche offendeth when
no meane is regarded.I hearde a pꝛeacher delityng much in
thys kynd of compoſition,who vſed ſo ofte to ende his ſenꝫ
tence with woꝛdes like vnto that whiche wente befoꝛe,that
in my iudgemente, there was not a doſen ſentences in hys
whole ſermon,but they ended all in ryme foꝛ the moſt part.
Some not beſt diſpoſed, wiſhed the Pꝛeacher a Lute,that
with his rimed ſermon he myght vſe ſome pleaſaunt meloꝫ
dye, and ſo the people myghte take pleaſure diuers wayes,
and daunce if they liſte. Certes there is a meane,⁊ no reaꝫ
ſon to vſe any one thinge at all times, ſeynge nothinge deꝫ

z.i.   liketh

liteth(be it neuer so good)that is alwayes vsed.

Quintilian likeneth the coloures of Rhetorique to a mannes eye sighte. And nowe(quod he)J woulde not haue all the bodye to be full of eyes,or nothinge but eyes: for the the other partes shoulde wante their due place and propor= cion. Some ouerthwartelye sette their woordes, placynge some one a mple frome his felowes, not contented with a playne and easye composition,but seke to sette wordes they can not tell howe, and therfore one not likynge to be called and by printe published Doctoure of Phisike, woulde nea= des be named of Phisike Doctour,wherin appeared a won= derfull composition(as he thought)straunge vndoubtedlye, but whether wise or no,lette the learned sitte in iudgement vpon that matter.

An other. As J rose in the mornynge (quod one) J mette a carte full of stones emptye. Belike the manne was fastinge,when the carte was full,and yet we see that thro= ughe straunge composition this sentence appeareth darke.

Some will tell one thinge.xx.times,nowe in,nowe out, & when a man would thinke they had almost ended,they are ready to beginne againe as freshe as euer they were. Such vayne repetitions declare both wante of witte,and lacke of learninge. Some are so homely in all their doynges,and so grosse for their inuention, that they vse altogither one ma= ner of trade, and seke no varietie to eschewe tediousnes.

Some burden their talke with nedelesse coppe, and will seme plentifull,when they shoulde be shorte.An other is so curious and so fine of his tongue, that he can not tell in all the worlde what to speake. Euerie sentence semeth commune,and euerye worde generallye vsed,is thought to be folyshe,in his wise iudgemente. Some vse so manye in= terposicions bothe in their talke and in their writinge,that they make their sayinges as darke as hell.Thus wha faul= tes be knowen,they may be auoyded : and vertue the soner may take place,when vice is forsene,and eschewed as euill.

Of Eronation.

Hen wee haue learned apte woordes and vsuall Phrases to sette forthe oure meanynge, and can orderlye place them without offence to the eare, we

we maye boldelye commende and beautifie oure talke wyth
diuers goodlye coloures, and delitefull tranflations, that
oure fpeache maye feme as bzyghte and pzecious, as a rylche
ftone is fapze and ozient.

Ezornation is a gozgioufe beautifynge of the ton=
gue with bozowed wozdes, and chaung of fentence
oz fpeache, with muche varietie. Firfte therfoze (as
Tullie fapthe) an Ozation is made to feme ryghte
excellente by the kinde felfe, by the colour and iuice of fpea=
che. Ther are.iij.maner of ftyles oz endiiinges, the great oz
mighty kind, whē we vfe great wozdes, oz vehemēt figures:

The fmal kinde, when we moderate our heate by meaner
wozdes, and vfe not the moft ftirring fentences:

The lowe kinde, when we vfe no Metaphozes, noz tranf=
flated wozdes, noz yet vfe any amplificatiōs, but go plaine=
lye to wozke, and fpeake altogether in commune wozdes.
Nowe in all thefe thzee kindes, the Ozation is muche com=
mended, and appeareth notable, when wee kepe vs ftyll to
that ftyle, whiche wee firfte pzofeffed, and vfe fuche wozdes
as feme fo: that kinde of wzitinge moft conuenient.

Yea, if we minde to encreafe, oz dininifh: to be in a heate,
oz to vfe moderatiō: to fpeake pleafauntly, oz fpeake graue=
lye: to be fharpe, oz to be fofte: to talke lozdlye, oz to fpeake
finelie: to ware auncient, oz familiar (which al are compze=
hended vnder one of the other thzee:) we mufte euer make
oure wozdes apte and agreable to that kinde of ftile, whi=
ch: we firfte ganne to vfe. Foz as frenche hodes do not be=
come Lozdes: fo Parliament Robes are vnfitting foz La=
dies. Comelines therfoze muft euer be vfed, and all thinges
obferued that are moft mete foz euery caufe, if we loke by at
temptes to haue our defire.

There is another kind of Ezornaciō ŷ is not equally fpar=
pled thzoughout ŷ whole ozatiō, but is fo diffeuered & par=
ted, as ftarres ftand in the firmament, oz floures in a gardē,
oz pzety deuifed antiques in a clothe of Araife.

What a fygure is?

A Figure is a certaine kinde, either of fentence, ozation,
oz wozde, vfed after fome new oz ftraunge wife, muche
vnlike to that, which men communely vfe to fpeake.

ſ.iij.   The

(marginal notes:)
Ezornation.

Thie maner of ftiles oz en= ditinges.

Ezornation by coloures of Rhetoziqu̅e.

The arte of Rhetorique.

The diuision of Fygures.

Here are thre kindes of figures, the one is when the nature of wordes is chaunged from one significa= tion to an other called a Trope of the Grecians: The other serueth for woordes when they are not chaüged by nature, but only altered by speaking, called of ç Grecians a Scheme: The third is wheu by deuersity of in= uention, a sentence is manye wayes spoken, and also mat= ters are amplified by heappynge examples, by dilatynge ar= gumentes, by comparinge of thynges together, by similitu= des, by contraries, and by diuers other like, called by Tullie Exornacion of sentences, or coloures of Rhetorique.

By all whiche figures, euerye Oration maye be muche beautified, and without the same, not one can attaine to be counted an Oratoure, thoughe his learninge otherwise be neuer so greate.

Of the fyrste vse of Tropes.

Tropes how they wer fyrst founded.

When learned and wise menne gan firste to enlarge their tongue, and sought with greate vtteraunce of speache to commende causes: they founde full ofte muche wante of wordes to set out their meanynge. And therfore remembrynge thinges of like na= ture vnto those wherof they spake: they vsed suche wordes to expresse their minde, as were most like vnto other. As for example. If I shoulde speake against some notable Phari= see, I might vse translation of wordes in this wise: Ponder man is of a croked iudgment, his wyttes are clowdie, he li= ueth in deepe darkenes, dusked altogether wyth blynde ig= noraunce, and drowned in the raginge sea, of bottomeles su= perstition. Thus is the ignoraunte set out, by callinge hym croked, clowdye, darke, blinde, and drownde in superstition. All whiche wordes are not proper vnto ignoraunce, but bo= rowed of other thinges, that are of lyke nature vnto igno= raunce. For the vnskilfull man hath his wytte set oute of
order

o2der,as a mannes bodye is set out of io2nte,and therupon it maye be sayde to be croked. Likewyse he maye be called clowdye,fo2 as the clowdes kepe the Sunne shiuynge from vs,so dothe his Igno2aunce kepe him blindefolde from the true vnderstandinge of thinges. And as when the eyes are oute,no manne can see anye thinge: so when perfecte iudge= mente is wantinge,the truthe can not be knowen. And so likewise of all other. Thus as necesstye hath fo2ced vs to bo2owe wo2des translated : so hath time and p2actice made theim to seeme mooft pleasaunt,and therfo2e thei are mucht the rather vsed. Yea, when a thynge full ofte can not be exp2effe by an apte and mete woo2de, we do perceyue (when it is spoken by a woo2de translated) that the likenes of that thynge whiche appeareth in an other wo2de, muche lighte= neth that, which we woulde most gladly haue perceyued.

And not onely do menne vse translation of wo2des (cal= led Tropes)fo2 nede sake, when thei can not finde other: but also when they maye haue mooste apte wo2des at hande, yet wyll they of a purpose vse translated wo2des. And the rea= son is this. Menne counte it a poynte of witte to passe o= uer suche woo2des as are at hande , and to vse suche as are farre fetcht and translated : o2 elles it is,becaufe the hea= rer is led by cogitacion vpon rehearsall of a Metapho2e, & thinketh mo2e by rememb2aunce of a wo2d translated, then is there exp2effe spoken : o2 elles becaufe the whole matter semeth by a similitude to be opened:o2 last of al,bicaufe eue= ry translation is commenly, & fo2 the most part referred to the senses of the body,& especially to the sense of seing,which is the sharpest and quickest aboue all other.ffo2 whe I shal saye that an angrye manne fometh at the mouthe , I am b2ought in remembraunce by this translation to remember a bo2e,that in fightyng vseth muche foming,the whiche is a fowle and lothelye sighte. And I caufe other to thinke that he b2ake pacience wonderfully, when I set out his rage co= parable to a bo2es fominge.

An other beinge offended wyth checkes geuen,will saye, I maruaile sir what you meane to be euer snarringe at me, wherein is declared a b2uttishenes, consideringe he speaketh

z.iij. bitynge

The arte of Rhetorique.

biting wordes, as muche without reason ⸫ as vncomelye, as a dogge dothe, when he snarreth, the whiche wee see is nothing semely. There is nothing in all the worlde, but the same maye haue the name of some other worde, the whiche by some similitude is lyke vnto it. Notwithstandinge there ought muche warenesse to be vsed in chosyng of wordes tanslated, that the same be not vnlike that thing, wherunto it is applied, nor yet that the translation be vncomely or suche as may geue occasion of any vncleane meaning.

A Trope.

Trope what it is. A Trope is an alteration of a word or sentence from the proper significatiō to that whych is not proper,

The diuision of Tropes.

Deuision of Tropes. Tropes are either of a word, or or a longe continued speche or sentence.

Tropes of a worde are these.

{
A Metaphore or translation of wordes,
A worde makinge,
Intellection.
Abusion.
Transmutation of a word,
Transumption,
Chaunge of a name,
Circumlocution.
}

Tropes of a longe continued speache or sentence are these.

{
An Allegorie, or inuersion of wordes.
Mountinge,
Resemblinge of thinges,
Similitude,
Example.
}

what is a Metaphore,

Metaphora A Metaphore is an alteration of a woorde from the proper and naturall meanynge, to that whiche is not proper, and yet agreeth therunto, by some lykenes that appeareth to be in it.

An

An Oration is wonderfullye enriched, when apte Meta=
phores are gotte and applied to the matter. Neither can a=
nye one perſwade effectuouſlye, and winne men by wepghte
of his Oration, withoute the helpe of woordes altered and
tranſlated.

The diuerſitye of tranſlations.

Irſte we alter a woorde from that which is in the
minde, to that which is in the bodye. As when we
perceyue one that hath begiled vs, we vſe to ſaye:
Ah ſirzha, I am gladde I haue ſmelled you oute.
Beinge greued with a matter, we ſaye communelye we can
not digeſt it. The Lawyer receiuing money more then nea=
deth oftentimes, will ſaye to his Client wythout any tran=
ſlation. I fele you wel, whē the pore man thinketh ỹ he doth
well vnderſtand his cauſe, and will helpe him to ſome good
ende. For ſo, communelye we ſaye, when we knowe a mans
minde in anye thinge. This kinde of mutation is muche v=
ſed, when we talke earneſtlye of any matter.

From the creature wythout reaſon, to that whyche hathe reaſon.

HE ſeconde kinde of tranſlation is, when we goo
from the creature wythout reaſon to that whiche
hathe reaſon, or contrarye from that whiche hathe
reaſon, to that whiche hath no reaſon. As if I ſho=
ulde ſaye, ſuch an vnreaſonable brawler, did nothinge elles
but barke like a Dogge, or like a Fore. Women are ſaide to
chatter, churles to grunte, boyes to whyne, and yonge men
to yell. Contrariwiſe, we call a Fore falſe, a Lyon proude,
and a Dogge flatteringe.

From the lyuynge to that whyche hath no lyfe.

ROm the liuynge to the not liuynge, we vſe many
tranſlations. As thus: you ſhall playe for almen
diſperſed throughoute the face of the earthe. The
arme of a tree. The ſyde of a Bancke. The lande
cryeth for vengeaunce. From the liuinge, to the not liuing:
Hatred buddeth emonge malicious men, his woordes flowe
out of his mouthe. I haue a whole world of buſines.
In obſeruing the woorke of Nature in al ſeueral ſubſtances
we

we maye finde tranflations at wyll, then the whiche nothinge is moze pzofitable foz anye one that mindeth by hys
vtteraunce to ftirre the hartes of menne either one waye oz
other.

wozd making.

A wozde makinge called of the Grecians Onomatopeia
is when we make wozdes of oure owne mynde, fuche as be
deriued from the nature of thinges. As to call one Watche
oz Cowlfon, whom we fee to do a thinge folyfhelpe, becaufe
thefe two in their time were notable foles. Oz when one is
luftye to fape Taratauntara, declaringe therby that he is as
luftye, as a Trumpette is delitefull, and fpzzinge: oz when
one woulde feme galaunte, to crye hoyghe, wherebye alfo is
declared courage. Boyes beynge greued will fape fome one
to an other, Sir I wyll cappe you, if you vfe me thus, and
withholde that frome me whyche is myne owne: meanynge
that he will take his cappe from him. Againe, when we fee
one gape and galaunte, we vfe to fape, he courtes it. Quod
one that reafoned in diuinitie wyth his felowe, I like well
to reafon, but I cannot chappe thefe textes in fcripture, if
I fhoulde dye foz it: meaning that he coulde not tell in what
chapiter thinges were contepned, althoughe he knewe full
well that there were fuche fapinges.

Intellection.

Intellection.

Intellection called of the Gretians, Synec-
doche. is a Trope, when wee gather oz Iudge the
whole by the parte, oz part, by the whole. As thus.
The king is come to London, meaning therby that
other alfo be come with him. The Frenche man is good to
kepe a Foste, oz to fkyzmifhe on horfebacke, wherby we declare the Frenchmen generally. By the whole y part, thus.
All Cambzidge foзowed foз the deathe of Bucer, meanînge
the moft parte. All Englande reiopfeth that pilgrimage is
banifhed, and Idolatrye foz euer abolifhed: and yet all England is not glad, but the moft parte.
The like phzafes are in the Scripture, as when the Ma-
gians came to Ierufalem, & afked where he was that was
bozne

bozne Kyng of the Jewes. Herode ſtarte vp beeyng greatly
troubled, and al the citie of Jeruſalem with hym, and yet al
the Citie was not troubled, but the moſt part. By the ſigne
we vnderſtande the thyng ſignified, as by an Juie garlande,
we iudge there is wyne to ſel. By the ſigne of a Beare, Bul
Lyon, oz any ſuche, wee take any houſe to be an Jnne. By
eatyng bzeade at the Communion, wee remember Chziſtes
death, and by faith, receiue hym ſpiritually.

❡ Abuſion.

Abuſion, called of the Grecians Catachzeſis, is when Abuſion.
foz a certaine pzoper woozde we vſe that whiche is
moſt nighe vnto it: As in callyng ſome water, a fiſhe
ponde, though there be no fiſſhe in it at all: oz elles
when we ſaie, here is long talke, and ſmall matter. Whiche
are ſpoken vnpzoperly, foz we cannot meaſure, either talke,
oz matter by length, oz bzeadth.

❡ Tranſmutacion of a woozde.

Ranſmutacion helpeth much foz varietie, the whi- Tranſmuta-
tion.
che is when a woozde hath a pzoper ſignification of
the owne, & beyng referred to an other thyng, hath
an other meanyng, the Grecians cal it Metonymia
the whiche is diuerſe waies vſed. When we vſe the authoz i.
of a thyng, foz the thyng ſelfe. As thus. Put vpon you the
Lozd Jeſus Chziſte, that is to ſay, be in liuyng ſuche a one,
as he was. The Pope is baniſhed England, that is to ſaie,
al his ſuperſtition, and Hyppocriſie, either is, oz ſhoulde be
gone to the Deuill by the Kynges expreſſe will, and commaundement. Againe when that whiche doeth contepne, is ii.
vſed foz that whiche is conteined. As thus. J haue dzonk an
hoggeſhead this weeke: Heauen may reiopce, and hell may
lament, when olde men are not couetouſe. Contrarywiſe, iii.
when the thyng conteined is vſed foz the thyng conteinyng.
As thus. J pzaie you come to me, that is to ſay, come to my
houſe. Fourthely, when by the efficient cauſe, the effecte is iiii.
ſtreight gatherde thereupon. As thus. The Sonne is vp,
that is to ſaie, it is day. This felowe is good with a long
bowe, that is to ſaie, he ſhouteth wel.

Aa.i.

Tranſ-

¶ Tranſumption.

Ranſumption is, when by digrees wee go to that, whiche is to be ſhewed. As thus: Suche a one lyeth in a darke doungeon, now in ſpeaking of darkeneſſe, we vnderſtand cloſeneſſe, by cloſineſſe, we gather blackeneſſe, and by blackeneſſe, we iudge depeneſſe.

¶ Chaunge of name.

Antonomaſia.

Haunge of a name, is when for the propre name, ſome name of an office, or other calling is vſed. As thus: the Prophete of God ſaith: Bleſſed, are they whoſe ſynnes be not imputed vnto them, meanyng Dauid. The Poete ſaieth: It is a vertue, to eſchew vice, wherein I vnderſtande Horace.

¶ Circumlocution.

periphraſis

Ircumlocution is, a large deſcription either to ſette forth a thyng more gorgeouſlie, or els to hyde it, if the eares cannot beare the open ſpeakyng: or when with fewe woordes we carnot open our meanyng, to ſpeake it more largely. Of the firſt thus. The valiaunt courage of mightie Scipio ſubdued the force of Carthage and Numantia. Henry the fifte, the moſt puiſſaunt Kyng of Englande, with ſeuen thouſand men toke the Frenſhe Kyng priſoner with al the flower of nobilitie in Fraunce. Of the ſeconde, when Saule was eaſyng hymſelfe vpon the grounde, Dauid toke a peece of his garment, tooke his weapon that laie by hym, and might haue ſlaine hym. Suche a one defiled his bodie with ſuche an euill woman. For the thirde parte, the large commentaries written, and the Paraphraſis of Eraſmus engliſhed: are ſufficient to ſhowe the vſe therof.

¶ What is an Allegorie.

N Allegorie is none other thyng, but a Metaphore vſed throughout a whole ſentence, or Oration. As in ſpeakyng againſt a wicked offendour, I might ſay thus. Oh Lorde, his nature was ſo euill, and his witte ſo wickedly bente, that he ment to bouge the ſhippe, where he hymſelfe ſailed, meanyng that he purpoſed the deſtruction of his owne countrie. It is euill puttyng ſtrong wine into weake veſſelles, that is to ſay it is euill truſtyng

ſome

some woorde with weightie matters. The English Prouer=
bes gathered by Jhon Heywood helpe wel in this behaulf,
the whiche commenly are nothyng elles but Allegories, and
darcke deuised sentences. Now for the other fower figures
because J mynde hereafter to speake more largely of them,
and Quintilian thynketh them more meete to be placed a=
mong the figures of Exornacion, J wil not trouble the rea=
der with double inculcation, and twyse tellyng of one tale.

¶ Of Schemes, called otherwyse sentences of a
woorde and sentence.

J Might tary a longe tyme in declaryng the nature of
diuerse Schemes, whiche are woordes or sentencies
altered, either by speakyng, or writyng, contrarie to
the vulgare custome of our speache without chaun=
gyng their nature at all: but because J knowe the vse of the
figures in woord is not so great in this our tôgue, J wil run
them ouer with asmuche haste as J can.

¶ The diuision of Schemes.

S Traunge vsyng of any woorde or sentence contrarie
to our daiely wont, is either when we adde, or take
away a sillable, or a woord, or encrease a sentence by
chaunge of speache côtrarie to the commune maner
of speakyng.

¶ Figures of a woorde.

T Hose be called figures of a word, when we chaunge
a woorde, and speake it contrarie to our vulgare and
daily speache. Of the whiche sorte, there are sire in
nomber.

- i. Addition at the first.
- ij. Abstraction from the first.
- iij. Interlacyng in the middest.
- iiij. Cuttyng from the middest.
- v. Addyng at the ende.
- vi. Cuttyng from the end.

OF Addition. As thus. He did all to berattle hym. Prosthesis.
wherein appereth that a sillable is added to this
woorde(rattle.)Here is good ale to sel, for good ale,

Aa.ij.   Of

Scheme what
it is.

The Arte of Rhetorique.

Apherefis. Of Abstraction from the first, thus. As I romed al alone, I ganne to thynke of matters greate. In whiche sentence, (ganne) is vsed, for beganne.

Epenthesis. Interlacyng in the middest. As. Relligion, for religion.

Syncope. Cuttyng from the middest. Idolatrie, for Idololatrie.

Proparaleptis Addyng at the end. Hasten your busines, for, Haste your businesse.

Apocope. Cuttyng from the end. A faire map, for, maide.

Thus these figures are shortely sette out, and as for the other Schemes, whiche are vtterde in whole sentences, and expressed by varitie of speache: I wil set them forth at large emong the coloures & ornamentes of Elocution, that folowe.

¶Of coloures and ornamentes to commende and sette forth an Oration.

Coloures of Rhetorique. NOW, when we are able to frame a sentence hand-somly together, obseruyng number and kepyng com-position, suche as shal lyke best the eare, & do know the vse of Tropes, and can applie them to our pur-pose: than thornamentes are necessarie in an Oratio, & sen-tences woulde bee furnished with moste beautifull figures. Therfore to thende that thay may be knowne, suche as most commende and beautifie an Oration: I wil set them forthe here in suche wise as I shal best be able, folowyng the order whiche Tullie hath vsed in his Booke made of a perfite Oratour.

¶Restyng vpon a poynte.

Commoratio. WHEN wee are earnest in a matter, and feele the weight of our cause, wee rest vpon some reason, whiche serueth best for our purpose. Wherin this figure appereth most, & helpeth muche to set forthe our matter. For if we stil kepe vs to our strongest holde, and make oftenrecourse thither, though we be driuē through by-talke to go from it nowe and than : we shall force them at length, either to auoide our strong defence, or elles to yelde into our handes.

¶An euident, or plaine settyng forthe of a thyng as though it were presently doen.

This

Illuſtris er‑
planatio.

This figure is called a deſcription, oꝛ an euident deſ‑
claratiõ of a thyng, as though we ſawe it euen now
doen. An example. Jf our enemies ſhall inuade, and
by treaſon wynne the victoꝛie, we al ſhal dye euery
mothers ſonne of vs, and our Citie ſhalbe deſtroied ſticke &
ſtoone. J ſee our childꝛen made ſlaues, our daughters rauiſ‑
ſhed, our wifes caried away, the father foꝛced to kil his own
ſonne, the moꝛher her daughter, the ſonne his father, the
ſucking child ſlaine in the mothers boſome, one ſtandyng to
the knees in anothers bloude, Churches ſpoiled, houſes
pluckte doune, and al ſet in fier rounde about vs, euery one
curſyng the day of their birth, childꝛen cryyng, women wai‑
lyng, and olde men paſſyng foꝛ very thought, and euery one
thynkyng hymſelfe moſt happy that is firſt ridde out of this
woꝛlde, ſuche will the crueltie be of our enemies, and with
ſuche hoꝛrible hatred wil they ſeeke to diſpatche vs. Thus
where J might haue ſaid, we ſhal al be deſtroied and ſaie no
moꝛe, J haue by deſcription ſette the euill foꝛth at large. Jt
muche auaileth to vſe this figure in diuerſe matters, the
whiche whoſoeuer can do, with any excellent gift, vndoub‑
tedly he ſhal muche delite the hearers. The circumſtaunces
wel conſidered in euery cauſe, geue muche matter foꝛ the
plaine opening of the thyng. Alſo ſimilitudes, examples, cõ‑
pariſons from one thyng to another, apte tranſlacions, and
heaping of allegoꝛies and all ſuche figures as ſerue foꝛ am‑
plifyng, do muche commende the liuely ſettyng foꝛthe of a‑
ny matter. The miſeries of the Courtiers lyfe might well
be deſcribed by this kind of figure. The commoditie of lear‑
nyng, the pleaſure of plowe men, and the care that a Kyng
hath. And not onely are matters ſet out by deſcription, but
men are painted out in their colours, yea buildynges are ſet
foꝛth, Kyngdomes, and Realmes are poꝛtured, places, and
tymes are deſcribed. The Engliſhe man foꝛ feedyng, and
chaung of apparel: The Duꝑtche man foꝛ dꝛynkyng: The
Frenche man foꝛ pꝛyde and inconſtaunce: The Spãpard foꝛ
nymblenes of bodie, and muche diſdaine: The Jtalian foꝛ
great witte and pollicie: The Scottes foꝛ boldenes, and the
Boeme foꝛ ſtubboꝛneſſe.

Deſcription of
outrage after a
battaile.

Diuerſitie of
natures.

Aa·iij. Many

The Arte of Rhetorique.

Many people are described by their degree as a man of good yeres is compted sober, wise and circumspect: a young man wilde, and carelesse: a woman babling, inconstant, and redy to beleue al that is tolde her.

By vocation of life, a souldiour is counted a great bragger, and a vaunter of hymselfe: a Scholer simple: a russed coate, sadde and sometymes craftie: a courtier, flatteryng: a citezen, ientle.

Description of persone.

In describing of persons there ought alwaies a commelinesse to be vsed, so that nothyng be spoken whiche may be thought is not in them. As if one shall describe Henry the sirth, he might cal hym ientle, milde of nature, ledde by perswasion, & redy to forgeue, carelesse for wealthe, suspectyng none, merciful to al, fearefull in aduersitie, & without forecast to espie his misfortune. Again for Richarde the third I might bryng hym in, cruell of harte, ambicioule by nature, enuioule of mynde, a depe dissembler, a close man for weightie matters, hardie to reuenge, and feareful to lose his high estate, trustie to none, liberal for a purpose, castyng still the worst, and hoping euer the best. By this figure also we imagine a talke for some one to speake, and accordyng to his person we frame the Oration. As if one should bryng in noble Henry the .viij. of most famouse memorie to enueigh againft rebelles, thus he might order his Oration. What if Henry theight were alyue, & sawe suche rebellion in this Realme, would not he say thus, and thus? yea me thynkes I heare hym speake euen now. And so set forth suche wordes as we would haue hym to saie.

Some tymes it is good to make God, the Countrie, or some one towne to speake, and loke what we woulde say in our owne person, to frame the whole tale to them. Suche varietie doth muche good to auoide tediousenes, for he that speaketh al in one sort though he spake thinges neuer so wittely shal sone wery his hearers. Figures therfore wer inuented to auoide sacietie, and cause delite: to refresh with pleasure & quicken with grace, the dulnesse of más braine. Who wil loke of a whit waul an houre together, where no workemanship is at al? Or who wil eate stil one kinde of meate, & neuer

The vse of figures.

neuer defire chaunge. Certes as the mouthe is daintie: fo
the wit is tickle, and wil fone loth: an vnfauery thing.

¶A ftop, oz half tellyng of a tale.

Stoppe is, whē we bzeake of our tale befoze we haue Precifio.
tolo it. As thus. Thou that art a young man of fuche
towardnes hauyng fuche frendes to plaie me fuche a
parte, wel, I will faie no moze, God amende all that
is amiffe. Oz thus. Dothe it become the to be, fhal I tel al,
Naie, I wil not foz verp fhame.

¶A clofe vnderftandyng.

Clofe vnderftandyng is, when moze map be gatherd Significa-
than is openly expzeft. A naughtie fellowe that vfed tio plus ad
muche robbery, founde hym felfe greeued that the intelligēdū
greate Dzatour Demofthenes fpent fo muche oyle q̄ dixeris.
wherby he watched from tyme to tyme in compaffyng matters foz the commune weale: In dede (quoth) Demofthenes Demofthenes.
darke nightes are beft foz thy purpofe, meanyng that he was
a great robber in the night. Dne alfo beeyng fet in a heate,
becaufe another had contraried hym foz the choife of mea-
tes, was muche moze greeued when he gaue hym this tauut.
Pou map boldely (q he) fpeake foz fifhe eatyng, foz my maifter pour father hath many a time z ofte wipt his nofe vpon
his ffeeue, meanyng that his father was a fifhemonger.

¶Shozte fentences.

Hen fhozte claufes, oz fentences are vfed when we Diftincte
fpeake at a wozde, parte of our minde, and next after concifa bre
fpeake as bziefely againe, vfyng to make almoft e- uitas.
uery wozde a perfite fentence. As thus. The man is
foze wounded, I feare me he will dye. The Phificions mi-
ftruft hym: the partie is fledde, none perfueth: God fende vs
good lucke.

¶Abatyng, oz leffenyng of a thyng.

We make our doynges appere leffe, whē with woz- Extenuatio
des we extenuate and leffen the fame. As when one
had geuen his fellowe a found blowe, beyng rebuked foz the fame faied he fcante touched hym. Likewife, when two haue fought together, to fap that the one
had his legge prickte with a fwozde, whē perchaunce he had
a great wounde,

wittp.

The Arte of Rhetorique.

A wittie iesting.

Illusio. Any pleasaunt ientlemen are well practised in merie conceited iestes, and haue both suche grace and
delite therin, that they are wonderfull to beholde,
and better were it to be sharpely chidde of diuerse
other, then pleasauntly taunted by any of thē. When a ientleman of great landes & small witte had talked largely at a
supper, and spake wordes scant worth the hearyng, an other
beeyng muche greeued with his foolie, saied to hym : Sir I
haue taken you for a plaine meanyng ientlemā, but I know
nowe, there is not a more deceiptfull bodie in al Englande:
with that, other beyng greeued with the young ientlemans
foolie, boldely began to excuse hym for deceipt, and therfore
said, he was to blame to charge hym with that fault, consideryng his nature was simple, and few can say that euer he
was craftie. Wel q thother, I must nedes say he is deceipt-
ful, for I toke hym heretofore for a sober wittie young man,
but now I perceiue, he is a foolish bablyng felowe, & therfore I am sure he hath deceiued me like a false craftie child,
as he is: with that they al laughed, and the ientleman was
muche abashed. But as touchyng sharpe tauntes, I haue
largely declared them in place, where I treated of laughter.

Digression, or swaruyng from the matter.

Digressio ab
re non longa. We swarue sometymes from the matter vpon iust
consideracions, makyng the same to serue for our
purpose as wel as if we had kepte the matter stil.
As in making an inuectiue against rebelles, & largely setting out the filth of their offence, I might declare by
the way of a digression, what a noble countrie England is,
how great commodities it hath, what trafike here is vsed, &
howe muche more nede other Realmes haue of vs, than we
haue nede of them. Or when I shal geue euidence, or rather
declame against an hainous Murtherer, I may digresse
from the offence doen, and enter in prayse of the deade man,
declaryng his vertues in moste ample wyse, that the offense
doen, may be thought so muche the greater, the more honest
he was that hath thus been slaine.

Notwith-

Notwithstanding this would be learned,that(whē we make
any suche digression)thesame maie well agre to the purpose
and be so set out, that it confounde not the cause,o? darken
the sense of the matter deuised.

¶ Proposicion.

Proposicion is a sho?t rehersall of that, wherof we Propositio
mynde to speake. I will tell you (y one) there is quid sis di-
none hath a wo?se name then this felow,none hath cturus.
been so often in trouble,he maie be fautelesse,but I
can hardely beleue it, there are enow that will testifie of his
naughtinesse,and auouche his euill demeanour to bee suche,
that the like hath not been hard heretofo?e.

¶ An ouer passage to another ma?ter.

When we go frō one matter to another,we vse this Seiunctio
kynde of ph?aise. I haue tolde you the cause of all ab eo quod
this euill, nowe I will tell you a remedy fo? the; dictum est.
same.You haue heard of iustificacion by faith one
ly,now you shal here of the dignitee of wo?kes,and how ne?
cessary thei are fo? euery ch?istian body.

¶ Of commyng again to the matter.

When wee haue made a digression, wee maie declare Reditus ad
our returne,and shewe that whereas wee haue ro? propositū.
ued a litle, we will now kepe vs within our boun-
des.In this kynd of digression, it is wisedome not
to wander ouer farre, fo? feare wee shall werie the hearers,
befo?e we come to the matter again.I knew a p?eacher,that
was a whole houre out of his matter,and at length remem?
b?yng hymself,saied, well,now to the purpose, as though al
that,whiche he had spoken befo?e, had been litle to the pur?
pose,whereat many laughed, and some fo? starke wearinesse
wer fain to go awaie.

¶ Iteratyng and repeatyng thynges said befo?e.

When a man hath largely spoken his mynd,he may re? Iteratio.
we peate in fewe wo?des,the somme of his saiyng . As if
one should be charged with felonie , that is a man of
welth and honestie, he might thus gather his mynd together
after a lōg tale told.First I wil p?oue there is no cause that
I should steale , again that I could not possible at suche a
Bb.i.   tyme

tyme ſteale, and laſt, that I ſtole not at all.

¶The concluſion, or lappyng vp of matter.

Rationis apta concluſio.

The concluſion, is an apt knittyng together of that, whiche we haue ſaid before. As thus. If reaſon can perſwade, if examples maie moue, if neceſſitee maie helpe, if pitee maie prouoke, if daungers foreſeen, maie ſtirre vs to be wiſe : I doubte not but you will rather vſe ſharpe lawes, to repreſſe offendours, then with diſſolute negligence, ſuffer all to periſhe.

¶Mountyng aboue the truthe.

Veritatis ſuperlatio, atq̃ traiectio.

Mountyng aboue the truthe, is when we do ſetfurthe thynges exceedyngly & aboue all mennes expectacion, meanyng onely that thei are very great. As thus, god promiſed to Abrahã, that he wold make his poſteritee, equal with the ſandes of the yearth. Now it was not ſo ſaid, that there ſhould be ſo many in deede, but that the nomber ſhould bee infinite. For, whether we ſhall vnderſtande thoſe, to bee the children of Abraham, that came of his ſtocke in fleſhe, or els take thẽ for the children of Abraham, that haue the faithe of Abraham: wee ſhall neuer proue the nomber of men, to bee equall with the ſandes of the ſea, though wee could reken all that haue been, from the beginnyng of the worlde. Therfore in this ſpeache, wee muſte vnderſtande there is a mountyng, called of the Grecians hyperbole: we vſe this figure muche in Engliſh. As thus. He is as ſwift as a ſwallowe, he hath a belly as bigge as a barrell, he is a giaunt in makyng. The whole Temneſe is litle enough to ſerue hym, for waſſhyng his handes. In all whiche ſpeaches wee mounte euermore a greate deale, and not meane ſo as the wordes are ſpoken.

¶Aſkyng other, and anſweryng our ſelf.

Rogatio.

By aſkyng other, and anſweryng to the queſtion our ſelf, we muche commende the matter, and make it appere very pleaſant. If I would rebuke one that hath committed a robberie, I might ſaie thus. I wonder what you ment to commit ſuche felonie. Haue you not landes? I knowe you haue. Are not your frendes worſhipfull? Yes aſſuredly. Were you not beloued of them? No doubt you were. Could you haue wanted any thyng ỹ thei had? If you would haue eaten golde, you might haue had it. Did not thei alwayes

The arte of Rhetorique.

pes bidde you ſeke to them,and to none other. I knowe thei
did. what euill happe had you then, to offende in ſuche ſorte
not goyng to your frendes,whiche would not ſe you want,
but ſekyng for that, whiche you ſhould not haue, endaunge=
ryng your ſelf by vntrue dealyng,to fele the power & ſtregth
of a law, whē otherwiſe you might haue liued in ſauegard.

The like kynd of writyng is al.o vſed,whē we make ano=
ther body to ſpeake,and yet not aſke them any queſtion at al.
As when D.Haddon had comforted the ducheſſe of Suffol=
kes grace for her childrē,and had ſaid thei wer happly gone
becauſe thei might haue fallen hereafter,and loſte that wor=
thy name,whiche at their death thei had: at laſt h: bringeth
in the mother,ſpeakyng motherlike, in her childrens behalfe
of this ſort,and anſwereth ſtill to her ſaiynges.But al theſe
euilles wherof you ſpeake (ꝙ ſhe) hadde not chaunced : yet
ſuche thynges doo chaunce. yet not alwayes:yet full ofte.
yet not to al:yetto a great many. yet thei had not chaun=
ced to myne: yet wee knowe not.yet I might haue hoped:
yet better it had been to haue feared.

☞·Snappiſhe aſkyng.

WE doo aſke oftentymes, becauſe we would knowe:
we do aſke alſo,becauſe we woulde chide,and ſette
furthe our grief with more vehemencie, the one is
called Interrogatio,the other is called Perconta=
tio.Tullie enueighyng againſt Catiline,that Romaine re=
bell,beginneth his oracion chidingly,queſtionyng with Ca=
tiline of this ſort.How long(Catiline)wilt thou abuſe our
ſufferaunce?How long will this rage and madneſſe of thine
go aboute to deceiue vs?

Percōtatio

☞·Diſſemblyng or cloſe teſtyng.

WHen we ieſt cloſely,and with diſſemblyng meanes,
grigge our felowe, when in wordes wee ſpeake one
thyng,and meane in hart another thyng,declaryng
either by our countenaunce,or by vtteraunce,or by
ſome other waie, what our whole meanyng is.As when we
ſe one boaſtyng himſelf,& vain glorious, to hold him vp with
ye and naie,and euer to ad more to that,whiche he ſaieth.As
I knowe one that ſaied hymſelf,to be in his awne iudgemēt

Diſſimuta-
tio, alia di-
centisac ſi-
gniſicantio

one of the beſt in all Englande,foʐ trying of metalles,ꝙ that
the counſaill hath often called foʐ his helpe, and cannot wāt
hym foʐ nothyng. In deede(ꝙ another)Englande had a ſoʐe
loſſe,if God ſhould call you.They are all Bunglers in cō=
pariſon of you,and I thynke the beſt of theim, maie thanke
you foʐ all that he hath:but yet ſir your cunnyng was ſuche,
that you bʐought a ſhillyng to nyne pence,naie to ſixe pence
and a grote to two pence, and ſo gaue hym a frumpe,euen to
his face,becauſe he ſawe hym ſo foliſhe.A gloʐious ientlemā
that had twoo ſeruauntes,and belike would be knowen not
onely to haue them,but alſo to haue mo, ſaid in the pʐeſence
of a woʐſhipfull man , I meruaile muche where all my ſer=
uauntes are? Marie ſir(ꝙ one)that thoughte to hitte hym
home:thei wer here al two,euen now. Thus he cloſly mockt
hym,and woʐthely.Foʐ, the nomber is not greate,that ſtan=
deth vpō.ij,and(all)is to muche,when we ſpeake of ſo fewe.

¶Doubtfulneſſe.

Dubitacio.

Doubtfulneſſe is then vſed, whē we make the hea=
rers beleue, that the weight of our matter cauſeth
vs to doubte,what were beſt to ſpeake.As when a
kyng findeth his people vnfaithfull,he maie ſpeake
in this wiſe.Befoʐe I begin,I doubt what to name ye.Shal
I call you ſubiectes? You deſerue it not.My frendes ye are
not.To cal you enemies wer ouerlitle,becauſe your offence
is ſo greate.Rebelles you are, and yet that name doeth not
fully vtter your folie.Traitoʐs I maie call you,and yet you
are woʐſe then traitoʐs,foʐ you ſeke his death, who hath ge=
uen you life.Thoffence is ſo great,that no man can compʐe=
hend it.Therfoʐe I doubt what to call you,except I ſhould
call you by the name of theim all.Another.Whether ſhall I
ſpeake,oʐ holde my peace? If I ſpeake, you will not heare,if
I holde my peace,my conſcience condempneth my ſilence.

¶Diſtribucion.

Diſtributio

Attribucion,is whē we apply to euery body,ſuche
thynges as are due vnto them, declaryng what e=
uery one is in his vocacion . It is the duetie of a
Kyng , to haue an eſpeciall care ouer his whole
realme.It is thoffice of his nobles,to cauſe the kynges will

to

The arte of Rhetorique.

to be fulfilled, and with all diligence to further his Lawes, and to fe iuſtice doen euery where.

It is the part of a ſubiect, faithfully to do his princes cõmaundement, & with a willyng hart to ſerue him at al nedes.

It is thoffice of a biſhop to ſetfurthe Gods worde,& with all diligence to exhort men to all godlineſſe. It is an huſbandes duetie to loue his wife,& with ientle meanes to rule her. It is the wifes office,hũbly to ſubmit her ſelf to her huſbãdes will. Seruauntes ſhould be faithfull to their maiſtres, not onely for feare of a law,but alſo for cõſcience ſake. Maſters ſhould vſe their ſeruauntes accordyngly,paiyng theim that,whiche is due vnto them. A father ſhould bryng vp his childrē in the feare of God. Childrē ſhould reuerẽce their fathers with all ſubmiſſion. It is alſo called a diſtribucion, when we diuide the whole,into ſeuerall partes, and ſaie we haue foure poyntes,whereof we purpoſe to ſpeake,comprehendyng our whole talke within compaſſe of theſame.

¶Correccion.

Correction, is when we alter a woorde or ſentence,or otherwiſe then we haue ſpokē before,purpoſyng therby to augmẽt the matter, and to make it appere more vehemẽt. Tullie againſt Verres,geueth a good example.

We haue broughte before you my Lordes, into this place of iudgement,not a thefe,but an extorcioner and violẽt robber, not an aduouterer, but a rauiſher of maides,not a ſtealer of churche goodes,but an errant traitor, bothe to God and all godlineſſe:not a common ruffin,but a moſte cruell eut throte ſuche as if a man ſhould rake hell for one, he could not finde the like. Again,if one would enueigh againſt backbiters,after this ſort. Thou haſt not robbed hym of his money,but thou haſt taken awaie his good name,whiche paſſeth all worldly goodes,neither haſt thou ſlaũdered thyne enemie, but thyne awne brother, & frende,that meant thee well,and hath doen thee pleaſures:nay thou haſt not ſlandred him,but thou haſt ſlain hym. For a man is halfe hanged,that hath loſt his good name. Neither haſt thou killed him with the ſworo,but poyſoned hym with thy tongue, ſo that I maie call it rather an enchanting,then a murther. Neither haſt thou killed one mã

alone

The arte of Rhetorique.

alone, but fo many as thou haft bought out of charite, with thy mofte venemous bacbityng yea, and laft of al, thou haft not flain a man, but thou haft flain Chrifte in his members, fo muche as laie in thee to do. But of this figure I haue fpoken heretofore, where I wote of amplificacion.

CReieccion.

Reieſtio.

R Eieccion is then vfed, when we lay fuche faultes frō vs, as our enemies would charge vs with all, faiyng it is foly to thynke any fuche thyng, muche moe to fpeake it: oz els to faie, fuche a mannes woode is no flaunder, oz it nedeth not to talke of fuche toyes. Oz thus. who wold thinke that I would doo fuche a deede? Oz is it like that I would do fuche a dede? Antony charged Tully, that he was the occafion of ciuill battaill. Nay (p Tullie) it is thou, it is thou manne and none other, that fettes Cefar on woke, to feke the flaughter of his countrey.

A Buttreffe.

premunitio

A Buttreffe is a fenfe made foz that, whiche we purpofe to hold vp, oz go about to compaffe. As thus. I hope my loes, bothe to perfwade this man by reafon, & to haue your iudgemēt in this matter. Foz wheras it is a foe thyng to be iuftly accufed, foz beaking frendfhip, then affuredly if one be wogfully flandzed, a man had nede to loke about him

A familiar talke, oz comunicacion vfed.

Communi‐ catio.

C Ommunicacion is then vfed, when we debate with oher, and afke queftiōs, as though we loked foz an anfwer, and fo go through with our matter, leauyng the iudgement therof to their difcrecion. As thus. what thinke you in this matter? Is there any other better meanes to difpatche the thyng? what would you haue doen, if you were in thefame cafe? Here I appeale to your awne confcience, whether you would fuffer this vnpunifhed, if a man fhould do you the like difpleafure.

Defcripcion of a mannes nature, oz maners.

Defcriptio

W E defcribe the maners of men, when we fet thē furthe in their kynd what thei are. As in fpeakyng againft a coueteous man, thus. There is no fuche pinche peny on liue, as this good felowe is. He will not lofe the paryng of his

The arte of Rhetorique.

his nailes.His heire is neuer ronned,for sparyng of money
one paire of shoen serueth hym a.rij.moneth,he is shod with
nailes like a horse.He hath been knowē by his cote this.rrr
winter. He spent ones a grote at good ale,beyng forced tho=
rowe companie,and taken short at his worde, wherevpon he
hath taken suche conceipt sins that tyme,that it hath almost
cost hym his life.Tullie describeth Pilo for his naughtines
of life,wonderfully to heare,yea,worse then J haue setfurth
this coueteous man.Read the Oracion against Pilo,suche
as be learned.

☞Error.

Error is, when wee thinke muche otherwise then the Errour truth is. As whē we haue conceiued a good opinion of
some one man,& are often deceiued,to saie, who would
haue thought, that he euer would haue doen so. Now of all
menne vpon yearth, J would haue least suspected hym.But
suche is the world.Or thus,You thinke suche a man a wor=
thy personage,and of muche honestie,but J will proue, that
he is muche otherwise: a man would not thynke it , but if J
do not proue it,J will geue you my hedde.

☞Mirthe makyng.

J Haue heretofore largely declared,the waies of mirth ma= king,& therfore J litle nede to renue thē here in this place

Anticipacion,or Preuencion.

Anticipacion, is when we preuent those wordes,that
another would saie,and disproue theim as vntrue,or
at least wise,answere vnto them.A Godly Preacher
enueighed earnestly against those , that would not haue the
Bible to bee in Englishe, and after earnest probacion of his
cause,saied thus:but me thynkes J heare one saie.Sir, you
make muche a doo,aboute a litle matter,what were we the
worse,if we had no scripture at al?To whom he answered:
the scripture is left vnto vs by Goddes awne will,that the
rather we might knowe his commaundementes, & liue ther=
after al the daies of our life.Sometymes this figure is vsed
when we saie,we will not speake this or that,& yet doo not=
withstandyng. As thus. Suche a one is an Officer, J will
not saie a briber . Righte is hyndered throughe mighte,

J

I will not saie, ouerwhelmed. Thus in saiyng we will not speake, we speake our mynde after a sort, notwithstandyng.
¶A Similitude.

A Similitude is a likenesse when. ij. thynges, or mo then two, are so compared and resembled together, that thei bothe in some one propertie seme like. Oftentymes brute beastes, and thynges that haue no life, minister greate matter in this behalfe. Therfore those that delite to proue thynges by similitudes, must learne to knowe the nature of diuerse beastes, of metalles, of stones and al suche, as haue any vertue in them, & be applied to mannes life. Sometymes in a worde appereth a similitude, whiche beyng dilated helpeth wel for amplificacio. As thus. You striue againste the streme, better bowe then breake. It is euill runnyng againste a stone wall. A man maie loue his house wel, and yet not ride vpon the ridge. By all whiche, any one maie gather a similitude, and enlarge it at pleasure. The prouerbes of Heiwode helpe wonderfull well for this purpose. In comparyng a thyng from the lesse to the greater, Similitudes helpe well to set out the matter. That if we purpose to dilate our cause hereby with poses and sentences, wee maie with ease talke at large. This shall serue for an example. The more precious a thyng is, the more diligently should it bee kepte, and better hede taken to it. Therfore tyme, (consideryng, nothyng is more precious,) should warely bee vsed, and good care taken, that no tyme bee lost, without some profite gotten. For if thei are to be punished, that spende their money, and wast their landes, what folie is it, not to thynke theim worthie muche more blame, that spend their tyme (whiche is the chiefest treasure that God geueth) either idlely, or els vngodly? For what other thyng doeth manne lose, when he loseth his tyme, but his life? And what can bee more deare to man then his life? If wee lose a litle money, or a ryng of golde with a stone in it, we compt that greate losse. And I praie you, whe wee lose a whole daie, whiche is a good porcion of a mannes life, shall wee not compte that a losse, consideryng though our money bee gone, wee maie recouer thesame again, but tyme lost can neuer be called backe again. Again whe we lose

our

our money,ſome boope getteth good by it, but the loſſe of
time turneth to no mannes auaple. There is no man that
loſeth in anye other thynge, but ſome boope gayneth by it,
ſaupnge onelpe in the loſſe of time. Pea,it hathe ſaued the
lpfe of ſome,to loſe al that thep hadde.ffoz riches be the oc=
caſion ſometimes of muche miſchiefe in this lpfe, ſo that it
were better ſometpmes to aſtefullpe to ſpende, then warelp
to keepe: by the loſſe of time,no man hath profited him ſelfe
anp thing at all. Beſides this,the better & moze pzecious a
thing is,the moze ſhame to ſpꝭd it fondlp.Though mꝭ kꝭpe
their goodes neuer ſo cloſe,and locke them vp neuer ſo faſt,
pet often times,either by ſome miſchaunce of fpze,oz other
thinge,thep are loſt,oz els deſperate Dickes bozowes nowe
and then againſte the owners wille, all that euer he hathe.
And now though ꝑ owner be vndone, pet is he not therfoze
diſhoneſt, conſiderpnge honeſtpe ſtandeth not in wealthe oz
heapes of monep: But the loſſe of tpme, ſepnge it happe=
neth thzoughe oure owne folpe, not onelpe dothe it make
vs wzetches,but alſo cauſeth menne to thinke that wee are
paſte all grace. A wonderfull kpnde of infamie, wһen the
whole blame ſhall reſte vpon none other mannes necke,but
vpon his onelpe that ſuffereth all the harme. Wpth monep
a manne mape bpe lande, but none can gette honeſtie of that
pzpce:and pet with well vſinge of tpme, a manne noꞇ onelp
might get him muche wozſhippe, but alſo mpghꞇe purchaſe
himſelf a name foz euer.Pea,in a ſmal time a man might get
greate fame,and liue in much eſtimation.By loſinge of mo=
nep wee loſe little elles:bp loſpnge of time,wee loſe all the
goodnes and grꝭces of GꝬꝬ, whiche bp laboure might be
hadde.

   Thus a Similitude mpghte be enlarged bp heappnge
good ſentences, when one thinge is compared wpth an oꞇ
ther,and a concluſion made therupon.

   Emonge the learned menne of the Churche, no one vſeth
this figure moze then Chziſoſtome, whoſe wzitpnges the
rather ſeme moze pleaſaunte and ſwete.ffoz ſimilitudes are
not onelpe vſed to amplifie a matter, but alſo to beautifie
the ſame,to delite the hearers, to make the matter plapne,
      Cc.i.   and

and to fhewe a certaine maiefiye wyth the reporte of fuche refembled thinges, but becaufe I haue fpoké of fimilitudes heretofore in the boke of Logique, I will furceffe to talke anye further of this matter.

Example.

Exemplum

HE that mynoeth to perfwade, mufte neades be well ftored with examples. And therfore muche are they to be commended whiche fearche Chronicles of all ages, and compare the ftace of our elders, with this prefente time. The hiftorye of Goddes boke to the chriftian is infallible, and therfore the rehearfall of fuche good thinges as are therin conteyned, moue the faythfull to all vpright doinge and amendmente of their lyfe. The Ethnicke aucthoures ftyrre the hearers, beynge well applyed to the the purpofe. For when it fhall be reported that they whiche hadde no knowledge of God, liued in a brotherlye loue, one towardes an other, detefted aduoutrye, banifhed periures, hanged the vnthanckefull, kepte the pole withoute meate, tyll they laboured for their liuynge, fuffered none extorcion, exempted Byphers frome bearynge rule in the commune weale: the Chriftians mufte neades be afhamed of their euyll behauiour, and ftudye much to paffe thofe, whiche are in callynge muche vnder them, and not fuffer that the ignoraunte and Paganes lyfe, fhall counteruaple the taughte chyldren of God, and paffe the Chriftians fo much in good liuynge, as the Chriftians paffe theim in good learninge. Vnequall examples commende muche the matter. I call theim vnequall, when the weaker is brought in againfte the ftronger, as if chyldren be faythfull, much more ought menne to be faythfull. If womenne be chafte, and vndefiled: menne fhoulde muche more be cleane, and wythoute faulte. If an vnlearned manne wyll do no wronge, a learned man and a preacher mufte muche more be vprighte, and liue without blame. If an houfholder will deale iuftlye with his feruauntes, a Kynge mufte muche the rather deale iuftelye with his fubiectes.

Examples gathered out of hiſtoꝛies and vſed in this ſoꝛt, helpe muche towardes perſwaſion. Pea, bꝛute beaſtes miniſter greate occaſion of righte good matter, conſideringe manye of theim haue ſhewen vnto vs, the paternes and pꝛmages of diuers vertues.

Doues ſeyng an haucke, gather all together, teachynge vs none other thing, but in aduerſitie to ſticke one to another. Doueꝗ

Craynes in the nyght haue their watche, warninge vs neuer to be careleſſe, foꝛ if their watche faile them, they al neuer leaue tyll they haue killed that one Crayne, teachyng vs that no traptours are woꝛthye to liue vpon earth. The watche foꝛ his ſafegarde, and becauſe he woulde not ſlepe: holdeth a ſtone in his foꝛe, the which falleth from him, whē he beginneth to waxe heauy, and ſo he kepeth him ſelfe ſtyll wakyng. Wherby wee maye learne that all menne in their vocation ſhoulde be right ware and watchfull. The Henne clocketh her chickens, feadeth them, and kepeth theim from the Kyte. Womenne muſt clocke their childꝛen, bꝛing them vp well, and kepe them from euill happe. Nowe I myght in ſpeakinge of ſome odious vyce, largelye ſette oute ſome example belonginge to the ſame, and compare it with oꝛher by heapinge of Chꝛonicles, and matchinge of thynges toꝛgether. Craynes

The vnthankefull in this age (whereof there is no ſmall number) can not haue enoughe ſaide againſte theim. And therfoꝛe I am minded to ſaye ſomewhat againſte theim, to the vtter abhoꝛrynge of all ſuche vnkynde dealynge. Foꝛ he that is vnthankeful, and foꝛ herty loue, ſheweth cankard hatred: wanteth all other Vertues, that are required to be in manne. The chiefe perfection and the abſolute fulfillyng of the Lawe, ſtandeth in the loue which manne oweth firſt to God, and nexte to his neighboure. Lette a m vnne haue fayth that he may be able to tranſlate mountaines (as ſaint Paule ſayeth:) yea, let him haue neuer ſo good qualities, oꝛ be he neuer ſo politique a manne foꝛ the ſaulfegarde of his Countrey, be he neuer ſo wiſe, ſo ware, and ſo watchful: yet if he wante Loue, he is nothynge elles but as a ſoundinge bꝛaſſe, oꝛ a tinckelinge Cymbal. vnthankefulnes how euil it is

Cc.ij. Nowe

Nowe he that is churliſhe and vnthankefull, muſte neades wante loue, and therfore wanteth he all other goodnes.

Vnthankeful⸗ nes puniſhed by the Perſi⸗ as with Death The Perſians therfore ſeyng the greatenes of this offence and that where it reſted, all vyces for euer were baniſhed: prouided by a law that ſuche ſhould ſuffer death as felons, which were founde faultye with vnthankefulnes.

And yet I can not ſee but they deſerue rather an exqui⸗ ſite kynde of Deathe (ſuche as fewe haue ſene, or fewe haue felte) then to ſuffer lyke Deathe with other, that haue not lyke offended wyth them.

But nowe becauſe this offence is an euill moſt odious, and the principal occaſion of all other miſchiefe, I will ſet forthe three notable examples, the one of a Dragon, the ſe⸗ conde of a Dogge, and the thirde of a Lyon (whiche all three in thankefulnes, if that be true whiche is reported of theim wonderfullye exceaded,) and the rather I ſeke to ſet theim oute, that the wycked herebye maye well knowe what they theim ſelues are, when bru te Beaſtes ſhall ſette theim al to ſchole.

Thankfulnes of a Dragon There was a manne (as Plinie writeth) whiche foſte⸗ red vp a pong Dragon, who ſeynge the ſame beaſte to waxe wonderfull greate, feared to kepe his Dragon anye longer within his houſe, and therfore he put him out into a wylde Forreſte. It happened afterwarde that the ſame manne traueylinge on hys iourney throughe the Forreſte, was beſette with thieues. And nowe beynge in this diſtreſſe, and lokinge for none other ende but death, made (as lothe to departe) a grea e ſhowte and an outerye: ſtrayghte vpon whoſe noyſe, and at the knowledge of his voyce, the Dragō came to him in all the haſte poſſible. Wherupon the thieues beinge greatelye afrayed, ranne cleane awaye to ſaue theim ſelues harmeles. Thus throughe the thanckefulnes of a Dragon, this mans life was ſaued.

Thankefulnes of a Dogge. The Dogge of the Romaine Fuluius is more wonderful This Fuluius traueylinge by the waye, was ſlayne wyth ſlaues that laye in wayte for him. Hys Dogge ſeynge his maſter deade, laye by him for the ſpace of two dayes. Wher⸗ vpon when the manne was miſſinge, and ſearche made for him, they founde him dead, with his Dogge lyinge by him.

Some

Some marueplinge to see the Dogge lye there by hys deade maister, ſtroke him, and woulde haue driuen him from the deade coiſe, and coulde not: ſome ſeynge ſuche kindenes in the Dogge, and pitiynge him that he ſhould lye there wt out meate, two or thre dayes before: caſt him a pece of fleſh, wherupon the Dogge ſtrayghte caried the meate to his mai ſters mouthe, and woulde not eate anye whitte him ſelfe, thoughe he hadde forborne meate ſo longe before. And laſt of all, when this deade bodye ſhoulde be caſte into the riuer, (accordinge to the maner of the Romaines)the Dogge ſkapt in after, and holdynge vp his maiſter ſo longe as he coulde, did chooſe rather to dye with him, then to liue without him.

The Lyon (wherof Appi in the Grammarian doth ſpea ke)is alſo ſtraunge for his kindenes, and almoſt incredible. A ſeruaunte that hadde runne awaye from his maſter, and hidde him ſelfe for feare in a caue, within a greate woodde, toke a thorne out of a Lions fote, whiche then came to him for ſuccour as he lay there. Now whē he had done, the Lion to requite his good turne, brought ſuche meate to the caue, as he coulde kyll in the woode. The whiche meate the Ser uaunte roſtynge againſte the Sunne, (beynge in the mooſte hotte countrey of all Affrica)did eate from time to time. At length yet being werye of ſuche a lotheſome lyfe, he left the caue, & came abrode, by meanes wherof, he was takē again, and beinge a ſlaue to his maſter (who hadde power of life & deathe ouer him)he was condempned to be caſt to the wylde beaſtes at Rome, there to be deuoured of a Lyon. The pore captife ſtode pitifullye in the ſighte of thouſandes, euer lo kinge when he ſholde be deuoured. It happened at theſame time, when this felow was thus adiudged to dye. that the ſame Lyon was taken, whoſe foote he healed in the wood. When the Lyon was putte to him, he came firſte very ter ribly towarde this felowe, and immediat ly knowyng what he was, ſtoode ſtyll, and at length fauned gently vpon him. The felow at firſte being amaſed, began to take harte vnto him afterwardes, as halfe knowing him likewiſe, and thus they began bothe to take acquaintaunce thone of thother, & played together a good ſpace withoute all daunger, wher

Cc.iij　　vpon

The arte of Rhetorique.

upon the people beynge amaſed, muche wondered at the ſtraungenes of this thinge. And ſtandinge thus aſtonied, they ſente to knowe of the ſlaue, what this matter ſhoulde meane. Unto whom this poore wretche opened the whole thynge altogether, euen as it happened. when the people hearde this, they not onely reiopſed much at the ſight ther= of, but alſo they made earneſt requeſt to his Maſter for his lpfe. His maſter marueylinge as muche as anye of them, at ſuche an vnwonte kyndenes: gaue him not onelye hys life, but alſo his fredome. And nowe to the ende he myght haue ſomewhat whereupon to lyue, the people gaue hym a fee for terme of his lyfe. The felowe by and by gotte him a lime and a coler, and caried the Lyon vp and downe the ci= tye in ſuche ſorte, as huntſmenne carye a Greyhounde, or a Spaniell, the people ſtyll wonderynge, and ſayinge euer as he came bye: Beholde a manne that hath cured a Lyon, be= holde a Lyon that hath ſaued a man.

The whiche example, the more ſtraunge it is, the more aſhamed maye they be that are vnnaturall, and maye learne kindenes of a bruite Beaſte. For ſuche menne beynge ouercome with kindnes by Beaſtes, are worſſe then Bea= ſtes, & more mete rather to be tormented with Deuils, then to liue with men.

Of enlargynge examples by coppe.

AND now becauſe examples enriched by Copy, helpe muche for Amplification: I will geue a taſte, howe theſe and ſuche lyke Hiſtories maye be encreaſed.

And for the better handelynge of theim, nedefull it is to marke well the circumſtaûces: that beynge well obſer= ued and compared together on bothe partes, they maye the rather be enlarged.

Example en=
larged.

As thus. That whiche bruite Beaſtes haue doone, ſhalt thou being a man ſeme not to haue done? They ſhew= ed them ſelues natural, and wilt thou appeare vnnaturall? May they ouercame nature, and wilte thou be ouercome of them? They became of beaſtes in bodye, men in nature, and wilt thou become of a manne in bodye, a Beaſte in nature? They beinge withoute reaſon, declared the propertye of reaſo=

The arte of Rhetorique Fol.104.

reasonable creatures, and wilte thou bringe a man endued
wyth reason, appeare in thy doynges altogether vnreaso=
nable? Shall Dogges be thankefull: and menne, yea, chri=
ctian menne warte suche a vertue? Shall woznes shewe
suche kindenes: and menne appearre gracelesse? It had ben
no matter if they had bene vnthankefull: but man can neuer
escape blame, seinge God hathe commaunded, and Nature
hathe graffed this in all menne: that they shoulde do to o=
ther, as they woulde be done vnto. Agayne, they foz meate
onelye shewed them selues so kinde: and shal man foz so ma=
ny benefites receiued, and foz such goodnes shewed, requite
foz good will, euil dedes foz hartie loue, deadlye hatred: foz
vertue, vyce: and foz life geuen to him, yelde death to other?
Nature hath parted man and beast: and shall man in nature
be no manner? Shamed be that wretche that goeth agaynst
nature, that onelye hath the shape of a man, and in nature is
wozse then a beast. Yea, wozthye are all suche rather to be
tozne with deuils, then to liue with men. Thus an example
might moste copiouslye be augmented, but thus muche foz
this time is sufficient.

The saiynge of Poets and all their fables are not to be
forgotten, foz by them we may talke at large, and winne mē
by perswasion, if wee declare befoze hande, that these tales
were not fayned of suche wise menne without cause, neither
yet continued vntyll this tyme, and kepte in memozie with=
out good consideration, and therupon declare the true mea=
nynge of all suche wzitinge. Foz vndoubtedlye there is no
one tale emonge al the Poetes, but vnder the same is com=
pzehended some thinge that perteyneth eyther to the amen=
demente of maners, to the knowledge of trueth, to the set=
tynge foorthe of Natures woozcke, oz elles to the vnderstan=
dinge of some notable thynge done. Foz what other is the
paynefull trauayle of Vlisses discribed so largelye by Ho=
mere, but a liuely picture of mans miserie in this life.

And as Plutarche sayth and likewise Basilius Magnus:
In the Iliades are described strengthe and valeantenes of
the bodye: In Odissea is set foorthe a lyuelye Paterne of
the minde.

The

The arte of Rhetorique.

Poets vnder culoures shew muche wisdome. The Poetes were wise men, & wished in harte the redresse of thinges, the whiche when for feare they durst not openly rebuke, thei didde in coloures paynte theim oute, and tolde menne by shadowes what they shoulde do in good south: or els becaule the wycked were vnworthy to heare the truth, they spake so, that none myght vnderstande, but those vnto whom they pleased to vtter their meaninge, and knewe the to be menne of honeste conuersation.

Danae

We reade of Danae the fayre damosel, whom Juppiter tempted full ofte, and coulde neuer haue his pleasure, tyll at length e he made it raine golde, and so as shee sate in her chimney, a greate deale fell vpon her lappe, the whyche shee toke gladly, and kepte it there: within the which gold Jup= piter him selfe was comprehended, wherby is none other thynge elles signified, but that women haue bene, and wyll be ouercome with money.

Ilis

Likewise Juppiter fanseinge the fayre maide Ilis could not haue his will, till he turned him selfe into a fayre whyte Bull, whiche signified that beautie may ouercome the best.

Tantalus

If a manne woulde speake agaynste couetous Captiues, can he better shewe what they are, then by settynge forthe the straunge plague of Tantalus, who is reported to be in Hell, hauinge water comminge styll to his chynne, and yet neuer able to drynke: and an apple hangyng before his mou= the, and yet neuer able to eate?

Icarus.

Icarus woulde nedes haue wynges and flye contrary to nature, wherupon when he hadde them sette together with ware, and ioyned to his syde, he mounted vp into the ayre. But so sone as the sunne hadde somewhat heated him, and his ware began to melte, he fel downe into a greate Riuer, and was drowned out of hande, the whiche water was euer after called by his name. Now what other thing dothe this tale shewe vs, but that euerye man should not meddle with thinges aboue his compasse.

Midas.

Midas desiered that whatsoeuer he touched, the same might be golde: wherupon when Juppiter hadde graunted hun his bounde: his meate, drinke, and al other thinges tur= ned into gold, and he choked with his owne desire, as al co=
uetous

conetoufe men lightelp ſhalbe , than can neuer bee content
when thep haue enough,

What other thyng are the wonderfull labours of Her⸗ Hercules la⸗
boures what
thep ſignified.
cules, but that reaſon ſhoulde withſtande affection, and the
ſpirite for euer ſhould fight, againſt the fleſhe? We Chriſti⸗
ans had like fables heretofore of iolp felowes,the Images
wherof were ſet vp (in Gods name)euen in our Churches.
But is anp man ſo mad to thpnk that euer there was ſuche
a one as S.Chriſtofer was painted vnto vs ? Marp God S.Chriſtofer
what he ſigni⸗
fied.
forbid.Aſſuredlp when he liued vpõ earth there were other
houſes builded for hpm, then we haue at this tpme, and I
thpnke tailers were muche troubled to take meaſure of him
for makpng his garmentes. He might be of kpnne to Gar⸗
ganteo, if he were as bigge as he is ſet forthe in Antwerpe.
But this was the meanpng of our elders(and the name ſelf
doth ſignifie none other)that euerp mã ſhould beare Chriſt
vpon his backe,that is to ſap,he ſhould loue his brother as
Chriſte loued vs, and gaue his bodp for vs : he ſhoulde tra⸗
uaile through hunger, colde,ſorowe,ſickenes,deathe,and al
daungers with al ſufferaunce that might be. And whether
ſhould he trauaile? to the euerliupng GOD.but how? In
darkenes? No forſooth,bp the light of his word. And ther⸗
fore Saint Chriſtofer bepng in the Sea, and not well able
to gette out(that is to ſap bepng almoſt drouned in ſpnne,¶
not knowpng whiche waie beſt to eſcape) an Heremite ap⸗
pered vnto hpm with a lãterne ⅋ a light therein,the whiche
dothe ſignifie none other thpng to the Chriſtian but the
true woorde of God,whiche lighteneth the hartes of men,⅋
geueth vnderſtandpng to the poungelinges(as the Prophet S.George on
horſe backe.
doth ſaie). Againe, Sainct George he is ſet on horſebacke ⅋
killeth a Dragon with his ſpeare , whiche Dragon woulde
haue deuoured a virgine, wherebp is none other thpng mẽt
but that a Kpng and euerp man vnto whom therecution of
tuſtice is committed,ſhould defende the innocent againſt the
vngodlp attemptes of the wicked, and rather kill ſuche de⸗
uilles bp marcial law, than ſuffer the innocentes to take a⸗
np wrong. But who gaue our clargie anp ſuche authoritie
that thoſe monſters ſhoulde bee in Churches as lape mens

Dd.i.   Bookes?

Bookes? God forbadde by expresse worde to make any graven Image, and shal we be so bolde to breake Gods wil for a good entent, and call these Idolles laie mens Bookes? I could talke more largely of examples,& heape a number here together, aswell of Ethnike Aucthours,as of other here at home:but for feare I should be tedious,these for this tyme shal suffise.

¶Of Fables.

Apologi.

The feigned fables,such as are attributed vnto brute beastes,would not be forgotten at any hand.for not onely they delite the rude & ignoraunt, but also they helpe muche for perswasion . And because suche as speake in open audience haue euer moe fooles to heare them than wise men to geue iudgement:I would thynke it not a-misse,to speake muche according to the nature and fansie of the ignoraunt,that the rather thei might be wonne through fables, to learne more weightie & graue matters. for al men cannot brooke sage causes,and auncient collacions:but wil lyke earnest matters the rather,if some thing be spoken there emong agreyng to their natures.The multitude(as Horace doth say)is a beast,or rather a monster that hath many heades

Fables how nedeful they are to teache the ignoraunte. and therefore like vnto the diuersitie of natures, varietie of inuencion must alwaies be vsed. Talke altogether of moste graue matters, or depely searche out the ground of thynges or vse the Quiddities of Dunce to sette forth Gods miste-ries:& you shal see the ignoraunt(I warrant you)either fal a slepe,or elles bid you farewel.The multitude must needes be made merp:& the more foolish your talke is,the more wise wil they counte it to be.And yet it is no foolishnesse,but ra-ther wisedome to wynne men by tellyng of fables to heare of Gods goodnesse. Undoubtedly fables well sette forthe, haue doen muche good at diuerse tymes, and in diuerse com-mune weales.The Romaine Menenius Agrippa alleggyng vpon a tyme a fable of the conflicte made betwixt the partes of a mans bodie , and his bellie:quieted a marueilouse stirre that was lyke to ensewe & pacified the vprore of sedicious rebelles, whiche els thought for euer to destroy their coun-trie.Themistocles perswaded the Atheniās not to chaunge
their

their Officers, by rehersyng the fable of a scabbed fore. For
(ꝗ he) when many flees stode feedyng vpon his rawe flesh,
ꝓ had wel fedde themselues, he was contented at anothers
persuasion, to haue them flapte away: whereupon their en=
sewed suche hungry flees afterwardes, that the sorie fore
beyng al alone was eaten vp almost to the harde boone, and
therefore cursed the tyme that euery he agreed to any suche
euil counsel. In lyke maner (ꝗ Themistocles) if you will
chaunge Officers, the hungry flees will eate you vp one af=
ter another, whereas now you liue beyng but onely bitten,
and lyke to haue no farther harme, but rather muche welth
and quietnesse hereafter, because they are filled, and haue e=
nough, that heretofore suckte so muche of your bloud.

Now likewyse as I gaue a lesson how to enlarge an er=
ample, so may fables also in lyke sorte be sette out, ꝓ aug=
mented at large by Amplification. Thus muche for the vse
of fables. Againe, sometymes feined Narrations and wittie
inuented matters (as though they were true in deede) helpe
wel to set forwarde a cause, ꝓ haue great grace in thē, beyng
aptely vsed ꝓ wel inuented. Luciane passeth in this pointe:
sir Thomas More for his Eutopia can soner be remēbred
of me, then worthely praised of any accordyng as the excellē=
cie of his inuenciō in that behaulf doth most iustly require.

Digestion.

Digestion is an ordely placyng of thynges, partyng Digestio.
euery matter seuerally. Tullie hath an erample
hereof in his Oration whiche he made for Sextus
Roscius Amarinus. There are three thynges (ꝗ
Tullie) whiche hynder Sextus Roscius at this tyme, the
accusacion of his aduersaries, the boldenes of them, and the
power that they beare. Erucius his accuser hath taken vpō
hym to forge false matter, the Roscians kinsfolke haue bold
ly aduentured, ꝓ wil face out their doynges, ꝓ Chrisogonus
here, that most can do, wil presse vs with his power.

A whisht, or a warnyng to speake no more.

A Whisht, is when we bid them holde their peace that Reticentia.
haue least cause to speake, and can do litle good with
their talkyng. Diogenes beeyng vpon the Sea emong

Diogenes.

a number of naughtie packes in a greate ſtorme of wether, whẽ diuerſe of theſe wicked felowes cried out for feare of drownyng, ſome with fained prayour to Iuppiter, ſome to Neptune, and euery one as they beſte fantaiſed the goddes aboue : whiſhte(q̃ Diogenes) for by Gods mother, if God hym ſelfe knowe you be here, you are lyke to be drowned euery mothers ſonne of you. Meanyng that they were ſo nought, and ſo fainedly made their prayour to falſe Godes without mynde to amende their naughtie lyfe, that the ly= uyng God woulde not leaue them vnpuniſhed though they cried neuer ſo faſt. Wee vſe this figure likewyſe, when in ſpeakyng of any man:we ſaie, whiſht, the woulſe it at hand: when the ſame man cometh in the meane ſeaſon, of whome we ſpake before.

¶ Contrarietie.

Contentio.

COntrarietie is, when our talke ſtandeth by contrarie wordes, or ſentences together. As thus wee mighte deſpraiſe ſome one man, he is of a ſtraunge nature as euer I ſawe, for to his frende he is churliſhe, to his foe he is ientle:geue him faire wordes, and you offende hym: checke hym ſharpely, and you wynne hym. Let hym haue his will, and he will flye in your face: kepe hym ſhorte, and you ſhal haue hym at commaundement.

¶Free-neſſe of ſpeache.

Liberavox

FReeneſſe of ſpeache, is when wee ſpeake boldely, & without feare, euen to the proudeſt of them, what= ſoeuer we pleaſe, or haue liſt to ſpeake. Diogenes herein did excel, and feared no man when he ſawe iuſt cauſe to ſaie his mynde. This worlde wanteth ſuche as he was, and hath ouer many ſuche, as neuer honeſt mã was, that is to ſay, flatterers, fawners, and ſouthers of mennes ſaiynges.

¶Stomake grief.

Iracundia.

S Tomake grief, is when we will take the matter as hote as a toſt. We nede no examples for this matter, hote men haue to many, of whom they may be bould and ſpare not, that fynde them ſelues a colde. Some tymes

we

we entreate earnestly and make meanes by praier to wynne Deprecatio
fauour. Somtymes we seke fauour by speakyng well of the Cōciliatio.
companie present. As. Thorowe your helpe my lordes this Læsio.
good deede hath been done. Some tymes we speake to hurte
our aduersaries, by settyng forth their euil behauior. Some Purgatio.
tymes we excuse a fault, and accuse the reporters. Somety= Optatio.
mes we wishe vnto God for redresse of euil. Sometimes we
curse the extreme wickednes of some pastgood roisters. In Execratio.
al whiche I thynke neither examples neede, nor yet any re=
hersal had been greately necessarie, considering al these come
without any great learnyng, sauing that for apt bestowing,
iudgement is right nedeful.

Of figures, in sentencies, called Schemes.

Hen any sentence vpon the placyng, or settyng of
wordes, is said to be a figure : thesaied is alwaies
called a Scheme, the whiche wordes beyng alte=
red, or displaced, the figure streight doth lose his
name, and is called no more a scheme. Of this sorte there be
diuerse, suche as hereafter folowe.

Doublettes.

Dublettes, is when we reherse one and thesame Geminatio
worde twise together. Ah wretche, wretche, that verborum.
I am. Tullie against Catiline inueighyng sore a=
gainst his traiterouse attemptes, saith after a long
rehersed matter, and yet notwithstandyng all this notouri=
ouse wickednesse: the man liueth stil, liueth? Nay mary he co
meth into the counsel house whiche is more. An other: Dar=
rest thou showe thy face, thou wretched theef, thou theefe I
saie to thyne owne father, darrest thou looke abrode? Thus
the ofte repeatyng of one worde doth munhe stirre the hea=
rer, and makes the worde seeme greater, as though a sworde
were ofte digged & thrust twise, or thrise in one place of the
bodie.

Alteryng parte of a worde.

A Lteryng parte of a word, is when we take a letter, or Paulum im=
sillable from some word, or els adde a letter, or silla= mutatum =
ble to a worde. As thus. William Somer seyng muche verbum.
a doo for accomptes makyng, & that the Kynges Maiestie of
Dd.iij.   most

The Arte of Rhetorique.

most worthie memorie Henry theight wanted monp suche as was due vnto hym: And ple se pour grace (q he) you haue so many frauditours, so many conuciers, and so many deceiuers to get vp pour money, that they get al to themselues, whether he said true, or no, let God iudge that it was vnhappely spoken of a foole, q I thynke he had some Schoolemaister: he shoulde haue saied Auditours, Suruepours, and Receauours.

CRepetition.

Repetitio a primo.

Repetition is when we begynne diuerse sentencies one after another with one and the same worde. As thus: when thou shalt appere at the terrible date of iudgemet before the high maiestie of God, where is then thy richesse? where is then thy deintie faire? where is thy thy great band of men? where are then thy faire houses? wher are then al thy landes, pastures, parkes, q forestes? I might saie thus of our soueraine lord the Kynges maiestie that now is. Kyng Edwarde hath ouerthrowne idolatrie: Kyng Edwarde hath bannished superstition: Kyng Edward by Gods helpe hath brought vs to the true knowlege of our creation: Kyng Edwarde hath quieted our consciencies, q laboured that al his people should seeke healthe by the death and Passion of Christ alone.

&Conuersion.

Conuersio eiusdem in extremum.

Conuersion is an ofte repeatyng of the last worde, q is contrarie to that which went before. when iust dealing is not vsed: welth goeth away, frendship goeth away, truth goeth awaie, all goodnes (to speake at a worde) goeth awaie. Where affections beare rule, there reason is subdued, honestie is subdued, good wil is subdued, q al thinges els that withstande euil, for euer are subdued.

CComprehension.

Conuersio in eadem.

Comprehension, is when bothe the aboue rehersed figures are in one kynd of speakyng vsed, so that bothe one first worde must ofte be rehersed, q likewise al one last worde. What winneth the hartes of men? Liberalitie. What causeth men to aduenture their lifes, and dye willyngly in defence of their maisters? Liberalitie. What continueth

The Arte of Rhetorique.

tinueth the state of a Kyng? Liberalitie. what becometh a
woman best, & first of al? Silence. what seconde? Silence.
what third? Silence. what fourth? Silence. Yea if a man
should aske me til dowmes day, I would stil crie, silence, silence, without the whiche no woman hath any good gifte,
but hauing the same, no doubt she must haue many other notable giftes, as the whiche of necessitie do euer folow suche
a vertue.

¶ Progression.

Progression standeth vpõ contrarie sentences which Progressio
answere one another. If we would rebuke a naugh-
ty boie, we might with cõmendyng a good boie, say
thus. what a boie art thou in cõparison of this fellow here. Thou sleapes: he wakes: thou plaies: he studies:
thou art euer abrode: he is euer at home: thou neuer waites:
he stil doth his attendaunce: thou carest fo? no body: he doeth
his dutie to al men: thou doest what thou canst to hurt al, &
please none: he doth what he can, to hurte none, & please all.

¶ Lyke endyng, and lyke fallyng.

Hen the sentences are said to ende lyke, when those Similiter
wordes do end in like sillables, which do lacke cases. desinens.
Thou liues wickedly, thou speakes naughtely. The Similiter
rebelles of Northfolke (y a most worthie man that cadens.
made an inuectiue against thē) through slauerie, slew Nobilitie: in dede miserably, in fashiõ cruelly, in cause deuilishly.

Sentencies also are said to fal like, when diuerse wordes
in one sentencie ende in lyke cases, & that in ryme. By great
trauaile is got muche auaile, by earnest affection, men learne
discrecion.

These .ij. kyndes of Exornacion are then most delitefull
when contrarie thynges are repeated together: when that
ones again is vtterde, whiche before was spoken: when sentencies are turned, and letters are altered. Of the first this
may be an example: where learnyng is loued, there labour
is estemed: but wher sleuth is thought solace, there rudenes
taketh place. A Kyng is honoured, that is a Kyng in dede.
wil you drink o? you go, o? wil you go o? you drinke. There
is a diffrence betwixt an horsemilne, & a milnehorse. He is a
meter

meter man to driue the Carte, than to serue in the Courte. Through labour cometh honour, through ydell lyuyng followeth hangyng. Diuerse in this our tyme delite muche in this kynd of writyng, whiche beeyng measurably vsed, deliteth muche the hearers, otherwyse it offendeth, and werieth mens eares with sacitie.

Augustine. S.Augustine had a goodly gifte in this behaulf, & yet some thinkes he forgot measure, and vsed ouermuche this kynde of figure. Notwithstandyng the people were suche were he liued, that they toke muche delite in rimed sentences, & in Orations made ballade wise. Yea thei were so nyce & so waiwarde to please, that excepte the Preacher from tyme to tyme coulde ryme out his Sermon, they

Tacitus. woulde not long abide the hearyng. Tacitus also sheweth that in his tyme, the iudges & sergeauntes at the lawe were driuen to vse this kynd of phrase both in their writyng, & also in their speakyng. Yea great lordes would thynk theselfes contemned, if learned men (when they spake before the)

Rymed sentences vsed without measure. sought not to speake in this sorte. So that for the flowyng stile, & ful sentence, crepte in mynstrelles elocution, talkyng matters altogether in rime, & for weightinesse & grauitie of wordes, succeded nothyng els but wantonnesse of inuencon. Tullie was forsaken, with Liuie, Cesar, & other: And Apuleius, Ausonius, with suche mynstrell makers were altogether folowed. And I thynke the Popes heretofore (seeyng the peoples folie to be suche) made al our Hymnes & Anthe-

Rymes made, to mocke the simple. mes in rime, that with the singyng of me, plaiyng of organes, ringyng of belles, & rimyng of Hymnes, & Sequencies the poore ignoraunt might thinke the Harmonie to be heauenly, & verely beleue that the Angels of God made not a better noise in heauen. I speake thusmuche of these two figures, not that I thinke folie to vse them (for thei are pleasaunt & praise worthie) but my talke is to this end, that thei shoulde neither onely, nor chefely be vsed, as I know some in this our time do ouermuche vse them in their writynges. And ouermuche (as al men know) was neuer good yet. Yea a man may haue ouermuche of his mothers blessyng if she wil neuer leaue blessyng. Therefore a measure is best, yea euen in the best thynges. And thus farre for these.ij.figures.

Egual

The arte of Rhetorique.

¶ Equal members.

EGuall members are suche, when the one halfe of the
sentence answereth to the other, with iust proporciõ
of nomber, not that the sillables of necessitee, should
be of iust nõbre, but that the eare might iudge them,
to bee so eguall, that there maie appere small difference. As
thus. Lawe without mercie, is extreme power, yet men tho=
rowe folie, deserue suche iustice. Learnyng is daungerous,
if an euill man haue it. The more noble a manne is, the more
ientle he should be. Isocrates passeth in this behalfe, who is
thought to write altogether in nomber, kepyng iust propor=
cion in framyng of his sentence.

*Paria pari=
bus relata.*

¶ Like emong themselfes.

SEntences are called like, when contraries are set
together, and the firste taketh asmuche as the other
folowyng: and the other folowyng taketh asmuche
a waie, as that did, whiche went before. As thus.
Lust hath ouercome shamefastenesse, impudencie hath ouer=
come feare, and madnesse hath ouercome reason. Or els sen=
tences are said to be like emong themselfes, when euery part
of one sentēce is eguall, and of like weight one with another
As thus. Is it knowen, tried, proued, euident, open, and as=
sured that I did suche a deede ? Another. Suche riote, Di=
cyng, Cardyng, pikyng, stealyng, fighting, ruffines, queanes
and harlottes, must nedes bryng hym to naught.

*Similia in=
ter se.*

¶ Gradacion.

GRadacion is when we reherse the worde that goeth
nexte before, and bryng another woorde thereupon
that encreaseth the matter, as though one should go
vp a paire of staiers, and not leaue til he come at the
toppe. Or thus. Gradacion is when a sentence is disseuered
by degrees, so that the worde, whiche endeth the sentence go=
yng before, doeth begin the nexte. Labour getteth learnyng,
learnyng getteth fame, fame getteth honour, honour getteth
blesse for euer. Another. Of slouthe cometh pleasure, of plea=
sure cometh spendyng, of spēdyng cometh whoryng, of who=
ryng cometh lacke, of lacke cometh thefte, of thefte cometh
hangyng, and there an ende for this world.

Gradatio.

Ee.i. Regres=

The arte of Rhetorique.

CRegreſſion.

Regreſſio. Hat is called regreſſion, when we repeate a worde eftſones, that hath been ſpoken, and rehearſed before, whether theſame bee in the beginnyng, in the middeſt, or in the latter ende of a ſentence.

In the beginnyng, thus. Thou art ordeined to rule other, and not other to rule thee.

In the middeſt, thus. He that hath money, hath not geuen it, and he that hath geuen money, hath not his money ſtill: but he that hath geuen thankes, hath thankes ſtill, & he that hath them ſtill, hath geuen them notwithſtandyng.

In the latter ende, thus. Manne muſt not liue to eate, but eate to liue. Man is not made for the Sabboth, but the Sabboth is made for man. If man do any filthy thyng, and take pleaſure therein: the pleaſure goeth awaie, but the ſhame tarieth ſtill. If manne do any good thyng with pain, the paines go awaie, but the honeſtie abideth ſtill.

Cwordes looſe.

Diſſolutnm Wordes louſe are ſuche, which as are vttred without any addicion of coniunccions, ſuche as knitte woordes and ſentences together. As thus. Obeye the Kyng, feare his lawes, kepe thy vocacion, doo right, ſeke reſt, like well a litle, vſe all menne, as thou wouldeſt thei ſhould vſe thee.

COut cryng.

Exclamatio Ut cryng is when with voyce we make an exclamacion. Oh Lorde, O God, O worlde, O life, O maners of menne. O death, where is thy Kyng? O hell where is thy victorie?

COft vſyng of one worde in diuerſe places.

L An he haue any mannes harte in hym, or deſerueth he the name of a man, that cruelly killeth a poore innocent man, who neuer thought hym harme.

CA cauſe geuen to a ſentence vttered.

I Feare not myne aduerſarie, becauſe I am not giltie. I miſtruſt not the Judges, becauſe thei are iuſte, the queſt will not caſt me, the matter is ſo plain.

CA cauſe geuen to thynges contrary.

Bb

BEtter it were to rule, then to serue: for, he that ruleth, liueth : because he is free. But he that serueth,
cannot be saied to liue. for where bondage is, there
is no life properly.

¶ Sufferaunce.

TAke your pleasure for a tyme, and do what you list, *Permissio.*
a tyme will come when accompt shalbe made. whē
thynges cannot be, that we would haue, we should
will that, whiche we can haue. Pacience is a remedy for euery disease.

¶ A doubtyng.

SHall I call hym foole, or shall I call hym var- *Dubitatio.*
let, or bothe? Another. what made hym to commit
suche a robberie? Lacke of money, or lacke of wit,
or lacke of honestie? I doubte whe.her to call hym
a foolishe knaue, or a knauishe foole . when muche matter
was here in Englande, for callyng the Pope, supreme hedde *A Spaniardes*
of the Churche (ꝙ a Spanyarde, that whilome was of the *doubte.*
Popes courte in Rome) you doubt muche here in Englande,
whether the Pope be hedde of the churche or no, and greate
variaunce there is emonges you, at the whiche folp of yours
I doo muche maruaill, for we doubte muche at Rome, whether he be a member of the Churche at all, or no.

¶ Reckenyng.

REckenyng, is when many thynges are nombred toge- *Dinumera-*
ther. There is no streat, no house, no man, no child, no *tio.*
shop, no lodgyng in all this toune, but he hath been in
it. There is no stone, no Diamōd, no Saphire, no Rubie, no
Chrystall, no Turcasse, no Emerode, but he knoweth theim
perfectly. By this figure we may enlarge that, by rehersyng
of the partes, whiche was spoken generally, & in fewe wor- *Sentence am-*
des. This maie be an example. Suche a gentle man beyng an *plified by seue-*
vnthrifte, hath spent all that euer he had. Thus the sentence *rall rehersyng*
maie be amplified, if we shew particularly what he had, and *of thynges.*
tell seuerally how he spent it. Loke what enheritaunce came
to him (whiche was no small thyng) by the death of his awn
kinne, and his wifes kinsfolk: What dower soeuer he had by
mariage of his wife, which by report was very greate thyng
Whatsoeuer he got by executorship: Whatsoeuer the kinges
Maiestie

Maiestie gaue hym. what booties soeuer he gotte in warre
fare, looke what money he had, what place, what apparell,
what householde stuffe, what lande and Lordeshippes, what
Shepe, goodes, Parkes, and Medowes, yea, whatsoeuer he
had, moueable, or vnmoueable, his house, and all that euer he
had: he hath so spent in fewe daies, so wasted it, & made suche
hauocke of all together, emong the beastly compagnie of filthy queanes, emong abbominable harlottes, with banque-
tyng from daie to daie, with sumpteous r[iare] suppers, with
drinkyng in the nighte, with daintees and delicates, and all
suche swete delites, with Dicyng, Cardyng, and all maner
of gamenyng: that he hath now left neither crosse nor cruci-
fixe, no not a dodkin in all the worlde, to blesse hymself with
al. Thus these wordes (he hath spent all his goodes in riot)
are dilated, and sette furthe at large, by rehersyng seuerally
euery thyng, one after another.

CReasonyng a matter with our selfes.

Disputatio

When wee reason the matter with our selfes, when
we aske questions of our selfes, and answere there-
vnto. As thus. Howe came this good felowe by all
that he hath? Did his father leaue hym any lande?
Not a foote. Did his frendes geue hym any thyng? Not a
grote. Hath he serued in any vocacion, to heape vp so muche
wealth? None hath liued more idlely. Doeth he not leane to
some noble man? Yea, but he neuer receiued more then .iiij.
marke wages. How then cometh he by all that euer he hath,
liuyng without labour, hauyng no frendes to helpe hym, hauyng so litle to take vnto by all outwarde apparaunce, and
spendyng so liberally, and owyng no man a grote in all the
worlde? Assuredly, it cannot be otherwise, but that he cometh
naughtily by moste of that, whiche he hath Another. Seyng
thou art so basely borne, so poore in state, so smally learned,
so hard fauoured, and hast no witte at al, what meanest thou
to vaunte thy self so muche, and to make suche bragges as
thou doest. What doeth make thee to waxe so proude? Thy
stocke wherof thou diddest come? Why manne, thei are very
base folke. Thyne owne wealth? tushe, thou art as poore as
Job.

Iob. Thy learnyng? Marie thou neuer camst yet where any learnyng did growe . Thy beautie ? Nowe in good sothe, a worse fauoured manne can there not be vpon yearth again. Thy witte? Now God he knoweth, it is as blounte as may bee . What other thyng then, is all this thy braggyng, but plain madnesse.

Resemblyng of thynges.

Esemblyng of thynges, is a comparyng or like: Imago.
nyng of looke, with looke, shape, with shape, and
one thyng with another . As when I see one in a
greate heate , and fiercely set vpon his enemie, I
might saie, he lette flee at hym like a Dragon. Or thus. He
lookes like a Tyger, a man would thinke he would eate one,
his countenaunce is so ougle. He speakes not, but he barkes
like a Dogge: he whettes his tethe like a Bore, he beates the
grounde with his foote, like a greate Horsse: he is as raun:
pyng as a Lion. By this figure called in Latine Imago, that
is to saie an Image, we mighte compare one manne with a:
nother, as Salust compareth Ceasar and Cato together, or
we mighte heape many men together, and proue by large re:
hersall, any thyng that we would, the whiche of the Logici:
ans is called induccion.

Answeryng to our self.

E are saied to answere our self, when wee seme to Sibi ipsi re:
tell our self, what we will do. Whedria in Terence sponsio.
beyng muche troubled and out of quiet, because he
was not receiued of his woman, but shutte out of
dores, when he was moste willyng to se her, made as though
he would not come to her afterwardes, nor yet se her at all,
when she did moste tently sende for hym. And therfore beyng
in his anger, thus he saied: Well, what shall I dooe? Shall
I not go, not euen now when she sendes for me, of her awne
accorde? Or shall I be of suche a nature, that I cannot abide
the despitefulnesse of harlottes? She hath shutte me out, she
calles me again. Shal I go to her? Naie I will not, though
she entreate me neuer so faire.

Order.

Ee.iij. Order

Ordo.

Rder is of twoo sortes, the one is, when the wor=
thier is preferred, and set before. As a man is sette
before a woman. The seconde is, when in amplifi=
cacion, the weightiest wordes are sette last, and in
diminishyng, thesame are sette formoste. With what looke,
with what face, with what harte dare thou do suche a dede?

☞ *Brief describyng, or circumscripcion.*

Circum-
scriptio.

Ircumscripcion, is a briefe declaryng of a thyng. As
thus. He is free, that is subiect to no euil. It is a ver=
tue to eschewe vice.

There are diuerse other colours of Rhetorique, to com=
mende and set furthe a sentence, by chaunge of wordes, and
muche varietee of speache, but I had rather offende in spea=
kyng to litle, then deserue rebuke in saiyng to muche. For,
asmuche as close silence maie soner be pardoned, then immo=
derate bablyng can want iust blame, & therfore thus an ende.

Of memorie.

S I haue labored to set out thother partes of Rheto=
rique, in suche ample wise as I thought moste nedefull
so it standeth me in hand, not to slacken myne endeuor,
now that I am come to speake of memorie. For, though man
haue vnderstandyng and iudgement, whiche is one parte of
wisedome: yet wantyng a remembraunce to apply thynges
aptly, when tyme and place shall best require: he shal do but
small good with al his vnderstandyng. And therfore it is said
not without reason, that thesame is memorie to the mynde,
that life is to the body. Now then what els must thei do that
esteme reason, and loue knowlege, but cherishe the memorie
from tyme to tyme, as an especiall and souereigne preserua=
tiue, against thinfeccion of cankard obliuion. The faulkners
saie, it is the first poynce of haukyng to hold faste. And yet I
cannot thinke otherwise, but that in al good learnyng also,
it is best & moste expedient, euermore to hold fast. For, what
auaile good thynges, if we cannot kepe theim, if wee receiue
theim in at one eare, and let theim out as fast again at the o=
ther eare? A good thriftie man will gather his goodes toge=
ther, in tyme of plentie, and laie theim out again in tyme of
nede

The arte of Rhetorique. *Fol. 112.*

nede: and shall not an Oratour haue in store good matter, in
the chest of his memorie, to vse and bestowe in tyme of ne=
cessitee? I doubte not, but all men desire to haue, a good re=
membraunce of thynges, the whiche what it is, how it is di=
uided, and howe it maie bee preserued, I will shewe in as
fewe woordes as I can.

what is memorie.

Memorie is the power retentiue of the mynde, to **Memorie**
kepe those thinges, whiche by mannes wit are cō= **what it is.**
ceiued, or thus. Memorie is the power of the mind
that conteineth thynges receiued, that calleth to
mynde thynges past, & reneweth of freshe, thynges forgotten.

The place of memorie.

The Phisicians declare, that in the former parte of
the hed, lieth the common sense, the whiche is ther=
fore so called, because it geueth iudgement, of al the
fiue outwarde senses, onely when thei are presently
occupied aboute any thyng. As when I heare a thyng, or see
a thyng, my common sense iudgeth, that then I doe heare, or
se the same. But the memorie called the Threasure of the
mynde, lieth in the hynder parte, the whiche is made moste
perfect by temperatnesse, and moderacion of qualitees in the
brain. For where humours excede or want, there must nedes
ensue muche weakenesse of remembraunce. Children there= **Children and**
fore beyng ouer moyst, and olde menne ouer drie, haue neuer **old men haue**
good memories. Again, where ouer muche cold is, & extreme **but euill me-**
moysture, there is euer muche forgetfulnesse. Therfore it a= **mories.**
uaileth greatly, what bodies we haue, and of what constitu=
cion thei bee compacte together. For suche as bee hotte and **Hot and moyst**
moyste, do sone conceiue matters, but thei kepe not long. A= **bodies sone**
gain, thei that bee colde and drie, dooe hardely conceiue, but **conceiue.**
thei kepe it surely, when thei ones haue it. And the reason is **Colde and drie**
this, heate beyng chief qualitee, dooeth drawe thynges vnto **kepe thynges**
it (as we maie se by the Sonne) the whiche notwithstādyng **sure.**
are sone after dissipated & resolued. Again, who hath seen a
print made in water of any perthly thing? Then though heat
and moysture together, drawe thynges vnto them, yet (we se
plainly)

plainly)thei cannot long hold theim. But when the brain is cold and drie, thynges are therfore the faster holden, becaufe it is the propertie of colde and drought, to thicken all thyn= ges, and to harden theim fafte together, as we fee the water through coldnesse, is congeled, and fofte thynges are frofen oftentymes, almofte as harde as a ftone. So that moyfture, through heate beyng chief qualitee, doth drawe: and drought through coldnesse, whiche is chief contrary to heate, dooeth harden and make thynges faft together. But now how dooe

Memorie in the latter part of the hedde.

wee knowe, that the memorie refteth in the latter parte of the hedde ? No doubte, experience hath proued, and confir= med this to be mofte true. For, there hath been fome, that be= yng hurt in that place, haue vtterly forgot their awne name I do remember one man, that (beeyng hurte in that place, at the infurreccion of the *Lincolne Shire* men, xv. yeres paft) could not deuife the makyng of fome Letters, in his Crofle rowe, when he tooke penne and ynke, to write to his frende, whereas before that tyme, he wrote bothe fafte and faire, and was learned in the *Latine*. And therefore when he wrote, he would ftande mufyng a greate while, before he could call to his remembraunce, howe he vfed to make a. P.a G.or fuche another letter, whereupon diuerfe muche marueiled what he would haue, or what he ment at the firft tyme. For beyng greued, and willing to afke help, he could not vtter his mea= nyng, for lacke of remembraunce, and yet his tongue ferued hym well otherwife, to vtter whatfoeuer came in his hedde.

¶ The diuifion of memorie.

Memorie diuided.

Memorie is partly naturall, and partly artificiall. Naturall memorie is, when without any precep= tes or leffons, by the onely aptenesse of nature, we beare awaie fuche thynges as wee heare. Where= in fome heretofore, did muche excell, and greatly paffe all o= ther. As *Themiftocles*, who had fo good a memorie, that when one proffered to teache hym the arte of memorie, naye by fainte Marie (qͬ he) teache me rather the arte of forget= tyng. Declaryng thereby that his memorie was paffyng good, and that it was more pain for hym, to forgette fuche thynges, as he would not kepe, then hard to remember fuche thynges

Themiftocles.

thinges as he would knowe.

Mithridates alſo hadde ſuche an excellente memorie, Mithridates
that whereas he was Lorde and ruler ouer. xxij. ſtraunge
countries that ſpake diuers ſpeaches one from an other: he
was able to talke wyth euerye one of theym in their owne
countrey language.

Likewyſe Cyrus Kynge of the Perſians, hauinge a Cyrus.
greate armye of menne, knewe the names of all his Soul-
diours.

Cyneas Ambaſſadoure for kinge Pyrrhus, called eue- Cyncas
rye one by his name that was in the Parliamente houſe at
Rome, the ſeconde daye after he came thither, the number
of them beyng foure times as many as they be, that belonge
vnto the Parliament here in Englande.

Julius Ceſar is reported that he coulde reade, heare, Julius Ceſar.
and tel one what he ſhould write, ſo faſt as his penne coulde
runne, and endite letters hym ſelfe altogether at one time.

Thus we ſee that naturallye menne haue hadde wonderfull memories, as contrarywiſe there haue bene hearde
of as ſtraunge forgetfull wittes. Some hathe not knowen
his right hande from his lefte. An other hath forgotte his Forgetful
wittes.
owne name. An other hath caried his knyfe in his mouth,
and hath runne rounde aboute the houſe ſekinge for it. An
other hath tolde a tale halfe an houre together, and immediatly after hath forgotte what he ſpake al that while.

Cicero telleth of one Curio, that where as he woulde
make a deuiſion of three partes, he woulde either foget the
thirde, or make vp a fourthe, contrarye to his firſte purpoſe
and entente.

This I remember beinge a Boye, that where as a prea- Belike thys
man had the
arte of forget-
tinge.
cher hadde taken vpon him to ſet forthe the. xij. Articles of
our beliefe, he coulde not in all the worlde finde oute paſte
nine. So that he was fayne to ſaye, he was aſſured there
was twelue, where ſoeuer the other three were become, and
he doubted not but the hearers knewe theim better then he
did, and therfore he woulde for his parte ſaye no more, but
commit them all to God, and thoſe nine (thought he) were
enoughe for him at that time, to ſet forthe and expounde for

ff.i. their

their vnderstandinge.

Nowe the beste meane bothe to mende an euil memozy and to pzeserue a good, is firste to kepe a diet, and eschewe surfites,to slepe moderatelye, to accompanye with women rarelye,and laste of all to exercise the witte with cunnynge of manye thinges without Booke, and euer to be occupied with one thinge oz other. Foz euen as by labôure the witte is whetted,so by lithernes the witte is blunted.

But nowe concerning the other kinde of memozye called artificiall,I had nede to make a long discourse, consideringe the straungenesse of the thinge to the English eare, and the hardnes of the matter,to the ignozaunte & vnlearned. But firste I will shew from whence it hath beginning,and vpon what occasion it was first inuented, befoze I aduenture to declare the pzeceptes that belonge vnto the same.

The firste founder of the arte of Remembzaunce.

THe inuention of this Arte is fatherde vpon Si;
monides,foz when the same manne(as the fable re;
cozdeth)had made in behalfe of a triumphãt Cham
pion called Scopas,foz a certaine summe of money a Ballade, suche as was then wonte to be made foz Con; querours:he was denied a piece of his rewarde, because he made a digression in his songe (whiche in those dayes was customablye vsed)to the pzaise and commendatiõ of Castoz and Pollur(who were then thoughte being Twinnes,and gotte by Iuppiter to be Goddes) of whom the Champion willed him to aske a pozcion, because he hadde so largelye set fozthe their woz̈thye doynges. Nowe it chaunced,that where as there was made a great feast to the honour of the same Victozye, and Simonides had bene placed there as a geiste,he was sodainely called from the table, and told that there was two yonge men at the doze,& bothe on hozsebacke whiche desiered moste earnestlye to speake with him oute of hande. But when he came out of the dozes,he sawe none at all, notwithstanding, he was not so sone out, and his fote on the thzesholde,but the Parlour fell downe immediatlye vpon theim al that were there, and so crusshed their bodies
toge;

together, & in such sorte, that the kinsfolke of those whiche
were deade, comming in, and desierous to burie them euery
one according to their calling, not onely could they not per=
ceiue them by their faces, but also they coulde not discerne
them by any other marke of any parte in all their bodies.
Then Simonides well remembringe in what place euerye
one of theim did sitte, tolde theim what euery one was, and
gaue them their kinsfolkes carkases, so many as were there
Thus the arte was first inuented. And yet (thoughe this be
but a fable) reason might beat thus much into our heades,
that if the like thinge had bene done, the like remembraunce
might haue ben vsed. For who is he that seeth a dosen sit at
a table whom he knoweth verye well, can not tell, after they
are all risen, where euery one of them did sitte before? And
therefore be it that some man inuented this tale: the matter
serueth well our purpose, and what nede we any more?

What thinges are requisite to get the Arte of Memorie.

They that wyll remember manye thynges and re=
hearse them together out of hande: muste learne to
haue places, and digest Images in them accordingly

A Place what it is.

A place is called anye rowme apt to receiue thinges.

An Image what it is.

An Image is any picture or shape, to declare some certayne
thing therby. And euē as in waxe we make a print with a seale
so we haue places wher liuely pictures must be set. The pla=
ces must be greate, of small distaunce, not one like an other,
and euermore the fifte place must be made notable aboue the
rest, hauinge alwayes some seuerall note from the other, as
some antique, or a hande pointing, or suche like, that the ra=
ther hauinge a greate number of places, we might the bet=
ter knowe where we are, by the remembraunce of suche no=
table and straunge places. And thus hauynge theim well
appoynnted, wee muste kepe theim fresche in oure memorye,
and neuer chaunge them, but vse them styll, whatsoeuer we
haue to saye. But the ymages we may chaunge as the mat=
ter shal geue iust cause, vsinge suche as shall serue beste for
the knowledge of thinges.

*Places howe
they must be.*

ff.ij.   The

Images how they muſt be.

The whiche Images muſte be ſette forthe as thoughe they were ſtirring, yea they muſt be ſometimes made raumping, and laſt of all, they muſte be made of thinges notable, ſuche as maye cauſe earneſt impreſſion of thinges in our mind. As a notable euill fauoured man, or a monſtruous horſe, ſuche as ſainte Georges horſe was wonte to be, or any ſuch like, helpe well for remembraunce.

- i. The places of Memory are reſembled vnto Waxe and Paper.
- ij. Images are counted lyke vnto letters or a Seale.
- iij. The placing of theſe Images, is like vnto wordes written.
- iiij. The vtteraunce and vſing of them, is like vnto readynge.

And therfore as we do reſerue paper, and yet chaūg our writynge, putting out wordes as occaſion ſhal ſerue, and ſettinge other in their rowme: ſo may we do for the Images inuented, chaunge our pictures ofte, and reſerue the papers ſtill. Some gather their places and ymages oute of the croſſe rowe, beginninge euerye letter with the name of ſome Beaſte, and ſo go thorowe the whole, makyng in euerye beaſte fyue ſeuerall places, where the impreſſion of thinges ſhalbe made, that is to ſaye, in the Heade, the Bealye, in the Taile, in the former parte of the legges, and alſo in the hinder part. So that bi this meanes, there ſhall be gathered, an hundreth and fiftene places.

Some againe will ſet their places in his heade or bodye with whom they ſpeake. As to make the noſe, the eyes, the forheade, the heere, the eares, and other partes, to ſerue for places. And for makinge places in anye houſe, churche, or other rowme, this leſſon is alſo geuen, that wee enter oure firſte places alwaies vpon the right hande, neuer returning backe, but goynge on ſtyll as I might ſaye in a circuite, til we come to that place where we firſt beganne. But firſt before the Images be inuented, the places muſte be learned
perfitely

perfitelye,and therfoꝛe one geueth coũſaple that we ſhould
go into ſome ſolitary place where no company is, and there
make our places, walking vp and downe foure oꝛ fiue times
and callyng ſtyll to our remembꝛaunce what and where the
places are. And not onely to do this once oꝛ twiſe, but to la=
boure in it two oꝛ thꝛe Dapes at ſeuerall times, vntil we ſhal
be able to tel our places vpon our fingers endes.

And nowe to make this harde matter ſomewhat plaine,
I will vſe an example. My frende (whom I toke euer to
be an honeſt manne) is accuſed of thefte, of aduoutrie, of rp=
ot, of manſlaughter, and of treaſon, if I woulde kepe theſe
woꝛdes in my remembꝛaunce, and rehearſe them in oꝛder as
they were ſpoken, I muſte appoynte fiue places, the whiche
I hadde neade to haue ſo perfeatlye in my memoꝛye, as
coulde be poſſible. As foꝛ example, I will make theſe in
my chamber. A doꝛe, a windowe, a pꝛeſſe, a bedſteade, and a
chimney. Now in ye doꝛe, I wil ſet Cacus the thefe, oꝛ ſome
ſuche notable verlet. In the windowe I will place Venus.
In the pꝛeſſe I will put Apitius ye famous glutton. In the
bedſteade I will ſet Richard the thirde kinge of England,
oꝛ ſome like notable murtherer. In the chimney I wil place
the blacke Smythe, oꝛ ſome other notable traytoure.
That if one repete theſe places, and theſe Images twiſe oꝛ
thꝛiſe together, no doubte, though he haue but a meane me=
moꝛie, he ſhal carpe away the woꝛdes rehearſed with eaſe.
And like as he maye do with theſe fiue wooꝛdes, ſo maye he
do wyth fiue ſcoꝛe, if he haue places freſhe in hys remem=
bꝛaũce, and do but vſe him ſelfe to this trade one foꝛtenight
together.

Therfoꝛe thoughe it ſeme ſtraunge and folyſhe to them
that knowe it not, yet the learned haue taken this waye, ꝫ
doubte not but maruayles maye be done, if one haue places
readye made foꝛ the purpoſe, and haue them freſhe in his re=
membꝛaunce. Foꝛ what other thinge els do they that ap=
poynt ymages in certaine places made foꝛ that purpoſe, but
wꝛite (as a manne woulde ſaye) vpon Paper, that which is
ſpoken vnto them? What maketh the olde manne (that foꝛ
lacke of naturall heate and moiſture, ſcante knoweth hys

right hande from his lefte) remember in the mouning where he layed his purse all nyght, but the beddes heade, whyche lyghtlye is the appoynted place for all mennes purses, espe-ciallie such as be wayfairers, and haue but little store.

Shall some gentilman playe blyndefolde at the chesse, and can not a learned man be able to rehearse vp a score or two of straunge names together? A Netcherde hauinge the charge and keppnge of .xviij. score heade of beastes in a wyld Fenne, that belonge to diuers menne, will not onelye tell, who be the owners of al suche cattell, but also he wil shew a manne twise a weeke where anye one is feading, and if he wante one amonge the whole, he will tell immediatly what it is, and whose it is that is wantynge. Then fonde are they that counte the Arte of Memorye so harde, seynge they will neither proue the hardenes of it, nor yet blowshe at the matter, when they see pore netcherdes go so farre be-yonde them. Howe many thinges dothe Memorie conteine marueylous to beholde, and muche more would, if we were not altogether slouthful, and as carelesse to kepe, as we are to gette, good thinges I meane, not goodes of thys world. Euerye Artificer hath through exercise and laboure, an ar-tificiall memorye, sauynge the learned man onely, who hath most nede of it aboue all other.

When we come to a place where we haue not bene many a daye before, we remembre not onely the place it selfe, but by the place, we call to remembraunce manye thinges done there. Yea sometimes a window maketh some remember that they haue stollen in their daies some thing out of it. Some-times a chimney telleth them of manye late drinkinges and sittinges vp by the fire. Sometimes a bedstead putteth thē in remembrance of many good morowes, sometimes a dore, & sometimes a parler. Thus we se places euē wout images, helpe oft the memorye, muche more then shall we remēbre, if we haue both places and Jmages.

But nowe because I haue halfe weried the reader with a tedious matter, I will harten him agayne wyth a merye tale. At the time of rebellion in Northfolke, there was a priest emong al other adiudged to dye vpō a gibet in a grene place,

The arte of Rhetorique　　　Fol.116.

place, a little from the hyghe waye side. This Prieste seinge the place of his laste ende, stode a whyle musinge wyth him selfe, and saide to the company there. Now Lord God God graunt al rebels lyke remembraunces. what a thinge is this. It comes to my remembraunce nowe that aboute fourtene yeres paste, I was merye here vpon thys Bancke wyth an other Prieste, and wallowynge me downe vpon the grasse, I said these wordes: Hæc requi. es mea in seculū seculi, hic habitabo quoniam elegi eam. The whiche Sentence beynge a Psalme of Dauid, is nothinge els in Englishe, But this is my restynge place for euer and euer, here shall be my dwellynge, because I haue chosen it. And nowe (quod he) I finde it to be ouer true, so that I thinke it be Goddes wyl I should dye, and therfore I take it in good worthe, and thus I desire you al to praye for me. Thus we see that the place brought hym in remembraunce of a sentence spoken .xiiij. yeres before.

Therfore this knoweledge is not to be neglected, no though we do contemne it, yet we haue the vse of it. For if we be fully disposed to remēber a thing, we do call vp the memorye, and styrre it to mynde thynges lyke thereunto. As Remembraūce of thinges lyke. if one be called Wingefeld, and I feare to forget this name I might remembre the winge of a byrde, and a grene feld to walke in. Sometymes we remēber the whole, by kepyng in mynde some parte of a word. As when one is called Crowcroft, I myght by remembring of a Crowe, the rather mind his name.

Notwithstāding ther be some (emōg whō is Erasmus) which like not this arte of Memorie, but saye it rather hindereth, then helpeth a mans wit. And yet Tullie the greateste Oratour emong the Romaynes, did wel alowe it, and proued it good by a naturall reason. For where as we knowe some thinges (sayeth he) onelye by vnderstandynge, and some by the sence of seyinge, those we kepe best in our mindes whiche we knowe by sight, & haue marked with our eyes. As for example. When I se a Lyon, the ymage therof abideth faster in my mind, thē if I should heare some report made of a Lyon Emong all the senses, the eye sight is most quicke, & cōteineth the impressiō of thinges more assuredly, thē any of the other senses do.

　　　　　　　　　　　　　　And

And the rather when a manne bothe heareth and seeth a thinge (as by artificiall memorye he dothe almoste se thinges liuelye) he dothe remember it muche the better. The sight printeth thinges in a mannes memorye, as a seale doth prynte a mannes name in waxe. And therfore heretofore Jmages were sette vp for remembraunce of Sainctes, to be layd mennes bokes, that the rather by seinge the Pictures of suche menne, they might be stirred to folowe their good liuynge. The whiche surely hadde bene well done, if God had not forbidden it. But seinge thinges muste be done not of a good entente, but euen as God hath commaunded, it is well doone that suche Jdolles are cleane taken oute of the churche. Marye for this purpose wherof we nowe write, they woulde haue serued gayly well. Thus the arte is sone tolde, but the practise of it is all. And therfore if one desire to excell herein, let him take paynes to gather his places together, and kepe them well in remembraunce, prouinge by halfe a score, how he shall be able to vse a hundreth. And no doubte, but time and exercise shall make hym perfecte.

For the beste arte of memorye that can be, is to heare muche, to speake muche, to reade muche, and to write much. And exercise it is that dothe all, when we haue saide al that euer we can.

Of Pronunciation.

Pronunciation is an apte orderinge bothe of the voyce, countenaunce, and all the whole bodye, accordynge to the worthines of suche woordes and mater as by speache are declared. The vse hereof is suche for anye one that liketh to haue prayse for tellynge his tale in open assemblie, that hauing a good tongue, and a comelye countenaunce, he shalbe thought to passe all other that haue the like vtterauce: thoughe they haue much better learning. The tongue geueth a certayne grace to euerye matter, and beautifieth the cause in like maner, as a swete soundynge Lute muche setteth forthe a meane deuised Ballade. Or as the sounde of a good instrumente styrreth

reth the hearers, and moueth muche delite, so a cleare soun=
dyng voice comforteth muche our daintie eares, with muche
swete melodie, and causeth vs to allowe the matter rather
for the reporters sake, then the reporter, for the maisters sake.
Demosthenes therfore, that famouse Oratour beyng asked
what was the chiefest point in al Oratorie, gaue the chiefe
and onely praise to Pronunciation, being demaunded, what 《Demosthenes saiyng of pronunciation.》
was the seconde, and the thirde, he stil made answere, Pro=
nunciation, and would make none other aunswere, till they
lefte askyng, declaryng hereby that Arte without vtteraunce
can dooe nothyng, vtteraunce without Arte can dooe right
muche. And no doubte that man is in outwarde apparaunce 《Aeschines.》
halfe a good Clarke, that hath a cleane tongue, and a comely
gesture of his bodie. Aeschines lykewyse beyng banished his
countrie through Demosthenes, when he had redde to the
Rhodians his owne Oration, and Demosthenes aunswere
thereunto, by force wherof he was banished, and all they
marueiled muche at the excellencie of the same: then (q Ae=
schines) you would haue marueiled muche more if you had
heard hymselfe speake it. Thus beyng cast in miserie & ban=
nished for euer, he could not but geue suche great reporte of
his most deadly and mortal ennemy.

¶The partes of Pronunciation.

Pronunciation standeth partely in fashionyng the
tongue, and partely in framyng the gesture.
    The tongue, or voice is praise worthie, if the vt=
teraunce be audible, strong, and easie, & apte to or=
der as we liste. Therfore they that mynde to gette praise in
tellyng their minde in open audience must at the first begin=
nyng speake somwhat softely, vse meete pausyng, and being
somewhat heated, rise with their voice, as the tyme & cause
shal best require. Thei that haue no good voices by nature,
or cannot wel vtter their woordes, must seeke for helpe else=
where. Exercise of the bodie, fastyng, moderacion in meate,
and drynke, gaping wyde, or singyng plaine song, & counter=
feityng those that do speake distinctly, helpe muche to haue
a good deliueraunce. Demosthenes beeyng not able to pro=

Gg.i.   nunce

pronounce the firſt letter of that Arte whiche he profeſſed, but would ſay, for, Rhethorique, Letolike, vſed to put litle ſtones vnder his tongue, & ſo pronounced, wherebp he ſpake at lengthe ſo plainelp as anp man in the worlde coulde doe. Muſicians in England haue vſed to put gagges in childrē mouthes that thep might pronounce diſtinctelp, but nowe with the loſſe and lacke of Muſicke, the loue alſo is gone of

Faultes in pronunciation bringpng vp childrē to ſpeake plainelp. Some therebe that either naturallp, or through folie haue ſuche euill voices & ſuche lacke of vtteraunce, & ſuche euil geſture, that it muche defaceth all their dopnges. One pipes out his woordes ſo ſmall through defaulte of his wpnde pppe, that pe woulde thinke he whiſteled. An other is ſo hource in his throte, that a man woulde thpnke he came latelp from ſcourpng of harneſſe. An other ſpeakes, as though he had Plummes in his mouthe. An other ſpeakes in his throte, as though a good Ale crūme ſtacke faſt. An other ratles his woordes. An other choppes his woordes. An other ſpeakes, as though his woordes had neede to be heaued out with leauers. An other ſpeakes as though his woordes ſhoulde be weped in a ballaunce. An other gapes to fetche wpnde at euerp thirde woorde. This man barkes out his Engliſhe Northrenlike with I ſap, and thou ladde. An other ſpeakes ſo finelp, as though he were brought vp in a Ladies Chamber. As I knew a Prieſt that was as nice as a Nonnes Henne, when he would ſaie Maſſe, he woulde neuer ſaie Dominus vobiſcum, but Dominus vobicum. In like maner as ſome now wil ſap, the Commendementes of God, blacke vellet, for Commaundementes and blacke veluet. Some blowes at their noiſtrelles. Some ſighes out their woordes. Some ſpnges their ſentencies. Some laughes altogether, when thep ſpeake to anp bodie. Some gruntes lpke a Hogge. Some cackels lpke a Henne, or a Jack Dawe. Some ſpeakes as thoughe thep ſhoulde tel a tale in their ſleeue. Some cries out ſo loude, that thep would make a mans eares ake to heare thē. Some coughes at euerp woorde. Some hēmes it out. Some ſpittes fier, thep talke ſo hotelp. Some makes a wrie mouthe, and ſo thep wreſte out their woordes. Some whpnes lpke a Pig.

Some

Some suppes their woordes vp as a poore man doth his porage. Some noddes their head at euery sentence. An other winckes with one iye, and some with both. This mã frowneth alwaies when he speakes. An other lookes euer as though he were mad. Some cannot speake, but thei must go vp and doune, o2 at the lest be stirryng their feete as though they stode in a cockeryng Bote. An other wil plaie with his cappe in his hande, & so tel his tale. Some when they speake in a great companie, will looke al one way, as I knewe a reader in my daies, who loked in lyke sorte when he redde to Scholers, whome one thought to disappoint of suche his constant lookes: and therefore against the nexte daie he painted the Deuil with hornes vpon his heade in the selfe same place where the Reader was wont alwaies to looke, the whiche straunge monster when the reader sawe, he was half abashed, and turned his face an other way. Some pores vpon the grounde, as though thei sought for pynnes. Tullie telles of one Theophrastus Tauriscus, who is saide to declaime arsee versee. Some swelles in the face & filles their chekes ful of wynde, as though they would blow out their woordes. Some settes forth their lippes two ynches good beyonde their teeth. Some talkes as thoughe their tongue went of patyns. Some showes al their teeth. Some speakes in their teeth altogether. Some leates their woordes fall in their lippes, scant openyng theim when they speake. There are a thousand suche faultes emong menne bothe for their speache, and also for their gesture, the whiche if in their young yeres they be not remedied, they will hartely be forgotte when they come to mans state. But the rather that these faultes may be redressed: I haue partly declared heretofore the righte vse of vtteraunce, and nowe I mynde by Goddes helpe to shewe the right vse of gesture.

What is gesture.

G esture is a certaine comely moderacion of the countenaunce, and al other partes of mans body, aptely agreeyng to those thynges whiche are spoken. That if wee shall speake in a pleasaunt matter, it is meete that the loke also should be chereful, and al the gesture stir-

Gesture what it is.

Gg.ij. ryng

ryng thereafter. The heade to be holden vpright, the fore-
head without frownyng, the browes without bendyng, the
nose without blowyng, the iyes quicke and pleasaunt, the
lippes not laid out, the teeth without grennyng, the armes
not muche cast abrode, but comely set out, as time, and cause
shal best require: the handes somtymes opened, and sometimes holdē together, the fingers pointyng, the brest laid out,
and the whole body stirryng altogether with a seemely moderacion. By the whiche behauiour of our body after suche
a sorte, we shal not onely delite men with the sight, but perswade them the rather the truth of our cause.

Hortensius.

M. Hortensius had suche delite to vse comely gesture, &
had suche grace in that behaulfe: that I doubt whether men
had a greater desire to see hym, than they had to heare hym.
His countenaunce so wel agreed with his wordes, and his
woordes were so meete for his contenaunce, that not onely he did please the iudgement of his hearers, and contented
their mynde: but also he pleased their iyes, and delited their
cares, so muche as could be wished.

Tullie saith well: The gesture of man, is the speache of
his bodie, and therfore reason it is, that lyke as the speache
must agree to the matter, so must also the gesture agree to
the mynde. for, the iyes are not geuen to man onely to se, but
also to shewe, and set forth the meanyng of his mynde, euen
as vnto a Boxe are geuen brisselles: to a Lyon, the taile: to a
horse, his eares : whereby their inclinacions and soubdeine
affections are sone espied. When we see a man loke redde in
the iyes, his browes bent, his teeth bytyng his vpper lip, we
iudge that he is out of pacience. Therfore as we
ought to haue good regarde for the vtteraunce of our wordes, so
we ought to take
hede
that our gesture
be comely, the whiche bothe
beyng wel obserued, shal encrease fame
and gette estimacion vni-
uersally.

But heare an end. And now as my wil hath been earnest to doe my beste : so I wishe that my paines may bee taken thereafter. And yet what needes wishyng, seeyng the good will not speake euill, and the wicked can not speake well.
Therfore beyng staied vpon the good, and assured
of their ientle bearyng with me: I feare
none, because I stande vpon a
saufe grounde.

';'

¶Faultes escaped in thenprintyng.

FOlio.viii.line.xxxii.i.reade,vaunte.
Fol.xxxiii.lyne.i.Reade,oʒ doe we.
Fol.lxxvi.line.vii.i.respecte.
Fol.lxxvi.line.viii.letter.
Fol.lxxxi.line.vii.seme.
Fol.lxxxvi.line.xv.ii.Rhetoʒician.

¶ A Table to fynde out suche matter as is conteined in this Booke, first by the Leafe, and nexte by the Page, or syde of the Leafe.

A.

B.

E.

Hh.j. Endyng

Hh.ij. Letter

Dh.iii.

Richardus Graftonus, typographus Regius excudebat.
Cum priuilegio, ad imprimendum solum.